A Basic Guide

to

Interpreting the Bible

Playing by the Rules

Second Edition

Robert H. Stein

Baker Academic
a division of Baker Publishing Group
Grand Rapids, Michigan

D1248993

© 1994, 2011 by Robert H. Stein

Published by Baker Academic
a division of Baker Publishing Group
P.O. Box 6287, Grand Rapids, MI 49516-6287
www.bakeracademic.com

Printed in the United States of America

Library of Congress Cataloging-in-Publication Data
Stein, Robert H., 1935–
    A basic guide to interpreting the Bible : playing by the rules / Robert H. Stein—2nd ed.
        p.   cm.
    Rev. ed. of: Playing by the rules : a basic guide to interpreting the Bible. c1994.
    Includes bibliographical references and indexes.
    ISBN 978-0-8010-3373-5 (pbk.)
    1. Bible—Hermeneutics. I. Stein, Robert H., 1935– Playing by the rules. II. Title.
BS476.S76 2011
220.601—dc22   2010051905

11   12   13   14   15   16   17   7   6   5   4   3   2   1

To
Steve and Liz

May the joys of your pilgrimage in life be multiplied
  because they are shared,
and may the sorrows along the way be lessened
  because they are borne together.

Contents

Preface to the Second Edition

Every author discovers in the very first reading of his or her published book things that he would like to add or change. With time this wish list continues to grow. As a result I was delighted when Baker Academic suggested that I do a revision of *A Basic Guide to Interpreting the Bible: Playing by the Rules*. This is not due to a change in my understanding of the basic goal of interpreting written texts. That goal remains the same. In fact it is held even more strongly in the revision than in the earlier edition. The basic goal of interpreting the Bible and other written texts should be to understand what their authors consciously sought to convey by what they wrote. It is the understanding of the authors' willed meaning, their communicative intent, that continues to be emphasized in this revision as the primary goal of biblical interpretation.

The most evident change in this revision involves the order of the chapters in part 2, "The Specific Rules for the Individual Games." Here the various genres making up the individual chapters have been rearranged according to their order of appearance in the Bible: biblical narrative, covenants and laws, poetry, psalms, proverbs, prophecy, idioms, parables, overstatement and hyperbole, and epistles and letters. In addition, the last chapter in the first edition—"The Games of Treaties, Laws, and Songs"—has been divided into two separate chapters, appearing as chapter 6 ("The Game of Rules: Covenants and Laws") and chapter 8 ("The Game of Songs: Psalms"). In addition, the content of each chapter in the revision has undergone considerable reworking, and two additional exercises have been added involving the use of the vocabulary for interpreting literature given in chapter 2. These exercises are then discussed in appendixes 1, 2, and 3.

I want to express my appreciation to numerous individuals who have read the revised manuscript and contributed to its improvement by pointing out errors and needed corrections, as well as by providing helpful suggestions and examples. These include my sons Keith and Steve, who read the first two chapters; my brother Bill, who lent his legal expertise to the reading of these chapters; and Dr. Daniel W. Taylor, professor of English at Bethel University, who also read these chapters and gave helpful advice concerning literary theory. I am also deeply indebted to four former students who for ten years have used *A Basic Guide to Interpreting the Bible* as a text for their classes in hermeneutics. Their familiarity with this text and their careful reading of the entire revised manuscript has resulted in a far better final product than would have come about otherwise. These are Dr. Barry C. Joslin, Dr. Robert L. Plummer, and Dr. Denny Burk of The Southern Baptist Theological Seminary; and Dr. Benjamin L. Merkle of Southeastern Baptist Theological Seminary. Needless to say, any weaknesses and errors of logic contained in this revision are mine and mine alone. A final word of appreciation must be expressed to Jim Kinney, associate publisher and editorial director of Baker Academic and Brazos Press, and to the editorial staff at Baker Publishing Group, who over the years have provided guidance and care in the editing of numerous manuscripts. I have been delighted to have had their assistance over the past twenty-four years in the publication of my books.

Preface to the First Edition

How can I justify writing a book on the study of the Bible when so many already exist? Both on the popular and the technical levels, there are numerous books on interpreting the Bible. How can I defend the publishing of still another? As a teacher I am well aware of the many books available on this subject. Many of them are well written. Yet for various reasons I believe there is a need for still another. This book is an attempt to present in a nontechnical way a text that will help the reader understand what the goal of reading the Bible should be and how this goal can be achieved.

In the first four chapters of this book I seek to demonstrate that the goal of reading the Bible is to understand what the biblical authors meant by their writings. Once this is understood, the next task is to discover the legitimate implications that flow out of this meaning, and how this applies today. To assist in this, I discuss and describe the roles that the author, the text, and the reader play in this process. A precise vocabulary is also provided in order to avoid confusion.

I then discuss the various kinds of literature found in the Bible. The description of a biblical text as being a proverb, a parable, a prophecy, or an epistle is of little value unless the "ground rules" governing these literary forms are understood. We know, for instance, that Luke 15:11–32 is a parable; Matthew 7:7–8 is a poetic form known as synonymous parallelism; and Jeremiah 4:23–26 is a prophecy. But what is the value of knowing this? How does this help us understand these passages? I have sought in this book to explain some of the rules that govern the interpretation of these various literary forms. How should prophecy be interpreted? Hyperbole? A biblical narrative?

The importance of interpreting the Bible correctly cannot be overemphasized. The claim that the Bible is inspired and that it is God's revelation to humanity is ultimately of little value without some understanding of how that divine revelation should be interpreted. When we describe the Bible as "infallible" or "without error," these terms are meaningless if we do not know how to interpret it. What do we mean when we say that the Bible is without error? What is it that is infallible? Is it my understanding of the Bible? Is it yours? Is it the particular translation of the Bible that I am using? Is it the Greek or Hebrew text that scholars use? Who gives meaning to a text? Can a text possess more than one meaning? Should we interpret the Psalms in the same way we interpret Romans? It is hoped that this work will provide the reader with answers to these and other questions.

The present work has been in process for nearly ten years. Much of it took shape in my teaching of a class called "Biblical Prolegomena," which has since been retitled "Hermeneutics." A great debt is owed to E. D. Hirsch Jr., whose *Validity in Interpretation* has made a lasting impact on my thinking. Much of what is said in the opening chapters has been greatly influenced by him. This is especially true with respect to the vocabulary I use. I trust that my use of much of his vocabulary will be understood as a compliment rather than a theft! I apologize, however, for any ineptness that appears at times in my expression of similar views.

I wish to express my appreciation to my students for their assistance in understanding more clearly what is involved in the task of interpreting the Bible. To Duane Tweeten, Gary Johnson, and Michael Welch I want to express my appreciation for reading and critiquing an earlier form of this work. I want to thank Gloria Metz, the faculty secretary, whose assistance has made my task in writing this book much easier and more enjoyable. I am grateful for her assistance over the years in my various writing projects. She has truly been a "gift" during this time. I especially want to thank my colleagues, Arthur H. Lewis and Thomas R. Schreiner, for their many helpful comments. I would also like to express my appreciation to Wooddale Church of Eden Prairie, Minnesota, for its part in the publication of the present text. It was through my teaching a course on biblical interpretation in their lay school that the writing of the present work had its start.

Abbreviations

esp.	especially
ESV	English Standard Version
KJV	King James Version
NAB	New American Bible
NASB	New American Standard Bible
NEB	New English Bible
NIV	New International Version
NLT	New Living Translation
NRSV	New Revised Standard Version
NT	New Testament
OT	Old Testament
p./pp.	page/pages
REB	Revised English Bible
RSV	Revised Standard Version

Introduction

Tuesday night arrived. Dan and Charlene had invited several of their neighbors to a Bible study, and now they were wondering if anyone would come. Several people had agreed to come, but others had not committed themselves. At 8:00 p.m., beyond all their wildest hopes, everyone who had been invited arrived. After some introductions and neighborhood chitchat, they all sat down in the living room. Dan explained that he and his wife would like to read through a book of the Bible and discuss the material with the group. He suggested that the book be a Gospel, and since Mark was the shortest, Dan recommended it. Everyone agreed, although several said a bit nervously that they really did not know much about the Bible. Dan reassured them that this was all right, for no one present was a "theologian," and they would work together in trying to understand the Bible.

They then went around the room reading Mark 1:1–15 verse by verse. Because of some of the different translations used (NIV, ESV, KJV, and NLT), Dan sought to reassure all present that although the wording of the various translations might be different, they all meant the same thing. After they finished reading the passage, each person was to think of a brief summary to describe what the passage meant. After thinking for a few minutes, they began to share their thoughts.

Sally was the first to speak: "What this passage means to me is that everyone needs to be baptized, and I believe that it should be by immersion." John responded, "That's not what I think it means. I think it means that everyone needs to be baptized by the Holy Spirit." Ralph said somewhat timidly, "I am not exactly sure what I should be doing. Should I try to understand what Jesus and John the Baptist meant, or what the passage means to me?" Dan told him that what was important was what the passage meant to him. Encouraged by this, Ralph replied, "Well, what it means

1

to me is that when you really want to meet God, you need to go out in the wilderness just as John the Baptist and Jesus did. Life is too busy and hectic. You have to get away and commune with nature. I have a friend who says that to experience God you have to go out in the woods and get in tune with the rocks."

Cory brought the discussion to an abrupt halt. "The Holy Spirit has shown me," he said, "that this passage means that when a person is baptized in the name of Jesus, the Holy Spirit will descend upon him like a dove. This is what is called the baptism of the Spirit." Jan replied meekly, "I don't think that's what the meaning is." Cory, however, reassured her that since the Holy Spirit had given him that meaning it must be correct. Jan did not respond to Cory, but it was obvious she did not agree with what he had said. Dan was uncomfortable about the way things were going and sought to resolve the situation. So he said, "Maybe what we are experiencing is an indication of the richness of the Bible. It can mean so many things!"

But does a text of the Bible mean many things? Can a text mean different, even contradictory things? Is there any control over the meaning of biblical texts? Is there such a thing as an invalid interpretation? If so, how does one distinguish an invalid interpretation from a valid one? Is interpretation controlled by means of individual revelation given by the Holy Spirit? Do the words and grammar control the meaning of the text? If so, what text are we talking about? Is it a particular English translation, such as the KJV or NIV? Why not the NRSV, ESV, or NLT? Or why not a German translation such as the Luther Bible? Or should it be the Hebrew, Aramaic, and Greek texts of the Bible that best reflect what the original authors, such as Isaiah, Daniel, Paul, and Luke, wrote? And what about the original authors? How are they related to the meaning of the text?

It is obvious that we cannot read the Bible for long before the questions arise as to what the Bible "means" and who or what determines that meaning. Neither can we read the Bible without possessing some purpose in reading. In other words, using more technical terminology, everyone who reads the Bible does so with a "hermeneutical" theory in mind. The issue is not whether one has such a theory but whether one's "hermeneutic" is clear or unclear, adequate or inadequate, correct or incorrect. It is hoped that this book will help the reader understand what is involved in the interpretation of the Bible. It will seek to do so by helping readers acquire an interpretative framework that will help them understand better the meaning of biblical texts and how to apply that meaning to their own life situation.

PART 1

The General Rules of Interpretation

1

Who Makes Up the Rules?

An Introduction to Hermeneutics

The term "hermeneutics" intimidates people. This is both unfortunate and unnecessary. The word comes from the Greek word *hermēneuein*, which means to explain or interpret. In the Bible it is used in John 1:42; 9:7; and Hebrews 7:2. In the ESV, Luke 24:27 reads, "And beginning with Moses and all the Prophets, he [Jesus] *interpreted* to them in all the Scriptures the things concerning himself" (italics added). The NIV reads, "And beginning with Moses and all the Prophets, he [Jesus] *explained* to them what was said in all the Scriptures concerning himself" (italics added). The word translated "interpreted" and "explained" in these two versions of the Bible is the word *di[h]ermēneuein*. A noun formed from this verb, *Hermes*, was the name given to the Greek god who was the spokesman or interpreter for the other gods. This is why in Acts 14:12 we read that after Paul healed a cripple at Lystra, the people thought that the gods had come to visit them. "Barnabas they called Zeus, and Paul, Hermes, because he was the chief speaker" (cf. Acts 9:36; 1 Cor. 12:10, 30; 14:5, 13, 26, 27, 28). The term "hermeneutics," which comes from these Greek words, simply describes the practice or discipline of interpretation and the rules involved. In interpreting the Bible, what are the rules governing this discipline?

The Game Itself: The Various Components Involved in Hermeneutics

In all communication three distinct components are necessary. If any one of these is lacking, communication is impossible. These three components are the author, the text, and the reader; or, as linguists prefer to say, the encoder, the code, and the decoder. And there are other ways of describing this: the sender, the message, the receiver; the speaker, the speech, the listener; and the world behind the text, the world of the text, and the world in front of the text. If we carry this over to the analogy of playing a game, we have the creator of the game, the game parts (pieces, cards, dice, board, etc.), and the players. Without these three elements, communication (the game) is impossible.

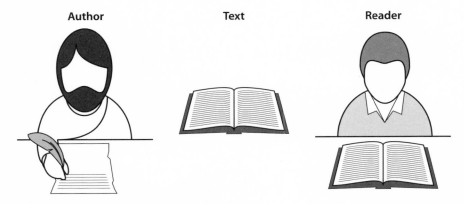

| Author | Text | Reader |

The main goal, or at least one of the main goals, of interpreting the Bible is to discover the meaning of the text being studied. We want to know what this text means (see the definition of "meaning" on pp. 31–33). Yet where does this meaning originate? Where does it come from? This is not self-evident. Some interpreters argue that it comes from one component, whereas others argue that it comes from another.

The Text (i.e., the Game Parts) as the Determiner of Meaning

Some have suggested that meaning is a property of the text. It is the text that determines what a writing means. We all have probably heard a pastor say in a sermon, "Our text tells us . . ." or "The Bible says . . ." Yet those who argue that meaning is a property of the text mean something very different from what the pastor meant by this. They claim that a literary text is autonomous and free standing. It possesses semantic autonomy in the sense that its meaning is independent of what its author meant when he or she wrote it. After a text is written, its author loses personal control of it. What the biblical author was thinking about and sought to convey by the text is essentially irrelevant with respect to the meaning of the text. Possessing autonomy, a text has a life of its own apart from its author or its reader. As a result, reading a related work such as Galatians in order to help us understand what Paul meant when he wrote Romans is of little value, for it is the present text that is the focus of attention. Furthermore, what Paul actually intended when he wrote Romans is of little value in determining the actual meaning of the present text of Romans, because Paul's thoughts are now inaccessible apart from the text (see below, pp. 15–18). According to text-centered critics, a text should be read independently of its real or hypothetical author. It has a life of its own and possesses its own meaning(s). T. S. Eliot has argued this strongly in his article "Tradition and the Individual Talent." He insists that the focus of the interpreter's attention should be the poetry itself and not the poet and his or her experience, the present writing and not the hypothetical author.

For most pastors preaching from a book like Romans, "The Bible says . . ." and "Paul means . . ." are synonymous. For those who argue that the text possesses its own meaning, however, these two things are not the same. Every text is perceived as an autonomous work of art that is to be interpreted independently of its author. It is as if it never had an author and simply materialized. According to this view, when a written work becomes literature, the normal rules of communication, in which hearers seek to understand what the speaker means by his or her words and readers seek to understand what the writer of a letter meant, no longer apply. What was once a piece of communication has been transformed into a work of art. Because it is art, the original composer no longer possesses control of it; the art possesses its own meaning completely apart from its creator. If in some way Paul could appear before those who argue for the semantic autonomy of the text and say, "What I meant when I wrote this was . . . ," the response of many new critics would essentially be, "What you say, Paul, is interesting but quite irrelevant. Your willed meaning of the text, what you intended to communicate in your writing, and what you actually communicated are not the same. Thus your intended meaning is no more authoritative than any other person's interpretation. Furthermore, after you wrote this text you lost all claim and control over it. It has since then become common property and a work of art rather than communication." Consequently, it is illegitimate to grant any serious authorial control over the meaning of the present text. This view was very popular among the "New Critics" and dominated academic circles from the 1930s to the 1960s.

This view is also popular within the US judicial system from the Supreme Court down to the lower courts. There is less concern today to seek what the authors of the Constitution and the nation that voted for it meant by the words found in it and its subsequent amendments. Instead, the Constitution and its amendments are seen as a "living," "growing," and "changing" document. Thus what the Constitution meant only fifteen years ago can change. This does not mean that an earlier ruling of the court was wrong and that the new ruling is the correct one. Rather, it is claimed that the Constitution *has changed*. (See the dissent written by Justice Scalia in Roper v. Simmons 543 U.S. [2005], p. 1.) The use of such terms as "living," "growing," and "changing" to describe the Constitution is unfortunate. The fact is that everything known to science is done to make sure that the original copies of the Constitution do not "live," "grow," and "change." These terms obviously are being used metaphorically, but exactly what they are intended to mean is unfortunately unclear. We should also note that these terms are not necessarily positive and need not imply improvement for the better. In certain contexts "growth" can serve as a synonym for cancer, and "living" and "changing" can describe something decaying and rotting. Traditionally at least, the Constitution has not been understood as "changing" by itself, but rather by the addition of amendments such as the repeal of slavery (thirteenth amendment), Prohibition (eighteenth), the right of women to vote (nineteenth), and the repeal of Prohibition (twenty-first). Thomas Jefferson argued strongly that it should not be by judicial decree that the Constitution was to "keep pace with the advance of the age of science and experience" but rather "by amendments."

The New Criticism brought several helpful insights and emphases to the study of texts. Its focus on the text itself avoided the previous preoccupation with psychoanalytical investigation of the mental experiences of the alleged author, the search for his or her sources, and the historical investigation of the text's subject matter. Instead, it focused on the close reading of the present text and the text as a whole. It helped point out the artistry and literary qualities of texts and focused on the final form of the text—a known entity that the reader possessed—rather than on such things as the hypothetical sources and stages of development that the text experienced. In the New Criticism formalistic critics discussed the real and actual texts, not the hypothetical and imaginary stages that led up to these texts.

Perhaps the biggest problem with this view, that the text itself is the determiner of meaning, involves what a "text" is and what "meaning" is. A written text is simply a collection of letters or symbols. Those symbols can vary. They can be English or Hebrew letters, Chinese symbols, or

Egyptian hieroglyphics. They may proceed right to left, left to right, up or down. They can be written on papyrus, animal skins, paper, stone, or metal. Yet both the letters and the material upon which they are written are inanimate objects. Meaning, on the other hand, is a product of reasoning and thought. It is something only people can produce. Whereas a text can convey meaning and emotions, it cannot "mean" or "emote," because it is an inanimate object. Only the authors and readers of texts can think. Thus, whereas a text can convey meaning, the production of meaning can only come from either the author in the writing of the text or the reader in the reading of the text.

The Reader (i.e., the Player) as the Determiner of Meaning

Some interpreters claim that the meaning of a text is determined by the reader. (In literary analysis this reader is sometimes called the "implied reader," the "competent reader," the "intended reader," the "ideal reader," the "real reader," etc.) The person who reads the text is seen as giving it its meaning and "actualizing" it. This should not be confused with thinking that the reader learns/deciphers/discovers/ascertains the meaning the text possesses in and of itself (the view described above). Nor should it be confused with the view that the meaning is determined by what the author meant when he or she wrote the text (the view described below). On the contrary, this view maintains that all written texts are essentially dead, or at least in hibernation. It is only through the reader that a text is actualized and comes to life as he or she breathes meaning into it. Each individual that reads the text creates the meaning. Reading a text does not involve the decoding of the original author's creative intention but rather a rewriting of the text, in which the reader now becomes the author and possesses authority over the text. Consequently, the meaning given to the text is a manifestation of the interpreter's own beliefs and desires. It is interesting to note that this view became very popular during the Vietnam War years, when there was a widespread revolt against authority in general. This new approach permitted the rejection of any authority over the reader in the area of interpretation. Readers did not have to submit to the authority of the text or its author as the determiner of meaning but rather claimed personal authority over both. Associated with this was a new worldview. Whereas the Ptolemaic, earth-centered understanding of the universe had been replaced by Copernicus's heliocentric understanding, now Copernicus's heliocentric understanding was replaced by an egocentric one. Now the individual saw himself or herself as the center of the universe and the determiner of its meaning. Thus it was not the Creator/Author of the universe who determined its meaning but the observer/reader.

According to this view (sometimes called "reception theory," "reception aesthetics," "reader-response or reader-centered criticism," "affective criticism," etc.), if different readers arrive at different meanings, this is because different readers respond to a text in different ways. Often these reader-centered meanings reflect to a great extent the readers' own values, likes, and dislikes. Readers in fact are encouraged to interpret texts in such a manner, for in so doing, more vibrant and relevant meanings are given to the text. Thus, for example, we come across Marxist, liberationist, postcolonial, feminist, egalitarian, complimentarian, green or ecological, homosexual, social-scientific, Calvinist, and Arminian "readings" or interpretations of a text. This does not necessarily mean that the reader has actually found in the particular text something that favors a Marxist, liberationist, feminist, or complimentarian interpretation. Rather, it means that the reader has chosen to read the words of the text in a particular way, apart from or even contrary to what the author may have meant. This view assumes that there are many legitimate meanings of a text, for each interpreter contributes his or her meaning to the text and in so doing actualizes it. The text functions somewhat like an inkblot onto which the reader projects his or her own meaning. Sometimes, in popular usage, we hear people say something like "What this biblical text means to me is . . ." or "This passage may mean something different to you but for me it means . . ." As we shall see later, in some instances such statements may describe different implications that readers see flowing out of the author's intended meaning. For those who hold to a reader-centered hermeneutic, however, this usually describes the meaning they choose to give to the text quite apart from and possibly even contradicting what the original author may have intended.

Reader-centered interpretation has contributed a number of insights into the study of texts. For one, it has emphasized the reader's contribution to the interpretive process. It has pointed out powerfully that readers do not approach texts with a mental tabula rasa. On the contrary, each reader brings to the reading of a text a preunderstanding consisting of their own interests and biases. This may bring distortion, a misreading of the text, and even a reading against the text, but it often brings passion and excitement to the investigation as well. In contrast to some author- and text-centered approaches, in which the reader appears to be a disinterested bystander, reader-centered interpretations are often practiced by people who have causes.

For many moderate reader-centered interpreters the presence of different and contradictory readings of a text is a serious concern. Unwilling to accept interpretative anarchy, they have sought certain restraints for the interpretation of texts. Thus they have raised the questions of how one can determine what kind of a reading is "richer," more "valuable" or "plausible." Perhaps the best known criterion is that of Stanley Fish, who appeals to the limitations that exist over readers by their "constraining community." Through the consensus of this community, various reader-oriented interpretations can be judged to be more valuable than others. Wolfgang Iser has suggested that the implied reader assumed by the text enables the present reader to arrive at the more plausible reading. In general, however, reader-centered interpretations oppose the pursuit of a single determinative meaning for a text and warn against any slavery to the text.

The Author (i.e., the Creator of the Game) as the Determiner of Meaning

In contrast to the preceding approach, which sees a text as a mirror by which readers seek to facilitate their own illumination and understanding, the more traditional approach to the study of the Bible, or any text, is to see it as a window through which the reader is able to see another world, the world of the author. Here the goal is to arrive at the creative intention of the original author contained in the words of the text. According to this view, the meaning of a text is what the author consciously intended to say by his text. Thus, the meaning of Romans is what Paul intended to communicate to his readers in Rome when he wrote his letter. This view argues that if Paul were alive and told us what he meant to convey in writing Romans, the issue would be settled. The text means what Paul just told us he meant. This is why in seeking to understand Romans it is more helpful to read Galatians, which Paul also wrote, than to read Ernest Hemingway's *For Whom the Bell Tolls* or Homer's *Iliad*. The reason for this is that the writer of Galatians thinks more like the writer of Romans than Hemingway does and uses the Greek language more like Paul in Romans than Homer does. Similarly, in seeking to understand the meaning of the Gospel of Luke, it is more helpful to read the book of Acts than the writings of Shakespeare or Charles Dickens.

This view argues that the Bible and other great works of literature are not to be treated as unique works of art possessing distinct rules supposedly appropriate only to art. On the contrary, they are to be interpreted in the same way that we normally interpret other forms of written or verbal communication. This is essentially the common sense approach to communication. All normal conversation assumes that the goal of interpretation is to understand the communicative intent of the speaker or writer contained in the words he or she has provided. We cannot even argue against this view without at the same time agreeing with it, for we must seek to understand what writers (or speakers) mean by their words in order to engage in conversation with them. For instance, in your attempt to understand this paragraph, are you not seeking to understand what I wanted to communicate by it?

This issue has become a major concern with respect to constitutional law. The basic issue at stake in recent Supreme Court nominations has not involved so much whether the nominees were liberal or conservative or their particular views on certain issues. It has involved a far more fundamental issue, for the issue of whether a nominee is liberal or conservative already assumes a particular understanding of who or what determines the meaning of the Constitution they will swear to uphold. It assumes that for a Supreme Court justice the determining factor in interpreting the Constitution will be their personal views (whether liberal, conservative, or other) on, for example, social, moral, and political issues, rather than what the framers of the Constitution meant by the words found in this precious document. An author-oriented approach seeks to decipher and understand what the framers meant by the words of the Constitution and judges all other laws and practices in light of this meaning. Thus, whether a Supreme Court justice is liberal or conservative is, at least theoretically, irrelevant, for the oath such a Supreme Court justice has taken is not "I swear to uphold the personal meaning that I choose to give to the words of the Constitution independently of what the original framers of the Constitution may have meant by it [i.e., reader-centered]." It is rather that, as the oath states, they swear to "administer justice without respect to persons . . . and . . . faithfully and impartially discharge and perform all duties incumbent upon me as [*title*] under the Constitution and laws of the United States. So help me God." The American people over the years have believed that in this oath the justices swear to uphold what the framers of the Constitution meant by the words contained in this foundational document of the nation—whether they agree with that meaning or not. This is an author-oriented hermeneutic. Thus the personal views of a Supreme Court justices should be essentially irrelevant. Far more important is whether they are good exegetes and can understand the meaning of the framers of the Constitution and whether they are committed to accepting their meaning as authoritative.

Recently, a Supreme Court justice stated that the desire to follow the original intent of the framers of the Constitution is "arrogance cloaked as humility" and that "it is arrogant to pretend that from our vantage we can gauge accurately the intent of the framers . . . to specific, contemporary questions." Far more important for him was the need to understand what the Constitution "mean[s] to us in our time," in light of the "overarching principle to changes of social circumstances." Yet the Federalist Papers are a rich source for understanding how the founders of the Constitution thought. If a justice cannot understand the intent of the framers of the Constitution, he or she is not demonstrating so much a lack of clarity in the Constitution itself as a disinterest in what the framers meant. Long ago James Madison argued that if "the sense in which the Constitution was accepted and ratified by the nation be not the guide in expounding it, there can be no security . . . for a faithful exercise of its power." And Thomas Jefferson argued, "Our peculiar security is in possession of a written Constitution. Let us not make it a blank paper by construction" (letter to William Cary Nicholas, September 7, 1803).

Ultimately, the question is whether the nation possesses in the Constitution a birthright offering protection and security, a document whose meaning is singular and rooted in history, or whether it possesses nine Supreme Court justices whose decisions are not necessarily rooted in what the original founders and citizens of the nation meant by it but rather in the wishes and desires (whether well-intentioned or not) and moral and social values of these nine Supreme Court justices, of whom only five need to agree. The infrequency with which Supreme Court justices say, "I do not agree with nor like what the Constitution says on this issue, but what it says is the law of the land and must be obeyed," as Chief Justice Oliver Wendell Holmes often did, suggests that all too often their interpretations of the Constitution may reflect the meaning that they choose to give to it. In a baseball game, should umpires call balls and strikes based on whose fans are the loudest? In empathy for a hitter in a slump, should an umpire narrow the strike zone? If the pitcher is in a slump, should he widen it? What if both are in a slump? Or should an umpire call balls and strikes according to what the authors of the baseball handbook meant? Similarly, should judges, and especially justices of the Supreme Court, make decisions according to what the authors of their handbook, the US Constitution, meant?

It has been argued that literature is to be interpreted differently from all other forms of written communication. In other written works, as well as in general communication, we are to seek the author's intended meaning, but when a work becomes literature, it is no longer to be treated in this manner. Literature does not fall under the rules of written communication but of art. As a result, the author's willed intention, what he or she meant when writing, is to be rejected or ignored, and meaning is to be determined either by the text itself or by the interpreter. Yet the idea that art is to be interpreted independently of the artist's intended purpose is belied by the fact that the artists, even those who create art for this purpose, usually not only place their names on their art but also give titles to assist viewers in understanding what they are seeking to portray. This indicates a desire to steer the viewers' interpretation of their work in a particular direction. A good example of whether art is to be interpreted according to the artist's intent or the viewers' can be seen in the renovation of the Sistine Chapel. These world-famous frescoes painted by Michelangelo in 1508–12 were in a serious state of disrepair when the Vatican began a multimillion dollar restoration process lasting twelve years. This involved some of the world's greatest restorers, art historians, conservationists, and cleaners. When the finished work was revealed to the public in 1992, there was an immediate outcry of horror. Numerous art critics protested that Michelangelo's great work had not been restored but radically changed. The new and brighter colors of the frescoes, they believed, no longer represented the original dark and more somber tones of Michelangelo's original work. The debate continues and will likely continue for many years. But does it matter if the readers (i.e., the interpreters/restorers/cleaners) of the text (the frescoes of the Sistine Chapel) changed the darker and more somber tones (the willed intention) of the author (the artist/Michelangelo) to lighter ones?

If one believes that the brighter tones of the restoration of the Sistine Chapel do not represent Michelangelo's original colors and that the restorers should not have changed them, it should be noted that we are then in fact attributing to the interpretation of art a more author-oriented interpretive approach than most reader-centered interpretations apply to the interpretation of literature. We would be condemning the unintentional (but mistaken) act of the restorers of the Sistine Chapel for changing the author's willed intention. Yet a reader-response approach discourages the pursuit of an author's consciously willed meaning, assuming that this is beyond our reach and of lesser importance. Instead, it favors rewriting (repainting?) the work of the author.

Yet who determines what is literature? There is no rule, law, or consensus that can be used to determine what is literature and what is not. (If, for example, we say that a work of literature is one that has been acknowledged over a period of time, then there is no such thing as late twentieth-century literature. If, on the other hand, we say that a work becomes literature when it has gained great popularity, then John Grisham is perhaps the greatest writer of English literature in the world!) The very fact that the classification of a work as "literature" is quite arbitrary indicates that interpreting such a work differently from all other written forms of communication is based on a debatable classification from the start.

Additionally, no one has yet been able to prove that "literature" should be interpreted by a different set of rules than other writings. There is no convincing answer to the question Why should this writing be interpreted differently from other writings? Surely the burden of proof lies with those who argue that a particular written work (arbitrarily called literature) should be interpreted differently from how all other works (nonliterature) should be interpreted. Yet such a proof has not been demonstrated.

To deny that the author determines the text's meaning also raises an ethical question. Such an approach appears to rob the author of his or her creation. To treat a text in complete isolation from its author's intended purpose is like stealing a patent from its inventor or a child from the parent who gave it birth. If we list a work under the name of its author, we are at least tacitly admitting that it belongs to its author. He or she owns this work. To take it and impose upon it our own meaning is a kind of plagiarism. There is a sense in which we have stolen what belongs to someone else. A text is like a will the author leaves for his or her heirs. For an executor to ignore what the author intended by his or her will is criminal and violates everyone's sense of fairness. For an interpreter to do the same with an author's literary work likewise seems unethical and disrespectful of the willed legacy of the author.

Objections to the Author as the Determiner of Meaning

Several objections have been raised against the view that the meaning of a text is determined by the author and that in seeking the meaning of a text we should try to understand what an author like Paul consciously willed to communicate by his text. One of the most famous of these objections is called the intentional fallacy. Made famous by William K. Wimsatt Jr. and Monroe Beardsley, it argues that it is impossible to climb into the mind of an author, such as Paul, and experience everything that was going through his mind when he wrote. A reader can never relive the experiences of an author. The innermost emotions, feelings, and motives Paul had as he wrote are simply not accessible to the reader, unless he chose to reveal them in his text. As a result of such considerations, it is argued that the meaning Paul willed is inaccessible.

But when reading a Pauline text, the primary goal is not to experience or reduplicate Paul's mental and emotional experiences when he wrote. It is not to get into the mind of Paul. Rather, the goal is to understand what Paul "meant," what he consciously sought to communicate to his readers by what he wrote. This objection confuses two different aspects of communication. The first involves the mental and emotional acts experienced by Paul in writing; the second involves what Paul wanted to communicate by his text. A careful distinction must be made between what Paul wished to convey in his text and his mental, emotional, and psychological experiences while writing. What Paul sought to convey by his text is in the public realm, for he purposely made this available to the reader in the text itself. On the other hand, the inner mental and emotional experiences of Paul, his mental acts, are private and not accessible to the reader unless Paul explicitly revealed them in his text. We do not have access to them (see the discussion of mental acts on pp. 47–49).

The intentional fallacy has also argued that an author at times may intend to convey a particular meaning but be incapable of adequately expressing this. The author may be linguistically incompetent. All of us at some time or other have realized that we may not have expressed adequately what we wished to communicate. Even very capable communicators can at times fail to express correctly or accurately what they meant. It is therefore quite possible that an author could fail to express in an understandable way what he or she sought to communicate. Authors could even mislead the reader by a poor or wrong choice of words. This objection, however, tends to be more hypothetical than real. Most writers, such as Paul, possess sufficient literary competence to express their thoughts adequately, so that their intended meaning is sufficiently perspicuous for the average reader to understand. In fact, those who write articles outlining this problem and drawing it to their readers' attention usually think that they are sufficiently competent to express their thoughts quite adequately. Otherwise, why would they write? Why then deny this competence to other writers?

For the Christian, an additional factor comes into play at this point. The belief that the Bible is inspired introduces a component of divine enabling into the situation. If in the writing of Scripture the authors were "carried along by the Holy Spirit" (2 Pet. 1:21), then it would appear that the authors of the Bible were given a divine competence in writing. This competence enabled them to express adequately the revelatory matters they sought to communicate (see chapter 3).

Another objection to the view that the reader should seek the authorial meaning of the text involves the psychological differences between the author and the reader. Since the psychological makeup of each individual is unique, it is argued that a reader cannot understand the thoughts, emotions, and feelings the author possessed when he or she wrote. The reader is simply too different psychologically. As a result, a reader can never understand what an author truly meant by his or her text.

A related objection is the view that a modern reader is not able to understand the meaning of an ancient author such as Paul. The radical difference between the situation of the present reader and that of the ancient author does not permit this. How can the modern-day reader, familiar with computers and megabytes, iPods, jet airplanes and international travel, television, heart transplants, human cloning, lunar landings, and nuclear power, understand an author writing thousands of years ago in a time of sandals, togas, and animal sacrifices? According to this view, the cultural distance between the author and the reader is so vast that it is impossible for a present-day reader to understand what an ancient writer meant. The author and reader live too many centuries, even millennia, apart.

These objections are well taken and should not be minimized. Not long ago I was watching a public television program in which an anthropologist related his experience of living for a number of years among a stone-age tribe of aborigines in New Guinea. He began by saying that it is impossible to understand how these people live and think because of the great cultural distance between them and us. Having said this, he then went on to explain to his viewers for the next fifty-five minutes how they live and think. The differences between the time and thought-world of an ancient author and the modern reader, as well as of developed and primitive cultures today in the example above, are very real. Far too often we tend to modernize ancient writers and assume that they thought exactly like twenty-first-century Americans. Consequently we misunderstand them. On the other hand, we can also overemphasize these differences. After all, we are not trying to understand the thoughts of worms or toads. The common humanity we share with the authors of the past and the fact that we both have been created in the image of God facilitate bridging this gap of time. The basic needs for food, clothing, warmth, security, love, forgiveness, and hope of life after death that the ancients had are still the basic needs we have today. Thus, while difficult, understanding an ancient author is not impossible. In a similar fashion the common possession of the image of God assists in overcoming the psychological differences between authors and readers as well.

One final objection that can be raised with regard to the interpretation of the Bible involves those texts in which an author appeals to a faith experience. One wonders how an atheist or unbeliever can "understand" the meaning of the psalmist when he states,

> Blessed is the one whose transgression is forgiven, whose sin is covered. Blessed is the man against whom the LORD counts no iniquity, and in whose spirit there is no deceit. For when I kept silent, my bones wasted away through my groaning all day long. For day and night your hand was heavy upon me. (Ps. 32:1–4a)

Whereas a believer may be able to understand the experience of faith that the author is talking about, how can an atheist? We must distinguish here between cognitively understanding what the psalmist meant by these words and actually experiencing the subject matter he is discussing. An atheist can acquire a correct mental grasp of what the psalmist is talking about concerning the joy of being forgiven by the LORD and the personal agony that preceded this. On the other hand, an atheist cannot understand the experience—that is, the subject matter—of which the psalmist is speaking. He or she may in fact seek to explain that subject matter via Freudian psychology because of not being able to accept the divine element involved in it. Yet an atheist can understand what the psalmist means by his discussion of this issue: the psalmist is speaking of the agony of guilt before a holy God and the joy of forgiveness. An atheist, however, cannot understand the truth of the experience of which the psalmist speaks (for further discussion, see pp. 60–66).

The Role of the Author

Texts do not simply appear in history. They do not evolve from trees or from papyrus plants or from animal skins. An ancient text did not come into existence because some animal lost its skin or some papyrus plant shed its bark and written symbols miraculously appeared on them. Someone, sometime, somewhere wanted to write these texts. Someone, sometime, somewhere willed to write something and have others read it. If this were not true, these texts would never have appeared. A thinking person consciously willed to write a text for the purpose of communicating something meaningful to a reader. Since this took place in past time, what the author willed to convey by the linguistic symbols used (whether the symbols were Hebrew, Aramaic, Greek, Latin, or Chinese is immaterial) possesses a meaning that can never change. What a biblical author willed by his text is anchored in history. It was composed in the past, and being part of the past, what the author willed to communicate back then can never change. What a text meant when it was written, it will always mean. It can no more change than any other event of the past can change, because its meaning is forever anchored in history.

Yet what an author such as Paul consciously willed to say in the past also has implications of which he was not necessarily aware, and those implications are part of the meaning of the text. For instance, when Paul wrote in Ephesians 5:18, "Do not get drunk with wine," he consciously meant that the Ephesian Christians should not become intoxicated with the mixture of water and wine (usually two or three parts water to one part wine) that they called "wine." This saying, however, has unforeseen implications that go beyond what Paul was consciously thinking. In this command Paul gives a principle or pattern of meaning that also has implications about not becoming drunk with beer, whiskey, rum, vodka, or champagne. If asked, Paul would state that although he was not consciously thinking of these other alcoholic beverages, he meant for Christians not to become drunk by using them as well. Certainly no one in Ephesus would have thought, "Paul in his letter forbids our becoming drunk with wine, but I guess it would not be wrong to become drunk with beer." Paul's text has implications that go beyond his own particular conscious meaning at the time. These implications do not conflict with his original meaning. On the contrary, they are included in and are part of the principle he sought to communicate. It is true that they go beyond his conscious thinking when he wrote, but they nevertheless are included in the principle Paul wished to communicate in this verse. Thus, what an author of Scripture stated in the past frequently has implications with respect to things he has not stated (beer) or that did not even exist at the time the text was written (whiskey, rum, vodka, champagne).

The purpose of biblical interpretation involves understanding not just the specific conscious meaning of the author but also the principle he sought to communicate. If Paul did in fact prohibit becoming drunk with whiskey and modern-day alcoholic beverages, does he also forbid in Ephesians 5:18 the unnecessary use and abuse of narcotics? Other statements of Scripture clearly forbid the abuse of the human body in such a manner. But does this specific passage forbid their use? If we understand Paul's command as involving a pattern of meaning, then the principle behind this command would be something like, "Do not take into your body substances like wine that cause you to lose control of your senses and natural inhibitions." If this is true, then the use of narcotics is likewise prohibited by this verse. If we were able to ask Paul about this latter instance, would he not reply, "I was not consciously thinking of narcotics when I wrote, but that's exactly the kind of thing I meant"? The fact is that every text has implications or inferences of which its author was unaware but that are nevertheless contained within the meaning willed in the text. Often the main concern of interpretation is to understand the legitimate, present-day implications of an author's meaning.

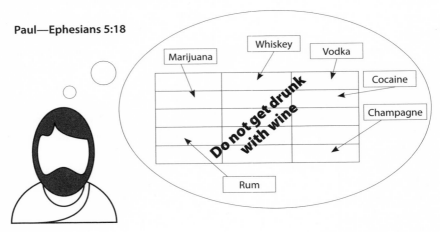

Is it possible that Jesus was thinking along these lines when he said, "You have heard that it was said to those of old, 'You shall not murder. . . .' But I say to you . . ." or "You have heard that it was said, 'You shall not commit adultery.' But I say to you . . ." (Matt. 5:21–48)? It appears that Jesus here describes what is involved in the higher righteousness referred to in Matthew 5:20 by bringing out the implications of several of Moses's commandments. Whether Moses was consciously thinking of these implications when he wrote these commandments is immaterial. They are legitimate implications of the principles he wished to convey by them.

At this point someone might raise the following objection: But isn't God the author of Scripture? This sounds devout and pious, but Scripture does not claim God as its immediate author. Paul's letters do not begin, "God, the Father, Son, and Holy Spirit, to the church at Rome, Galatia, and so on." No book of the Bible claims God as its immediate author. Christians believe that behind the books of the Bible stands the living God, who inspired his servants in the writing of these works. But the Scriptures were physically written by men, not God. As a result, to understand the meaning of the biblical texts we must understand what their human authors consciously willed to convey by their texts. The divine meaning of the biblical texts is the conscious, willed meaning of God's inspired prophets and apostles. (For the role of the Holy Spirit in writing and interpreting the Bible, see chapter 3.) To understand the divine meaning of Scripture, then, is to understand the conscious meaning of God's inspired servants who wrote it. It is in, not behind or beyond, the meaning the biblical author wished to share that we find the divine voice of God in the Scriptures. (The instances in which a biblical author may not have understood the meaning of what he wrote—perhaps in describing a vision or writing down a prophecy—are quite rare.)

The term "conscious" has been used on several occasions with respect to the willed meaning of the author. Although this may seem awkward, it is intentional. The reason for this is to avoid two errors. One involves those interpreters who argue that myths are present throughout the Bible. According to this view, the miracle stories found in Scripture are to be understood not as historical accounts but as fictional stories or myths. The meanings of these myths, it is argued, involve subconscious truths and values that were at play in the subconsciousness of the early church and the Christian writers. Thus the meanings of these myths are not found in what the authors of Scripture consciously sought to express in what they wrote. On the contrary, the meaning of these myths was totally unknown to them and is independent of any conscious meaning they wished to convey. The meaning lies in their subconsciousness, which gave rise to these myths. They, however, were completely unaware of this. Attributing the meaning of a text to the conscious willed meaning of the author avoids this error.

The term "subconsciousness" must not be confused with what is referred to as the "unconscious" meaning of the text. An unconscious meaning or implication is indeed unknown to the author, but it falls within his conscious, willed meaning. The subconscious meaning sought in this mythical approach, however, has nothing to do with what the author consciously wished to convey. In fact, it is usually quite opposed to the author's willed meaning, because the author believed in the facticity of the events he was reporting and wished to share the meaning of those events with his readers. (This will be discussed at greater length in chapter 2, under "Implications.")

The second error that reference to the conscious meaning of the author seeks to avoid involves the opposite claim that the Bible should be interpreted literally at all times. This too is an error, for it loses sight of the fact that the biblical writers used various literary forms in their works, such as proverbs, poetry, hyperbole, and parables. They never intended that their readers should interpret such passages literalistically. They intended for them to be interpreted according to the literary rules associated with such forms. What the Reformers meant when they argued that the Bible should be interpreted literally was not that it should be interpreted literalistically but that it should be interpreted according to the original, grammatical meaning of the authors. Thus, the conscious willed meaning of Luke when he quoted Jesus's words, "If anyone comes to me and does not hate his own father and mother and wife and children and brothers and sisters, yes, and even his own life, he cannot be my disciple" (Luke 14:26), is not that Jesus's followers must literally hate their parents. It means rather that to be a follower of Jesus one must place him before everything and everyone else. The meaning of Luke 14:26 is therefore what Luke consciously sought to communicate by these words and not the literal meaning of the words without regard to the literary form (exaggeration) in which it is found. Similarly, the parable of the rich man and Lazarus (Luke 16:19–31) is to be interpreted as a parable and thus according to the rules governing the interpretation of parables. It is not to be interpreted as a historical account. (Luke reveals this by the introduction "A certain man . . . ," which he uses throughout his Gospel to introduce parables [cf. Luke 10:30; 14:16; 15:11; 16:1; 19:12]. This is clearer in the Greek text than in most translations.)

The danger of unknowingly reading one's own biases and prejudices into texts is a continual problem in an author-oriented as well as a reader-response hermeneutic. In the former, however, this is done unwittingly. In the latter it is done knowingly and willingly. When discovered in an author-oriented approach, it results in embarrassment and, hopefully, recantation. In a reader-response approach, it is boldly acknowledged and defended. For those following an author-oriented approach to interpretation, the following advice applies: (1) Be aware of this danger. The greater your awareness of the danger of reading your biases and prejudices into the author's meaning, the less likely you will be to do this. (2) Be aware of your biases and prejudices. If you find them in your understanding of a text, double-check that they are really there. (3) Master the world of the author. Know his emphases, vocabulary, and grammar. Know how the intended audience would (or should) have understood what the author meant. The better we understand the world and mind of an author, the better our chance is of understanding that author's creation. (4) Pursue with single-mindedness the goal of understanding what the author consciously wanted to say by the text. Do not let your focus shift from the pursuit of the author's meaning to the various subject matters discussed in the text until after you have come to understand the meaning of the text.

There are several benefits to an author-centered hermeneutic. For one, it coincides with the basic aim of most communication. In such communication we seek to ascertain information such as, What does the person speaking seek to communicate by his or her words? What does the writer of this letter seek to convey to me by it? What does the president of this company seek to tell me by this report? What does the radiologist seek to inform me of by this report? Second, this approach respectfully recognizes the rightful ownership of the author over his or her text. Third, it provides the best, if not the only, objective basis for judging the validity of an interpretation. Attempts to judge the validity of an interpretation in a text-centered or reader-centered hermeneutic are far more subjective. In fact, many practitioners of text-centered and reader-centered interpretation deny that there is a single meaning latent in a text, and others, while not denying this possibility, deny that such a meaning is accessible to the reader.

The Role of the Text

A text consists of a collection of shareable symbols. These symbols can be various kinds of letters, punctuation marks, accents (Greek), vowel pointings (Hebrew), and so on. A biblical author could have used any symbols he wanted to write his text. In fact, he could have invented a language that only he, and those whom he chose, knew. Special codes are created for this purpose. A secret code is a text whose meaning the author wants to keep hidden from others and to be understandable only to those who know the code. In times of war such codes are especially important. When others break that code, as US naval intelligence did in World War II at the Battle of Midway, this may have disastrous consequences for those assuming that only their side (the Japanese navy) understands the code.

However, if authors wish to convey their meaning to as many people as possible, as the biblical authors usually did, they will choose a code (a collection of verbal symbols) that their readers will understand. This code will involve consonants, vowels, punctuation, words, idioms, and grammar that the author and readers share in common. In writing, an author therefore creates a text that possesses shareability. Shareability is the common understanding of a text's words and grammar possessed by both author and reader. Apart from this a reader cannot understand what an author wills to say. As a result, an author purposely submits himself or herself to the conventions and understanding of language possessed by the readers. Thus, if we understand how the author's intended audience would have understood the text (or should have understood it, for at times the original audience misunderstood what the biblical author meant, cf. 2 Thessalonians and 2 Corinthians), we, as readers today, can also understand the meaning of that same text. Because we can learn how a contemporary of Paul would have understood the Greek words (vocabulary), grammatical construction (syntax), and context of the text, we can also understand Paul's meaning, for the apostle purposely confined himself to the semantic range of possible meanings allowed by the language of his readers.

Because of the need for shareability, an author will abide by the rules of the language he is using and use the words and grammar in a way understandable to his audience. If he uses a word in an unfamiliar way, a good author will explain this in some way to his reader. (Cf. how the author of Hebrews explains in 5:14b what he means by "mature" in 5:14a; how John explains in 2:21 what Jesus meant by "temple" in 2:19–20, and in 7:39 what he meant by 7:37–38.) Within the semantic range of a language, however, words can possess a range of possible meanings. We can discover this range of meanings in a dictionary or lexicon. When an author uses his words, he is aware that they must possess one of these meanings, and when he uses these words, he provides a context that assists readers in narrowing down the possible meanings to just one: the specific meaning found in the statement itself (see below, pp. 52–54).

For example, the word *love* can mean a number of things. It can mean such things as profoundly tender, passionate affection; warm personal attachment; sexual intercourse; strong predilection or liking; a score of zero in tennis; and a salutation in a letter. In the sentence "He lost six to love," however, it can only mean a score of zero in tennis. The sentence "Let us love one another," on the other hand, is quite ambiguous. It can mean one thing when found in the context of Jesus's teachings and quite another thing in the context of a pornographic movie. Authors reveal the specific meanings of their words through the specific context that they provide for their verbal symbols—the sentence in which these symbols occur, the paragraph in which they are found, the chapter in which they are placed, the book in which they occur. Linguists sometimes use the French word *langue* to describe the semantic range of possible meanings that a word possesses within a language and the French word *parole* to describe the specific meaning of the word as it is used within the sentence.

Because of the shareability of the verbal symbols the biblical author uses, a text can communicate his meaning. A text, however, can communicate a great deal more. A text can open up to the reader vast areas of information. By reading a text, a reader may learn all sorts of historical, psychological, sociological, cultural, and geographical information. A text can be a storehouse of information or subject matter, and a reader can investigate a text to acquire such information. We can read the Gospel of Mark, for instance, to learn about the historical Jesus, about the shape and form of the Jesus traditions before they were written down, about the Markan literary style. We can study the book of Joshua to learn about the geography of Palestine or second-millennium military strategy. We can study the book of Psalms to learn about ancient Hebrew poetry or Israelite worship. All this is both possible and frequently worthwhile, but when this is done, we should always be aware of the fact that this does not involve the central focus and intention of the text. The meaning or communicative intention found in those texts is what the authors of Mark, Joshua, and the Psalms willed to teach their readers by recounting such history, traditions, geography, or poetic forms.

As a result, when investigating an account such as Jesus calming the sea (Mark 4:35–41), we must be careful to focus our attention on the meaning of the account rather than on its various subject matters. The purpose of this account is not to help the reader acquire information concerning the topography of the Sea of Galilee (a lake surrounded by a ring of high hills) and how this makes it prone to sudden, violent storms (4:37). Nor is it primarily about the lack of faith on the part of the disciples (4:40) or the shape and size of boats on the Sea of Galilee in the first century (4:37). On the contrary, Mark has revealed in the opening verse of his Gospel that this work is about "Jesus Christ, the Son of God." This account, therefore, should be interpreted in light of this. The meaning that Mark sought to convey is also clear from the account itself. The account reaches its culmination in the concluding statement, "Who then is this, that even the wind and the sea obey him?" (4:41). The meaning of this account, the communicative intention of Mark, is therefore that Jesus of Nazareth is the Christ, the Son of God. He is the Lord, and even nature itself is subject to his voice.

Perhaps the greatest need in reading the Bible is to distinguish the vast amount of information that we can learn from the biblical texts, especially those involving biblical narrative, from the meaning the authors sought to convey through this information. This will be dealt with at greater length in succeeding chapters (see esp. pp. 41–43).

The Role of the Reader

Using the verbal symbols of the author (i.e., the text), the reader seeks to understand what the author meant by these symbols. Knowing that the author intentionally used shareable symbols, the reader begins with the knowledge that the individual building blocks of the text, the words, fit within the semantic range of possibilities that the language of the original readers permitted. This means that when reading the works of Shakespeare, we must use a seventeenth-century English dictionary rather than a twenty-first-century English one. This also means that when reading the Greek NT, we must use a Koine Greek lexicon rather than a classical Greek one. Seeing how the words are used in phrases and sentences, how the sentences are used within paragraphs, how paragraphs are used in chapters, and how chapters are used in the work, the reader seeks to understand the author's communicative intent in writing this work. This process is called the hermeneutical circle. This expression refers to the fact that the whole text helps the reader understand each individual word or part of the text; in turn, the individual words and parts help us understand the meaning of the text as a whole. This sounds more confusing than it really is, for all of this goes on simultaneously in the mind of the interpreter. The mind is able to switch back and forth from the part to the whole without great difficulty. It is like the task that is completed by a parallel computer, where many individual processors continuously share and communicate information in order to complete a shared task. Similarly, the mind switches back and forth from the meaning of the individual words and the general understanding of the whole text until it comes to a successful resolution of the text's meaning.

Because the reader is interested in what a biblical author meant by his text, he or she is interested in his other writings as well, for these are especially helpful in providing clues to the specific meaning of the words and phrases in the text. Other works written by people of similar conviction and language are also helpful, especially if they were written at the same time. The writings of people who had different convictions but lived at the same time may also be helpful, but less so, in revealing the rules of the language under which the author worked. As a result, to understand what Paul means in a particular verse in Romans, we should look at the context he provides for us, beginning with the immediate context and proceeding to the more distant. Thus we seek help from what Paul says in the verses surrounding that text, in the neighboring chapters, in the rest of Romans, then in Galatians (which is the Pauline writing most like Romans), then in 1 and 2 Corinthians, and then in the other Pauline writings. After having worked through the Pauline materials, the reader can also look elsewhere. Probably the order of importance after the Pauline materials would be the rest of the NT, the OT, the intertestamental literature, the rabbinic literature, the early church fathers, and then contemporary Greek writers.

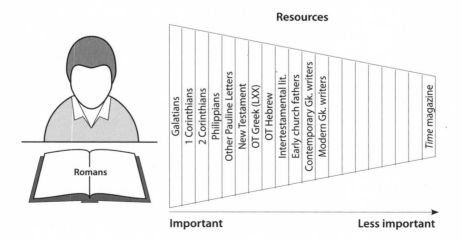

This order is determined by which of the other sources best reflects the way Paul thought. In a similar way, a verse in the Gospel of Luke is best interpreted by the verses surrounding it, the paragraphs and chapters surrounding that verse, the rest of the Gospel of Luke, and then the book of Acts. Acts reveals how Luke thought better than Matthew, Mark, or John does, but other Gospels are more useful than the Epistles, which in turn are more useful than Isaiah, which in turn is more useful than Josephus (a Jewish historian of the first century), and so on.

It is also important for the reader to understand the particular literary form being used by the author, for different forms of literature are governed by different rules. If the author has expressed his willed meaning in the form of a proverb, we must interpret that proverb by the rules governing this literary form. If he has used a parable, we must interpret the parable in light of the rules associated with parables. The careful argumentation of Paul in Romans must be interpreted differently from the poetic form in which the psalmist has expressed his meaning. What is common in the interpretation of every literary form, however, is that in each instance we are seeking to understand the meaning the author willed. Furthermore, since he sought to share that meaning with his readers, we can assume that he was abiding by the common rules associated with the particular literary form he was using. The second part of this book (chapters 5–14) addresses such rules for interpreting the various literary genres found in the Bible.

Once we know the meaning of the author, we will need to seek out those implications of that meaning that are especially relevant (see pp. 33–38). If the principle Paul willed when he wrote Ephesians 5:18 is "Do not take into your body substances like wine that cause you to lose control of your senses and natural inhibitions," what implications arising out of this principle are most relevant for the reader? Paul's text has far-reaching unforeseen implications of which he was not aware. Although the meaning of a text never changes because it is locked in past history, the recognition of its various implications is always growing. This is why some people claim that the Scriptures have different meanings. Yet a text does not have different meanings, for an author like Paul willed a single specific pattern of meaning when he wrote. (The instances in which an author willed a double-meaning pun are quite rare.) A text, however, has different *implications* for different readers. For example, the words of Jesus, "And you will be my witnesses in Jerusalem and in all Judea and Samaria, and to the end of the earth" (Acts 1:8), have a single meaning. Luke sought to share with his reader that Jesus wanted the message of the gospel to be spread throughout the entire world. Yet the relevant implications will no doubt vary for each reader. For me, it has involved teaching in a theological seminary; for my daughter and son-in-law, it involves going overseas to a foreign land to share the good news with an unreached people; for my sons and their wives, it involves working in their local church and sharing the good news with neighbors and friends. For others, it may involve working in a rural church or in the inner city or witnessing about Christ at work. For a non-Christian, it no doubt would involve a rejection of the meaning. There is one meaning to a text, that meaning consciously willed by the author, but the particular way that meaning affects the readers—its specific implications—may be quite different.

Questions

1. Is there such a thing as "the meaning" of a text? If so, where is this meaning to be found? Who or what determines it?
2. How can we determine what constitutes a good translation of the Bible? Does this have any bearing on what is discussed in this chapter?
3. Why do people learn Greek and Hebrew (and Aramaic) in order to study the Bible? What does this say about where a text's meaning is to be found?
4. In the desire to communicate their message, how do writers restrict themselves? How does this restriction aid us in interpreting the Bible?

2

Defining the Rules

A Vocabulary for Interpretation

One of the major problems encountered in interpreting and discussing written texts is the use of imprecise terminology. If in the process of interpretation terms are used inaccurately, confusion will result. This is even more so if the same term is used in different or contradictory ways. Terminological precision leads to clarity; terminological imprecision leads to fog. One of the values of a precise vocabulary is that it helps us obtain a clearer picture of what is involved in the process of interpretation. Such a vocabulary also enables us to understand better what others are saying when they use less-precise terminology. This is because we can retranslate their terminology into our clearer terminological framework.

This works well in other areas too. For example, in the study of theology it is very helpful to master a theological system such as Calvinism, even if one is not a Calvinist. If we know this theological system well, we can then compare other theological views to this known system. As a result, we will understand the new theological views better when we compare them to a known theological system. Similarly, it is easier to understand how other governments function if we possess a clear understanding of how our own government functions. This will permit us to make comparisons such as "Their X functions like our House of Representatives, but they do not have a Senate." In this chapter a precise hermeneutical vocabulary will be presented in order to help us understand better what is involved in the process of interpretation. This will prove useful even if one does not agree with some of the definitions given, for the consistent use of a common, well-defined vocabulary will assist in bringing clarity.

Meaning

> *The meaning of a text is the principle that an author consciously willed to convey by the words (shareable symbols) used.*

Some other terms that are used to describe this "principle" are "paradigm," "type," "template," "pattern of meaning," and "communicative intention." It should be noted that all three components of communication are present in our definition: The *author* is represented in the consciously willed intention contained in the principle communicated by the text. The *text* is represented by the words or symbols the author used to express this principle. The *reader* is represented by the shareable or communicative nature of those words or symbols. This is because the author wrote his text with his reader(s) in mind and purposely submitted himself to the semantic range of possible meanings of the words that he shared with his reader.

The meaning of a text depends on the specific, conscious intention that the author willed in the past when the text was written (i.e., on his communicative intent when he wrote). It is the biblical author who is the determiner of the text's meaning. Since this principle originated in the past when the text was written, the meaning of a text can never change. It is determinate, for it is locked in history. It can no more change than any other historical event of the past can change. Even the author cannot change the meaning of the text, because he cannot change the past. In the first book I wrote I incorrectly made the statement that the best English translation for Jesus's use of the word *abba* for God was a baby's cry of "Daddy." Whereas I could recant of this statement, this would not alter the fact that this statement in the book still meant and would always mean what I willed it to mean when the text was written. Fortunately, in a revised edition I could correct the original statement. I could not make the old text mean something different now. I could, however, point out in the revised edition that both children and adults used this intimate term of affection to address their father and that the privilege of Christians addressing God as *abba* in prayer indicated the unique relationship that Jesus's followers have with God. The fact that such recantations produce new revisions or editions is tacit testimony to the fact that the willed meaning of old texts cannot change. If an author wishes to argue for a different meaning, he must produce a revision or new edition to express this new willed meaning.

In this sense, the US Constitution is not a "growing" document, as is often stated. Everything possible is done to keep it from growing, that is, from becoming contaminated with mildew and mold. The Constitution does not take on new and different meanings simply with time, independent of its authors' intended meaning. Our definition of meaning locks a text's meaning to its creation in the past and does not allow this possibility. What the Constitution meant when it was written can only change by the addition of amendments, which produce a revised edition now containing the desired change.

That said, it should also be noted that what the biblical authors and the framers of the Constitution meant has implications of which they were not aware. Every law has unforeseen implications of which the original lawmakers were unaware. The task of the courts is to determine which alleged implications of these laws are legitimate and which are not. The framers of the Constitution were not consciously aware of all the legitimate implications flowing out of the various principles contained in this great work. These implications are nevertheless part of the meaning of this great text, and the role of the Supreme Court is to discover such implications. In the same manner, the authors of Scripture, led by the Holy Spirit, willed patterns of meaning containing implications that go beyond the specific meaning they were thinking of when they wrote.

Recent speech-act theory has emphasized that the act of communication not only involves the passing on of information (theological or historical material) but is often action-motivated and seeks to "do" something by bringing about a desired action (with a request, teaching, or command). This communicative act is seen as consisting of three parts: the locutionary act (the text), the illocutionary act (the meaning or creative intent of the author), and the perlocutionary act (the response or action of the reader). These correspond to the roles of the text, author, and reader in communication. Unfortunately, some advocates of speech-act theory seem to attribute to an inanimate object—the words and symbols of the text—the ability to "act" and "do" something. We noted above (see pp. 8–9) that, whereas a text can convey meaning, this meaning comes not from the inanimate paper and ink making up the text but from the author who willed the meaning conveyed by the text. It is not inanimate words and symbols that set into motion the desired act. Rather, it is the meaning given to the symbols by the author, which often has both a cognitive and volitional element, and the conviction and divine enabling of the Holy Spirit that "do" this (see chapter 3).

Implications

Implications are those inferences in a text of which an author may or may not have been aware but that nevertheless legitimately fall within the principle he willed.

The specific meaning that an author like Paul willed when he wrote is often only the tip of the iceberg of his meaning. Far more of his willed principle may lie below the surface of his specific meaning than above. Most visible, of course, is the specific meaning Paul consciously sought to convey. Yet this specific meaning usually involves a principle or pattern of meaning that contains numerous implications, and Paul was probably not aware of the majority of them. Paul's specific meaning lies within his principle, but that specific meaning is only part of all the implications contained in that principle. For instance, in our earlier discussion of the principle willed in Ephesians 5:18 (see pp. 19–20), we noted that Paul prohibited drunkenness that results from drinking any alcoholic beverage, not just wine. The command not to be drunk with wine is part of that principle, of course, but that principle also involves all later alcoholic beverages, as well as drugs used for nonmedical purposes. Although Paul was thinking primarily of drinking wine, he also meant by implication becoming drunk by consuming alcoholic beverages or by taking drugs intravenously, even though he had no idea of how such substances could enter the body in this manner.

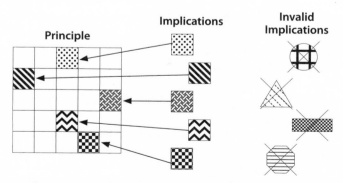

Note: The principle is represented by a square, and the implications are therefore subsquares that fit the "squareness" of the principle.

Other terms sometimes used to describe such implications are "infer-ences," "nuances," "subtypes," "consequences," "deductions," "emana-tions," and "submeanings." (The term "unconscious meaning" is also used by some as a synonym, although, if we want to be precise, it is somewhat less inclusive than the term "implication." When writing, an author may be consciously aware of various implications of his specific meaning even though he does not state them.) The pursuit of a text's implications involves the process of contextualization, in which readers seek to derive present-day inferences from the past willed meaning contained in a text. Thus, Paul was no doubt aware that Ephesians 5:18 also forbade being drunk from beer, because this was an existing alcoholic beverage. However, he was not aware of distilled alcoholic beverages such as whiskey, vodka, rum, sake, and gin. These were unknown to the ancient world and became available only with the technology of the seventeenth and eighteenth centuries. Nevertheless, they also are included within the willed meaning of Paul.

This is evident if we imagine the following scenario. Let us assume that Paul visited the church in Ephesus after sending his letter. Upon discovering drunkenness among its members, he then asked, "Did you not read in my letter not to be drunk with wine?" If one of the members replied, "Paul, we are not drunk with wine. Ever since you wrote your letter we have switched to beer," would Paul have responded, "Well that's all right, so long as it was not wine"? Of course not. He would have said something like, "You know that I meant not to be drunk with beer also." Or imagine that Paul visited a church today and found drunkenness among its members. If he asked, "Did you not read in my letter not to be drunk with wine?" and someone replied, "We are not drunk from wine but from whiskey," would he not, after learning what whiskey is, respond, "Well, if I said not to be drunk from wine, I certainly also meant not to be drunk from whiskey as well"?

The goal of biblical interpretation is to understand not just the spe-cific meaning of the authors of Scripture but also, by understanding their willed principle, to understand the various implications. These implica-tions are not determined by the interpreter, however. On the contrary, they are determined by the author. By his willed principle the biblical author has delineated what the legitimate implications of his meaning are. The interpreter of Scripture ascertains or discovers these implications, but it is the author alone who has determined them. The interpreter seeks to dis-cover the various implications of an author's meaning much like a miner digs into a mountain to discover gold. Even as a miner does not create the gold in the mountain, so the interpreter does not create the implications in a text's meaning. Both miner and interpreter seek to discover what is already there. The miner seeks to discover the gold God created that lies in the mountain. Similarly, the interpreter seeks to discover the implications the biblical author created that lie in his willed principle. What both miner and interpreter seek lies in a past event of creation. Just as God created the gold in the past, so the author created the implications of his meaning in the past.

The legitimate implications of a statement such as "Oak trees are wonderful" are determined by the author who spoke/wrote it and the context he or she provided. Thus, if it was spoken by a child climbing a tree, a contractor building a house, an artist painting a landscape, a civil engineer in charge of flood control, or a biologist teaching photosynthesis, the implications will be quite different. For a child, an implication such as "Oak trees are wonderful for climbing because of their many branches" would be legitimate, whereas the strength and beauty of oak trees for housing construction, the beautiful proportions of a certain oak tree, the value of oak trees for preventing erosion and for breaking the momentum of a flooded river, or the ability of an oak tree to convert nutrients through photosynthesis would not be. On the other hand, these other implications may be legitimate for a contractor, an artist, an engineer, or a biologist. Which of these possible implications flow justifiably from the statement "Oak trees are wonderful" will be determined not by the hearer but rather by the speaker whose willed meaning is accessible from the context he or she provides.

An example of how this works is found in Galatians 5:2. There Paul states, "Look: I, Paul, say to you that if you accept circumcision, Christ will be of no advantage to you." The specific meaning that Paul had in mind is clear. He wanted the Galatian Christians to know that, if they as Gentiles submitted to being circumcised under pressure from the Judaizers, they would be renouncing their faith. They would no longer be trusting God's grace in Christ alone but would instead be seeking to establish a relationship with God that ultimately depended on their own actions or works (i.e., on their having submitted to circumcision). Paul wanted his readers to know that they could not mix a faith that rests on God's grace alone with a righteousness based on one's works. For the Gentiles in Galatia to accept circumcision was therefore the equivalent of renouncing Christ.

Yet such a specific teaching is of little value today, unless Paul willed a principle by this teaching that has implications of which he may not have been aware. Circumcision is not an issue within the Christian church today. Yet throughout the history of the church, the implications of this verse have proved most useful. Luther saw in this text a very relevant implication for his day. He saw buying indulgences and doing penance as a sixteenth-century attempt to establish a relationship with God that depended on one's works. Such actions were contrary to the biblical teaching that salvation is based purely on the grace of God and is mediated by faith alone. Certainly Paul was not thinking of the sixteenth-century abuse of indulgences or works of penance when he wrote Galatians, but Luther was correct in seeing these as implications contained in Galatians 5:2.

I remember very clearly a situation when the implications of this text possessed great relevance for me personally. Confronted by some religious zealots who warned me that to be saved I needed to worship on a particular day of the week, I responded, "My only hope of salvation is that when I stand before God, he will remember that Jesus died for me and that because of his atoning death, he will forgive me. Are you saying that if I do not worship on the day of the week you worship on, God will not accept me?" Their reply was, "If you do not worship on the day of the week we worship on due to ignorance, God may forgive you." To this I replied, "But I am not doing this out of ignorance. I worship on the first day of the week because this is what the early church did." "Then," they responded, "you are damned!" The implications of this Pauline text were very relevant for me. We cannot mix grace/faith with works of law. It is by grace alone, not grace plus circumcision, not grace plus indulgences, not grace plus penance, not grace plus Sabbath worship, that we are saved.

In a similar way, the commands not to kill and not to commit adultery in Exodus 20:13–14 have implications that go beyond the conscious meaning of the biblical author. Jesus understood this when he said that anger violated the meaning of the command not to kill and that looking at a woman lustfully violated the meaning of the command not to commit adultery. In Matthew 5:21–48 ("You have heard that it was said. . . . But I say . . ."), Jesus was not contradicting the meaning of Moses's words in Exodus (cf. Matt. 5:17–20). Rather he was bringing out various implications contained within the willed principle of Moses's meaning. Similarly, the commandment "eye for eye, tooth for tooth" found in Exodus 21:23–25 has such implications as not cutting off the hand of a person for stealing a loaf of bread and not executing a person for killing a deer in the king's forest preserve. This is because the intended principle was that a punishment must fit the crime. Cutting off a hand for stealing a loaf of bread or executing a person for killing a deer on the king's preserve are much too excessive and go far, far beyond a fitting penalty.

It is evident that the meaning of a text goes beyond the specific conscious meaning of its author. It also includes all the implications or inferences contained in the principle he is teaching, whether he was aware of them or not. It includes both the specific meaning that the author consciously willed to convey by the shareable symbols he used, as well as all the implications that fit within his principle and communicative intent. This is why the implications of biblical writers can go far beyond their conscious thinking at the time. These implications, however, are controlled and bounded by the writer's willed meaning. If we visualize Paul's principle in Galatians 5:2 as a square, then only those possible submeanings that are also square in nature are legitimate.

Circular submeanings are not legitimate, nor are triangular submeanings. Similarly, if the principle willed in Ephesians 5:18 is visualized as rectangular in nature, then only those possible submeanings that are rectangular in nature are valid implications. It is necessary, therefore, to have a clear and carefully defined understanding of the willed principle of the author in order to delimit the true implications of the text. Thus, whereas alcoholic and narcotic substances fit within the meaning of Ephesians 5:18 in that they cause people to become intoxicated and lose control over their behavior, gluttony does not. There are texts of Scripture that speak about gluttony, but the principle willed by Paul in Ephesians 5:18 does not.

A similar relationship with respect to meaning and implication in propositions can be found in the relationship of past events in history (types) to later events in history (antitypes). For example, certain historical connections can be seen between some events, persons, and things in the OT and similar events, persons, and things in the NT. Such typological interpretations assume the unity of the Bible and a correspondence between OT and NT events based on the conviction that an unchangeable God is working out his divine purpose and will consistently within history. It also assumes that NT writers understood that certain OT events had analogous implications for the future (cf. Rom. 5:14; 1 Cor. 10:6 ["examples" = *typoi*]; 1 Pet. 3:21 ["which correspond to this" = *antitypon*]). For example, the good qualities and characteristics of a godly king in the OT would of necessity be expected to foreshadow the moral and spiritual qualities of the coming messiah.

Significance

Significance refers to how a reader responds to the meaning of a text.

Whereas implications involve unexpressed inferences of the author's willed meaning and are cognitively ascertained by readers, significance involves the reader's willed response to the author's meaning ("perlocution" in speech-act theory) and is volitional in nature. It should come after, not before, the understanding of an author's meaning. For Christians there is a close relationship between the significance and the implications of a biblical text. The reason is that Christians attribute positive significance to the implications of such texts. But a non-Christian might agree that X and Y are legitimate implications of a biblical text and simply say, "I don't believe this!" or "So what! I don't care!" Significance involves a person's attitude toward the meaning of a text and its implications. It is a reader's critique of the willed meaning of the author. Another way of saying this is that significance is the effect that a text's meaning has on a reader. It may be positive, but it may also be negative. Because Christians believe that the Bible is the Word of God, a legitimate implication of the meaning of a biblical text usually receives a positive response (significance).

Frequently, people make a distinction between what a text meant and what a text means. (The expressions "past meaning" and "present meaningfulness" are also used.) The former refers to what the biblical author meant when he wrote the text, his willed principle. The latter, on the other hand, refers to the significance of the text for the present-day reader. Such terminology, although popular, is confusing, because the verb *mean* is being used in two quite different ways. What a text "meant" refers to the meaning willed by the author and its implications. It is cognitive and controlled by the author. What it "means" refers to the reader and involves his or her will and volitional response. Thus the same verb is used to describe two different people (author vs. reader) and two different areas (cognition vs. volition). For the sake of greater clarity, it is wiser to refer to the "meaning" of the text and the "significance" of the text. Meaning belongs to the author; significance belongs to the reader. Thus, the expression "what a text meant" corresponds to what is defined as "meaning" in this chapter. The expression "what a text means (to me) . . ." will not be used but will be replaced by "The *significance* of this text (for me) is . . ." This will also avoid the erroneous suggestion, created by the use of "meant" and "means," that the meaning of the text has changed over time.

It has been pointed out that there is only one meaning of a text, that of the author. Because it is located in the past, that meaning is unchangeable. Significance, however, is multifaceted. The significance of a text for one person may be quite different from its significance for another person. The significance of the Great Commission in Matthew 28:19–20 for one person may involve obeying one of its implications by becoming a pastor; for another it may involve obeying one of its implications by becoming a missionary; and for still another it may involve obeying one of its implications by sharing the good news of the gospel with one's neighbors. All these are positive responses to legitimate implications of the willed principle found in that commission, and they are all different. On the other hand, for some the meaning of this passage will be ignored or rejected. The meaning of the Great Commission, while singular, has numerous implications and invites many responses (i.e., significances).

The significance of a text's meaning must be distinguished from the implications of the text's meaning. Significance is something that readers do as they respond to the meaning of the text. The reader is the master of significance, because he or she can say yes or no. Implications, however, lie outside the domain of the interpreter. They are determined by the author. They are only discovered or learned by the reader. Once discovered, however, the reader becomes master of the situation, for the reader can say yes or no to these implications. He or she can obey or reject them. We therefore should not confuse the implications of the author's willed

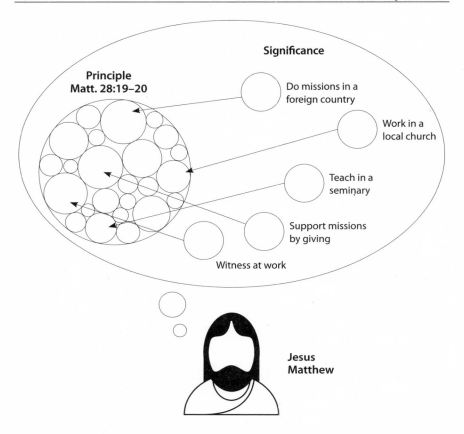

meaning with the interpreter's response to those implications. Significance refers to the response of the interpreter and involves the will. It does not refer to the reader's mental perception of the various implications of the author's willed meaning, that is, the reader's understanding (see below).

The term "application" is sometimes used to describe significance. Application, however, is not a single element in the interpretative process but a compound of two distinct elements: implication (the cognitive understanding of the author's meaning and its inferences) and significance (the volitional response of the reader). It intermixes the roles of the author and the reader. Unfortunately, when people speak of "the application of this text for me," they are sometimes referring to what we have here defined as significance and at other times to what we have defined as implication. We shall therefore avoid using the term "application" because of its ambiguity and refer instead to "implication" and "significance," which are less ambiguous and more specific.

Subject Matter

> *Subject matter refers to the content, or "stuff," talked about in a text, without regard to how it is used by the author to convey meaning.*

The subject matter of a text involves the different kinds of information found in the text. Some examples of subject matter are as follows:

Genesis 1–3: The creation of the world, ancient traditions about creation, the literary and oral sources used by the author (note the discussion of J, E, D, P with respect to the Pentateuch), authorship, and date.

Ezra: The history of the Jews in the fifth century BC, the political situation of the Middle East in that century, the geography or archaeology of Jerusalem, authorship, and date.

Psalms: Hebrew poetry, ancient Jewish liturgical formulas, Jewish worship, the classification of psalm forms, authorship, and date.

Proverbs: Ancient Near Eastern Wisdom literature, the literary genre of proverbs, authorship, and date.

Jeremiah: The history of Judah in the sixth century BC, the rise of the Babylonian Empire, the life of Jeremiah, the literary genre of prophecy, how prophetic traditions were circulated, authorship, and date.

Gospels: The life of Jesus, the teachings of Jesus, the literary relationship of the Gospels (note the discussion of Mark, Q, L, M), the classification of the Gospel pericopes according to their form, the history of the oral traditions, authorship, and date.

Galatians: Greek epistolary form, the ancient genre of rhetoric, the geographical location of Galatia, the chronology of Paul's life, the relationship between Galatians 2:1–10 and Acts 15:1–35; the problem in Galatia, authorship, and date.

As can be seen from the above, a text can be investigated for numerous reasons. The ones listed are only a sample of some of the legitimate and interesting areas of study that are possible, but none of these deal with the author's communicative intent in sharing this information with his readers. A clear distinction must be maintained between the subject matter found in the text and the principle or meaning that the author seeks to convey through this subject matter. At times this subject matter may be descriptive without being prescriptive (cf. John 13:1–20; 1 Cor. 16:20b).

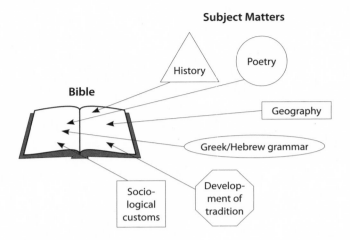

An example may be helpful. In Mark 2:1–12 we find the account of the healing of the paralytic. This account contains a vast amount of subject matter that can be investigated. Some of this includes the historical questions of when in the life of Jesus this event occurred or what exactly took place (the quest for the historical Jesus), the architectural design and construction of first-century homes in Galilee, medical questions as to the kind and causes of paralysis in first-century Galilee, the relationship of illness and sin in Jewish theology, the form-critical classification of this account, and the history of this account during the oral period of tradition. None of these, however, deal specifically with the meaning of this text.

The meaning of Mark 2:1–12 is what the evangelist sought to teach by his use of this subject matter. What he sought to teach his readers by this passage is clear from Mark 1:1. The Gospel according to Mark is about the "gospel of Jesus Christ, the Son of God." In the text itself this emphasis is seen in several places: in the questions "Why does this man speak like that? . . . Who can forgive sins but God alone?" (2:7); in Jesus's statement that the Son of Man has authority to forgive sins (2:10); in the performance of a miracle to demonstrate this authority; and in the conclusion, "We never saw anything like this!" (2:12). Here lies the meaning of this passage. Mark wants to show his readers by this text that Jesus is the Christ, the Son of God. There has never been anyone like him, for only he and God have divine authority to forgive sins.

The meaning of this text involves the great christological truth that Jesus is the Son of God and possesses the divine authority to forgive sins. One legitimate implication is that Jesus is an all-sufficient Savior. Another is that Jesus has authority to forgive me of my sins. Still another is that

Jesus is able, if he so wills, to heal us. On the other hand, the meaning of the text is not about the building construction materials of Galilean houses in the first century or whether we should classify this account as a miracle story or as a pronouncement story. The meaning willed by Mark concerns Jesus Christ, the Son of God, who has divine authority to heal and to forgive sins.

Frequently, with respect to narrative texts scholars make a distinction between the "text" and the "event." In this terminology, text is related to event as meaning is related to subject matter. When we are investigating the text, we are seeking to ascertain the communicative intention that the author willed to convey by his record of this event. When we investigate the event, we are investigating the historical subject matter referred to in the text. In studying the Gospels, the investigation of the event involves learning what actually happened in the life of Jesus. When investigating the text, we are investigating what the evangelist is seeking to teach by recounting this event in the life of Jesus. In other words, the "text" is the meaning the author attributes to the "event" (subject matter).

Whereas the significance of a text (Significance^{Text}) involves the reader's response to the authorial meaning of the text, a reader can also at times find significance in the subject matter (Significance^{SM}) contained within a text, such as in the teachings of the historical Jesus. Unless specified, the word *significance* in this book will always refer to the significance of a text. The same is also true with respect to implications contained within the subject matter of the text (Implication^{SM}). In this book *implication* will always refer to the implication of a text (Implication^{Text}) and not of its subject matter, unless specified.

Understanding

Understanding refers to the correct mental grasp of an author's meaning by the reader.

The understanding of a text involves the correct mental perception of a text's meaning by the reader. Another way of saying this is that understanding involves the reader's correct, cognitive grasp of the principle or communicative intent of the author. Since the author willed a single meaning, each individual who understands this meaning will have the same mental grasp of the author's principle. Some understandings may be more complete than others because of a greater perception of the various

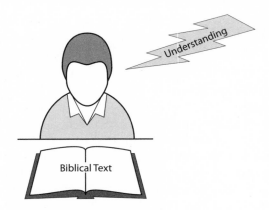

implications and subject matters involved, but if an understanding is to be correct, it must have the same mental grasp of the author's meaning as any other understanding. Thus, although one person's understanding of the meaning may be greater or more exhaustive than another's, every correct mental grasp of the author's meaning, or understanding, will be the same.

If we visualize the author's willed principle as a circle, then every (correct) understanding grasps that the author willed a circle. Each person's understanding is the same—the author willed a circle. However, what is involved in that circle (all its implications) is not understood equally. Also, an individual's expression of that understanding (his or her interpretation) will vary. One person may express the meaning as a circle; another as a perfect roundness; another as a 360-degree curve; another as a two-dimensional, round sphere; still another as a closed plane curve of which all points are at an equal distance from the center; and so on. Regardless of how this understanding may be expressed, every understanding involves a correct mental grasp of the meaning of the text.

Because understanding is defined as a "correct" mental grasp of meaning, there cannot be an "incorrect" understanding. This would be a contradiction of terms. To be precise we shall speak of an incorrect mental grasp of meaning as a misunderstanding. This will enable us to use the term "understanding" without qualification.

Interpretation

> *Interpretation refers to the verbal or written expression of a reader's understanding of an author's meaning.*

Interpretation is the verbal expression of one's cognitive understanding of an author's meaning. Whereas there is a single meaning of a text and a single correct understanding of that meaning, there are an almost infinite number of ways of expressing this understanding because there are many ways of explaining the same perception of meaning. We can use different kinds of examples to express our understanding. In his ministry Jesus taught that the kingdom of God had come, but he used several different parables to teach this. We can also rephrase and use different vocabulary to express the same thought or understanding. The multiplicity of correct interpretations is demonstrated whenever we say something like, "Another way of saying this is . . ." or "Another example that will illustrate this is . . ." or "Perhaps a better way of stating this is . . ." The purpose of exegesis is to understand (to obtain a correct mental grasp of) the principle willed by an author (the specific meaning and its implications) and interpret (express) this effectively for others.

Some interpreters argue that there is no such thing as a perfect synonym or a perfectly synonymous expression. Yet an author can consciously will to use one term to mean the same thing as another term, because within the norms of language these synonyms can refer to the same thing. I have often used a thesaurus to find a synonym to express the same thing in order to avoid overusing a certain word. Within the semantic range of a language (see below) a word possesses a range of possible meanings. For the sake of analogy, let us conceive of the possible semantic range of a term as consisting of a circle. Two closely related words, such as *observe* and *see*, have their own circle of meanings, but these two circles overlap. In this overlapping area, *observe* and *see* can mean the same thing. Thus, an author can choose to select the same possible meaning for *observe* as for *see*. He or she may mean the exact same thing by "I observed the accident" as "I saw the accident." Within this very chapter, I have done this; I have used *inference, nuance, deduction, submeaning, consequence, subtype,* and so on in order to avoid overusing the word *implication*. In this book, these terms are functioning as synonyms.

Although understanding and interpretation are closely related, they are quite different. Understanding precedes interpretation. Understanding involves thinking and is mental, whereas interpretation is verbal. That they can be separated is witnessed to by those occasions when we understand something quite well but cannot find the words to express that understanding. For example, I understand what German-speaking people mean by the word *gemütlich* but find it difficult to express this verbally. It usually expresses a feeling of well-being one might associate with relaxing at home, sitting on the patio with old friends on a summer evening, or enjoying coffee and fresh baked goods for breakfast.

Interpretation should not be confused with translation. The latter is an attempt to express the author's conscious meaning using the verbal symbols of another language. Because both interpretation and translation must be preceded by understanding and involve the verbal expression of that understanding, the boundary between them is somewhat vague and unclear. Translation seeks, however, to reproduce the meaning of the author as closely as possible in a different language; it seeks to restate the author's words in another language. Interpretation, on the other hand, need not involve two different languages and is free to use radically different images, terms, and metaphors to explain an author's meaning.

Translation can be based on a word-for-word or a thought-for-thought philosophy. For the English Bible, the following translations reflect a word-for-word philosophy in translating the biblical texts: Tyndale, Coverdale, Geneva, King James Version, American Standard Version, Revised Standard Version, New American Standard Bible, New Revised Standard Version, English Standard Version. (However, in its attempt to use gender-neutral terminology, the New Revised Standard Version tends to reflect a more thought-for-thought translation when replacing "man" and masculine pronouns with generic equivalents.) Other popular modern translations, such as the New English Bible, the Revised English Bible, the New International Version, and the New Living Translation, follow a thought-for-thought philosophy.

The weakness of the first approach is that no two languages and cultures have exact word equivalents. We need only attempt to translate Joseph's relationship to Mary in Matthew 1:18–20 to see this:

> Now the birth of Jesus Christ took place in this way. When his mother Mary had been betrothed to Joseph, before they came together she was found to be with child from the Holy Spirit. And her husband Joseph, being a just man and unwilling to put her to shame, resolved to divorce her quietly. But as he considered these things, behold, an angel of the Lord appeared to him in a dream, saying, "Joseph, son of David, do not fear to take Mary as your wife, for that which is conceived in her is from the Holy Spirit."

Were Joseph and Mary "betrothed," that is, engaged (1:18)? If so, why is Joseph described as her "husband" (1:19)? Why is he considering "divorcing" her (1:19)? The problem we encounter is that we have no equivalent term in our culture to describe the relationship of Joseph and Mary. In their culture they possessed a relationship that could only be broken by divorce (1:19). In this relationship any outside sexual relationship would have been considered adultery. However, no marriage ceremony had yet taken place (cf. Matt. 25:1–13), and there had been no sexual consummation (1:25). There are no English terms that are exact equivalents to describe this situation. We have a similar problem in trying to find an English equivalent for the German word *Gymnasium*. This is the word for a school, grades 5–13, that prepares students to enter the German university system, in contrast to the *Hauptschule* and *Realschule*, and we have no equivalent English term. Furthermore, the fact that the German word *Hochschule* (literally, "high school") refers more to what we would call "college" compounds the problem.

The thought-for-thought model for translation also has its weaknesses. This is most evident when we seek to trace how an author uses the same term in different places. The value of a concordance is compromised in such a translation even more than in a word-for-word translation. I have been frustrated on a number of occasions when I have referred to other passages in the NIV in which a biblical author uses the same word with the exact same meaning, but the NIV does not translate this word similarly. This is also a problem in a word-for-word translation but decidedly less so. It should be noted that all of these translations of the Bible are essentially based on the same understanding of its meaning!

Mental Acts

Mental acts refer to the experiences of an author while writing the text.

Although the principle that an author willed to convey to readers is available through the text, his or her inner emotional and mental experiences while writing are not. At times people confuse the meaning of a text with these mental acts. This is evident in the intentional fallacy, which states that it is impossible to experience what authors were going through when they wrote.

When we seek to understand the meaning of a text, however, we are not seeking to experience the mental acts of its author. We are interested rather in what the author wished to convey by the text given to us (i.e., in the communicative intention of the author revealed in the consciously willed symbols he or she has written). Understanding what Paul willed to

Galatians 3:1ff.

convey by his words is quite possible apart from knowing his mental acts while writing. His meaning he has provided by the shareable symbols of his text; his mental acts, however, he has not.

In an illuminating article titled "Fern-Seed and Elephants" (in *Fern-Seed and Elephants* [Glasgow: Fontana/Collins, 1975]), C. S. Lewis warns against the attempt to reconstruct the mental acts of an author. In reviews of one of his earlier articles, various commentators speculated on what had prompted him to write this article and what had been going through his mind as he wrote. This caused him to note how reviewers frequently had sought to reconstruct his writing experiences as well as the experiences of other authors whom he knew. He noted how reviewers, often with great confidence and certainty, spent a great deal of their reviews explaining what had caused a particular author to write a work and what the circumstances were that had given rise to it. In analyzing such reconstructions of the mental acts of works by authors he knew well, as well as those of his own works, Lewis's impression was that they were not simply wrong at times, or wrong half the time, but always wrong. He later qualified this somewhat by stating that this impression might be incorrect because he did not keep a written record, but he could not remember a single instance when reviewers had been correct in regard to such speculations.

If Lewis is correct concerning the inability of critics, who were reared in the same country, culture, and educational system, to understand the mental acts of their contemporaries when writing, this should give us pause. How then can we hope to understand what ancient authors were experiencing and the circumstances that led them to write? If as contemporaries, who share the same culture, mother tongue, and background, we are not able to climb into the minds of present-day authors and ascertain their mental acts, how can we ever hope to do so with authors living thousands of years ago whose culture, training, language, and worldview are radically different from ours? What these authors consciously willed to convey to their readers we can know. Their willed meaning is available to us and can be understood, because we possess their texts. But their private experiences are not. Unless an author chose to share such experiences with his readers in his written text, they are inaccessible, and Lewis rightly suggests that such investigation is highly speculative and of little value.

Semantic Range

The semantic range is the limit of possible meanings allowed by the words (verbal symbols) of a text.

Within a language, a word can possess a range of possible meanings. This is seen most clearly in a dictionary, in which such possible meanings are listed. Although a word is limited to certain meanings, an author may choose any of these meanings listed in the dictionary. If authors wish to communicate with their readers, however, they cannot go outside these possibilities. Since they want to be understood, they are willing to submit to these limitations. If they use a word in a way not permitted by the semantic range of the language, they must reveal this to their readers or they will not be understood. The word *love*, for example, has a limited range of possible meanings: intense affectionate concern, intense sexual desire, strong fondness, a zero score in tennis, a complimentary close of a letter, an affectionate nickname, and so on. The word *love* can possess any of these meanings and several more as well that fall within the parameters of its semantic range, but it cannot mean cheeseburger or dandruff. Its semantic range of possible meanings does not permit this. Likewise, a dictionary reveals that the semantic range of the word *trunk* permits it to mean the main stem of a tree, a sturdy chest for holding or transporting clothes, a storage compartment in a car, the torso of a person or animal excluding the limbs, the snout of an elephant, the main channel of a river/railroad/highway/canal, and so on, but it cannot mean pizza or submarine.

The word *faith* possesses a range of meanings in the NT. It can mean, along with other possibilities, a mere mental assent to a fact, a wholehearted trust, or a body of beliefs. Its semantic range permits any of these possible meanings, but it does not permit "faith" to mean bacon and eggs.

Semantic Range
Dictionary

Perhaps the classic example of this issue is found in Lewis Carroll's *Alice in Wonderland*, where Alice and Humpty Dumpty have the following conversation:

> "There's glory for you!"
>
> "I don't know what you mean by 'glory,'" Alice said.
>
> Humpty Dumpty smiled contemptuously. "Of course you don't—till I tell you. I meant 'there's a nice knockdown argument for you!'"
>
> "But 'glory' doesn't mean 'a nice knockdown argument,'" Alice objected.
>
> "When I use a word," Humpty Dumpty said, in a rather scornful tone, "it means just what I choose it to mean—neither more nor less."
>
> "The question is," said Alice, "whether you can make words mean so many different things."
>
> "The question is," said Humpty Dumpty, "which is to be master—that's all."

There is a sense in which Humpty Dumpty is correct. He can make a word mean whatever he wants it to mean. But—and this is critical—if he wants to communicate his meaning to others, he must submit himself to the semantic range of possibilities allowed by the language he shares with his hearers. He can create a new word or a new meaning for an old word, of course, but if he wants to communicate his meaning, he must explain such an unusual usage. Thus Alice, too, is correct. Whether he likes it or not, if Humpty Dumpty desires to communicate, he cannot arbitrarily create unique meanings for words unless he informs his hearers/readers that he has done so. For communication to take place an author's text must possess shareability; that is, the meaning of the symbols of the text must fall within the semantic range of the language or code shared with the intended readers.

As pointed out in chapter 1, codes are a good example of this. In a code the encoder seeks to communicate the intended message only to certain potential decoders. He does this by communicating via the semantic range of the language (the rules of the code) known only to him and friendly decoders. The encoder intends that unfriendly decoders not be able to understand the message, and this is made possible by withholding from them the specific semantic range of the symbols used in the code.

Biblical scholars study NT Greek and OT Hebrew (and Aramaic) because the biblical writers wrote and willed their meaning using the semantic range of meanings of these languages. And NT scholars study Koine Greek rather than classical or modern-day Greek because the authors of the NT assumed that their readers knew and would interpret their works according to the Greek of their day, Koine Greek, rather than earlier, classical Greek or later, modern-day Greek. Similarly, interpreters of the King James Version of the Bible and the works of William Shakespeare use English dictionaries and grammars of the sixteenth and early seventeenth centuries rather than modern-day English dictionaries and grammars to understand the range of possible meanings of the English words used by Shakespeare and the KJV translators.

Specific Meaning

The specific meaning is the particular meaning that an author has given to a word, phrase, sentence, and the like, in a text.

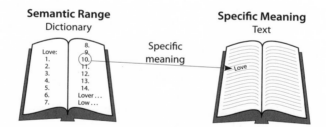

Whereas a word or combination of words possesses a specific limit of possible meanings within its semantic range (*langue*), when an author uses a word in a text, it usually means only one thing. The task of interpretation is to understand and explain this one specific meaning (*parole*). Fortunately, the semantic range of the language used by the author limits the number of possibilities. We can assume that authors are keenly interested in conveying their meaning to their intended readers. (Why else would they write?) As a result, the biblical authors chose carefully the words and grammar they used, and they confined themselves to the semantic range of possibilities permitted by the language they were using. They did so in order to assist their readers in understanding what they meant. Through the context the biblical authors have provided, they assist their readers in narrowing down the possible meanings allowed by the language to the one specific meaning they willed. Thus, although the term "sleep" can mean numerous things, in 1 Thessalonians 4:13a the expression "those who are asleep" can only mean "those who died," as the context indicates. (Note that those sleeping create the possibility of grieving [4:13b]; they are contrasted with those who are "alive" [4:15]; and they are referred to as being "dead" [4:16b].)

Whereas a dictionary or lexicon provides an interpreter with the range of possible meanings for a word and a grammar provides the range of possible meanings for a phrase or sentence, a concordance is useful for narrowing down the range of possible meanings to the specific meaning of a statement. See pp. 192–99 for how this is done.

Literary Genre

> *Literary genre refers to the literary form being used by an author and the rules governing that form.*

In chapters 4 and following, it will become evident that the biblical materials contain many different literary genres. The writers of the Bible sought to share their meaning with their readers. Thus, they worked within the literary conventions of their day that controlled the particular literary forms they used. Recognizing the genre used by an author creates certain expectations for the reader, and the author built on these expectations to help assist his readers in interpreting his text. It thus controlled the author in writing and guides the reader in interpreting the text. Apart from a correct analysis of the literary form of a text and a correct application of the rules governing that genre, it is impossible to correctly understand the author's meaning. Beginning in chapter 5, we shall investigate the norms and conventions of several of the more important literary genres found in the Bible.

Context

> *Context refers to the willed meaning that an author gives to the literary materials surrounding a passage in a text.*

Authors help readers understand the meaning they seek to convey by providing a context. It is quite common to hear people say such things as "The meaning of a passage is determined by the context" or "We know what

Paul means here from the context." Yet what exactly is this "context"? If we say that the context of a passage is composed of the words, sentences, paragraphs, and chapters surrounding it, we may be attributing to such verbal symbols a meaning in and of themselves. Such a context possesses no more semantic autonomy than a passage or the text in which it is found (see pp. 6–9), for such symbols cannot will a meaning. Apart from the willed meaning of the author, the verbal symbols that make up the context possess no meaning. The context, like the passage itself, is simply a collection of verbal symbols. Lacking personhood, such verbal symbols are inanimate markings and cannot will a meaning. As a result, we must understand the literary context not simply as the verbal symbols surrounding a passage but rather as what the author meant by these shareable symbols. Therefore, when we refer to "context" in this book, we are referring to the communicative intent of the author found in the words, sentences, paragraphs, and chapters surrounding a passage. Thus, the context of Romans 3:20–21 is what Paul meant by the words that appear before Romans 3:20–21 and what he meant by the words that appear after Romans 3:20–21. Good authors, of course, seek to assist their readers by providing a context whose meaning will be easily understood and help clarify the meaning of a passage.

A context is valuable because it assists the reader in understanding the meaning the author has given a passage. It can do this because the author has willed a meaning to this context that aids in understanding the meaning of the passage. The immediate literary context surrounding a passage is the most valuable context available. Other literary contexts are of value to the degree that their authors thought like and used terms and grammar like the writer. Social, political, and economic contexts are far less valuable. This is evident in that, out of identical contexts, a person may write as an anarchist or a monarchist, a theist or an atheist, a revolutionary or a loyalist, a fatalist or a libertarian, and so on. What biblical writers believed, wished, and meant by their texts can be known with certainty only from the texts they have written and the literary contexts they have provided. (See pp. 27–28 for a discussion and evaluation of various literary contexts helpful for studying biblical texts.)

Great confusion can result if we do not pay careful attention to context. For instance, both Paul in Romans 4:1–25 and James in 2:14–26 use the term "faith [*pistis*]." Yet we will misunderstand Paul if we assume that he means "a mere mental assent to a fact," and we will misunderstand James if we assume that he means "a wholehearted trust." It is evident from the context that Paul means the latter (cf. Rom. 4:3, 5) and that James means the former (cf. 2:14, 19; see pp. 197–98).

Questions

1. Define the following terms using your own words: meaning, implications, significance, subject matter, understanding, interpretation, mental acts, semantic range, specific meaning, literary genre, and context.
2. How can an author "mean" something concerning things about which he knew nothing?
3. How are "meaning" and "implication" alike? How are they different?
4. What is the difference between interpretation and understanding?
5. Do most sermons on the Gospels (or Acts, or Genesis to Esther) focus on the meaning or on the subject matter of the text? Can you give an example?
6. Distinguish between the specific willed meaning, the principle, and the implications of Paul's command to "greet one another with a holy kiss" (1 Cor. 16:20).
7. Are there any implications of Deuteronomy 24:19–22 for people who do not live in a rural community?
8. Was Isaiah specifically thinking of Jesus's audience in Mark 7:6–7 when he wrote Isaiah 29:13? Can our definition of "implications" help us in answering this?

Exercise in Definition

Which of the terms used in this chapter best describes each of the following statements? For answers, see appendix 1.

1. "What does Acts teach us in this chapter about the early church?"
2. "Oh, now I know what Paul meant!"
3. "Although Paul only told Timothy that women should dress modestly and not wear pearls (1 Tim. 2:9), he probably would also accept the view that women should not wear large amounts of any kind of expensive jewelry."
4. "What Paul means in Galatians 3:1–6 is that since the Galatians had received the Holy Spirit, the earnest of their salvation, by faith, this proves that God had already accepted them and there was therefore no need for them to be circumcised."
5. "Evidently, Paul was thinking of his past background as a Pharisee when he wrote this."

6. "This passage cannot mean what you are suggesting because the present participle in the text cannot be interpreted in this manner."

7. "What Jesus meant when he said, 'Render to Caesar the things that are Caesar's, and to God the things are God's,' is that you and I should obey our government and pay our taxes."

8. "This passage was not meant to be interpreted literally but figuratively."

9. "From Paul's use of the term elsewhere it is clear that it also means 'to declare righteous' here in Romans 3."

10. "Moses probably was not thinking of this, but it seems to be applicable."

11. "Our text tells us that Jesus performed his first miracle in Cana of Galilee."

12. "What this passage tells us is that Jesus is also able to forgive our sins if we put our faith in him."

13. "The word Paul uses in this text can mean a number of different things."

14. "What we find in 1 Corinthians 15:3–7 is an early church creed concerning the resurrection that Paul is quoting."

15. "What Paul says here is interesting, but I do not think that it has any value for us today."

3

Can Anyone Play This Game?

The Spirit and Biblical Interpretation

In the previous two chapters we discussed the three components involved in all written communication (author, text, reader) and discussed various terms that are helpful for defining the process of communication. No mention, however, has been made of the role of the Holy Spirit in this process. Yet throughout the entire process of interpreting the Bible, the Holy Spirit is intimately involved. He was involved at the very beginning in the inscripturation of the biblical materials, for it was under his divine inspiration that the biblical authors wrote the Scriptures. He was involved in the preservation of these inspired writings and in the recognition by the church of which books were inspired and part of the sacred Scriptures (the development of the canon). The Spirit is also involved at the end of the interpretative process, as the believer seeks to understand and apply the biblical teaching to his or her life.

The Role of the Spirit in Inspiration

The Bible is the product of divine inspiration (2 Tim. 3:16–17; 2 Pet. 1:20–21). As a result, the Bible is the Word of God and reveals what Christians are to believe (matters of faith) and how they are to live (matters of practice). The terms "infallible" and, more recently, "inerrant" are often used to describe the reliability of the Bible. The former term focuses on the doctrinal reliability of the Bible, the latter on its factual reliability. ("Plenary" is often used to indicate that this divine inspiration extends to the very words chosen by the biblical authors to express their meaning.) It is not always understood, however, that these terms are essentially meaningless apart from an explanation of *what* is infallible and inerrant.

When Christians say that the Bible is infallible or inerrant, what does this mean? Does it mean that the spiritual or existential messages being taught in the Bible are true even if the accounts are not accurate descriptions of what took place, that is, that the accounts are not historical but mythical? Whereas certain existentialist interpreters might agree with this statement, this is not what Christianity has traditionally meant by these terms. Does it perhaps mean that the ethical (or "substructural") realities, lying beneath the plain or surface meaning of what the author meant, are true? Whereas some people (such as structuralists) might agree with this view, this too is not what Christianity has meant by these terms. Does it mean that the facts of the Bible are true? Yet what is a "fact" of Scripture?

We can resolve such confusion once we realize that such terms as "infallible" and "inerrant" are judgments about propositions. They are evaluations of statements of meaning. Thus, the Christian claim that the Bible is infallible or inerrant means in essence that what the authors of Scripture willed to convey by their words (their proposition or pattern of meaning) is true. The term "infallibility" means that what the authors willed to convey with regard to matters of faith (doctrine) and practice (ethics) are true and will never lead us astray. The term "inerrant" means that what the authors willed to convey with regard to matters of fact (history, geography, science, etc.) is also true and will never lead us astray. What is determinative at all times, however, involves what the author, led by the Spirit, sought to convey by his text.

An illustration of this is found in Isaiah 11:12, where the prophet states that God will "gather the dispersed of Judah from the four corners of the earth." What does he mean by this statement? Does he will to tell his readers, "I want you to know that the earth contains four corners and God will bring his people back from these four corners"? Or does he will to tell his readers, "I want you to know that God will bring his people back from the ends of the earth"? (Notice how I use the expression "ends of the earth," even though I believe that the earth is round and has no "ends.") If Isaiah meant to teach geography in this verse, then the verse is errant, not inerrant, because it would contain an error of geography. The earth has no "corners." However, if Isaiah did not will to teach geography, but wanted rather to teach the future regathering of God's people from throughout the world, then his statement can be infallible and inerrant.

Inspiration involves the role of the Holy Spirit in guiding the authors of Scripture as they sought to convey their pattern of meaning in writing. As they wrote, they were "carried along by the Holy Spirit" (2 Pet. 1:21), so that their writings are the only infallible rule of faith and practice for the Christian. Various passages reveal that this divine superintendence extends to the very words (verbal symbols) used by the authors (cf. Matt. 5:18; Gal. 3:16). The question of *how* the Spirit guided the authors in their writing, however, is far from clear. At times he may have done this through a vision (Obad. 1; Nah. 1:1; Hab. 2:2; Rev. 1:11) or through a voice (Exod. 17:14; Jer. 30:1–2; 36:2; Rev. 1:12), but how Paul or Luke was guided by the Spirit in their writing is unclear. The style and theological emphases of the individual writers shine through their writings. This indicates that the Spirit worked with and through the personality of the human authors. As a result, Christian theologians have seldom argued in favor of a dictation form of inspiration by the Spirit. Such statements as Luke 1:1–4 and Romans 16:22 argue strongly against such a view.

The Role of the Spirit in the Formation of the Bible

The process by which the sixty-six books that make up the Bible came to be collected and recognized as the Word of God involves the question of "canon." The term itself is a Greek word that referred to a staff or straight rod used as a means of measurement. The term soon came to mean a rule or standard. In the history of the Christian church the term came to be used with respect to the books that were judged to be the standard by which the church should live.

In the process of recognizing which of the various books were part of the canon, several factors played a role. It should be pointed out, however, that in this process the church did not *make* these books into the Word of God but rather *recognized* which books were in fact the Word of God. It was through the inspiration of the Holy Spirit that the books of the OT and NT became the Word of God. Thus, the canon of Scripture was closed when the last book of the NT was written. Whereas at the time of Jesus there was a general consensus that the OT canon consisted of the present books in the OT (the status of the books of the Apocrypha is debated), the recognition of which books made up the NT canon took time.

One of the factors that aided the church in recognizing which books were part of the NT canon was apostolic authorship or association with an apostle. Thus, the Pauline, Petrine, and Johannine epistles were assumed to be part of the canon due to their being apostolic. This was true also of the Gospels of Matthew and John. Luke-Acts was associated with Paul; Mark with Peter; and Hebrews with Paul as well. Another factor that played a role in the church's recognition of which books were part of the NT canon was antiquity and continuous usage throughout the church. Thus, those books that were written late and had a limited and only local history of usage within the church were not recognized as canonical. Still another factor was the unity and agreement of these books with the rest of Scripture. The church rightly assumed that the Spirit who inspired such works as the Gospels and the Pauline Letters could not have inspired works that contradicted them. (From this it is evident that they were able to "harmonize" Paul and James in a way that Luther was not.)

Along with these, another important factor was the divine superintendence of this process by the Holy Spirit. Through his leading the church recognized which books belonged to the canon of Scripture. It is difficult for Christians to assume that the God who sent his Son to be the Savior of the world would have stopped his providential rule of creation at that point. The NT teaches that God through his Spirit then went on to inspire the interpretation and recording of that great redemptive event. Thus, God sovereignly ruled over not only the birth-life-death-resurrection of his Son but also the interpretation and recording of that event. In the sovereign rule of God, the Spirit then led the church to recognize which of those books were divinely inspired and the infallible rule of faith and practice of the church. (This is true even if some of the church's reasoning was flawed, in that not all NT books were written by apostles and many books of the Bible are anonymous.)

God's Superintendence and the Spirit's Guidance

| Revelatory events and message | Understanding of events and message by author | Recording of events and message by author | Collection of inspired writing (canon) |

Although it cannot be proved, it also seems reasonable to think that in his providential rule God likewise saw to it that those inspired texts were not lost or corrupted in any major way. The existence of over six thousand Greek manuscripts of the NT (from small fragments to entire copies of the NT), tens of thousands of manuscripts of early translations (in Latin, Syriac, Coptic, Armenian, Gothic, and Ethiopic), thousands of lectionaries (church Scripture readings), and over one million quotations throughout the writings of the early church fathers strongly suggests the providential concern of God in making sure that the text of Scripture would not be lost but carefully preserved.

The Role of the Spirit in the Interpretation of the Bible

In the previous section we described how the Spirit was active in guiding the biblical writers in the process of inscripturation. As the writers chose the words and grammar by which they sought to express their meaning, they were led by the Spirit. Yet is the Spirit also active in guiding and aiding the reader in the process of interpretation? If so, where in the process does this take place? Is it in the understanding of the text's meaning? In discovering the various implications? In the evaluation of the text's meaning (i.e., in its significance)? Is the Spirit involved in all these areas?

As Luther, Calvin, and the other Reformers reflected on how the Spirit was involved in the interpretation of Scripture, they spoke of the Holy Spirit's inner work of illumination and conviction. This view is also expressed at times by saying that apart from the Spirit we cannot "fully" or "truly" understand the Bible. Using the terminology discussed in chapter 2, it would appear that what the Reformers called "illumination" refers to understanding the meaning of the text (cognition), and what they called "conviction" refers to the attribution of a positive significance to the text (persuasion). In other words, the Spirit helps the reader understand the principle that the author willed and convinces the reader as to the truth and personal relevance of that teaching.

Textual support for this view is frequently seen in 1 Corinthians 2:14, where Paul states, "The natural person does not accept the things of the Spirit of God, for they are folly to him, and he is not able to understand them because they are spiritually discerned." This is interpreted as meaning that, apart from the Spirit, a person cannot understand the meaning of biblical texts. Without the Spirit these texts are simply foolish riddles. Yet before we assume that Paul, and his English translators, are using the term "understand" in the same sense in which we defined the term in chapter 2, we must look more closely at this verse.

What does Paul mean when he says that apart from the Spirit these things are "folly"? Does he mean that a person without the Spirit is unable to come to a correct mental grasp of what biblical texts mean? Is Paul saying that apart from the Spirit the biblical teachings are incomprehensible?

The meaning of the term "folly" in 1 Corinthians 2:14 is best understood by observing how Paul uses it elsewhere. In 1 Corinthians 3:19 the term is used as follows: "For the wisdom of this world is folly with God." Here, it should be noted, something is folly to God. Clearly, Paul does not mean that God cannot arrive at a correct mental grasp of what this world calls wisdom. God is omniscient; he understands everything. God, of course, understands what this world calls wisdom. He rejects it, however, as folly. The term "folly" in 1 Corinthians 3:19 refers not to what we have called "understanding" but rather to "significance." God understands perfectly well what this world calls wisdom, but he critiques it. He evaluates it. He condemns it as folly. In 1 Corinthians 1:20 the verbal form of this word is used, and Paul states similarly, "Has not God made foolish the wisdom of the world?" Here (1:20), in the chapter before 1 Corinthians 2:14, as well as in the chapter following (3:19)—that is, the immediate context—Paul uses the expressions "folly" and "made foolish" to refer to the significance or value judgment that God places upon this world's wisdom.

Should this same meaning be attributed to the term in 1 Corinthians 2:14? It would appear so, for Paul is not saying that unbelievers cannot arrive at a correct mental grasp of the things of the Spirit. They can and do, but they attribute to this understanding of the author's meaning a negative significance. They reject it as folly. Thus, in the first three chapters of 1 Corinthians we have the following parallel: The unbelieving world can understand the things of the Spirit—that is, what the biblical text means—but what it understands it rejects as folly. Similarly, God understands the wisdom of this world but rejects it as folly. In both instances, there is a correct mental grasp of what is meant (understanding), followed by a rejection of its value (negative significance).

In a similar way it would appear that the words translated "understand" in 1 Corinthians 2:12 and 14 are best understood as meaning something other than simply acquiring a correct mental grasp of meaning. They refer rather to embracing these biblical truths as true. It is probably best to see the expressions "does not accept," "folly," and "not able to understand" as referring to various ways in which the unbeliever critiques the divine revelation. This critique (negative significance) is based on a cognitive understanding of what the biblical author meant by the text. This understanding of the text, however, is rejected in different ways: (1) it is not accepted, not received eagerly or welcomed, because it is opposed to human wisdom (cf. 1 Cor. 1:18–25); (2) it is judged to be folly because it conflicts with a human sense of wisdom and truth; and (3) it is not believed as being true because only the Spirit can convince a person of the truth of the gospel message. It would appear that whereas 1 Corinthians 2:14 refers to the work of the Spirit in "conviction" or "significance," it does not deny but rather assumes that an unbeliever can "understand" the gospel message. In a similar way, the disciples are described in Mark 9:32 as "not understanding" Jesus's passion prediction found in the previous verse. Yet if asked what Jesus meant by this passion prediction, they could have said something like, "Jesus just said that he was going to be killed and after three days rise from the dead." They possessed a correct mental grasp of Jesus's words, but as in 1 Corinthians 2:14 they judged what he said as "folly" or nonsense.

Can a person understand the Bible apart from the Spirit? Let us assume for a moment that we are able to form two groups of college students with equal intelligence, background, and dedication to getting good grades. One group consists of Christians, the other of non-Christians. They are assigned the task of describing in eight to ten pages what Paul meant by Romans 3:20–21. Would their grades be sufficiently different? Would Christians be able to understand and then interpret their understanding in ways that would cause them to receive a higher grade than the non-Christian group? Would the Spirit assist the Christians in obtaining a correct mental grasp of the meaning and thus enable them to obtain better grades? (It might be argued that Christians would have an advantage because of greater familiarity with the Bible, but perhaps they would also possess the disadvantage of bringing with themselves numerous misunderstandings as well. What Bible teacher in college or seminary has not encountered strange interpretations that some Christian students bring to class?)

I would suggest that the grade curve for both groups, all other things being equal, would be quite similar. Non-Christians can arrive at a correct mental grasp of the meaning of the Bible. They can understand the Scriptures. This is why we try to explain the gospel message to them. This is why Paul reasoned every Sabbath in the synagogues (Acts 18:4) and sought to explain the gospel message and persuade his audience in the synagogues at Thessalonica, Corinth, and Ephesus (Acts 17:2–3; 18:4; 19:8). Why would someone today seek to explain the "four spiritual laws" or John 3:16 to their friends, unless they were convinced that the listener was capable of understanding these laws and John 3:16? A Christian defense of the faith to unbelievers is based on the assumption that they are capable of understanding the teachings of Scripture.

Where, then, does the work of the Spirit come into play? Could it be in revealing the implications of the author's principle? Certainly a Christian has far greater desire to understand such implications than a non-Christian. This may be true, but is a non-Christian capable of understanding the implications of the meaning of a biblical text? Let us again imagine that the same two groups of students are asked to write an eight- to ten-page paper on the modern-day implications of Jesus's words in Matthew 6:24, "No one can serve two masters, for either he will hate the one and love the other, or he will be devoted to the one and despise the other. You cannot serve both God and money [lit., *mammon*]." Would there be any significant difference in the grading of these two groups of papers? Assuming the same intelligence and dedication to grades, this is unlikely. (If it is assumed that the Christians will work with greater devotion on their papers because of their love for God, it is also unfortunate but probably true that the desire of some non-Christians to achieve good grades may be every bit as great as the devotion of some Christians to God.)

Some might protest and say, however, "But an unbeliever cannot 'truly,' 'really,' 'fully,' 'savingly' [etc.] understand the Bible." But the addition of such adjectives creates a new expression in which "truly/really/fully/savingly understand" is distinguished from and possesses a different meaning from our definition of "understand" given in chapter 2. There we defined understanding as being a correct mental grasp of an author's willed meaning. This is possible for both believer and unbeliever alike. The newly created expressions, such as "truly understand," involve both a correct cognitive understanding of the biblical author's meaning and the recognition and joyous acceptance of its truthfulness. It adds a positive significance ("truly") to a correct mental grasp of the meaning (understanding) of the text. (There are also times when unbelievers can be convicted by the Holy Spirit of the truthfulness of the gospel message and their need to repent and believe but nevertheless refuse to do so. Significance involves the value one attributes to meaning, and that can be either positive or negative.)

There are several important consequences that arise from the universal ability of people to understand the meaning of a biblical text. The first is that Christians can study the works of non-Christians with profit. It is simply not true to claim that only believers can understand biblical teachings. If by "understand" we mean "to possess a correct mental grasp of the meaning of the text," it is quite apparent that evangelical Christians do not have a corner on understanding the Bible. I must confess that I have frequently learned more from reading the works of nonevangelicals than those of evangelicals. When I went to seminary, many of the best texts and commentaries available were written by scholars who made no claim to be evangelical Christians. There were not many well-researched, scholarly works available that were evangelical in nature. Today this has changed significantly. Evangelical scholarship has made remarkable progress in recent years, and some of the very best texts available today have been written by evangelicals. Yet it must still be admitted that many of the best works in biblical studies are being written by those who make no claim to be evangelical Christians. Even without the Spirit, they are able to describe accurately and well what the authors of Scripture meant in their texts, and we can benefit from their labors. However, there will be a great difference in Christians' and non-Christians' evaluations of what the biblical authors meant.

One point that has not been dealt with up to this point is the problem of how sin affects humans' ability to understand the biblical teaching. How do the fall and the resulting depravity of humanity affect the ability of people to understand divine revelation? Has the reasoning ability of humanity been so affected as to require a divine enabling to counter and overcome the results of sin? Without minimizing the effect of the fall, we must also guard against exaggerating its effect. The image of God has been tarnished and spoiled but not destroyed. It has been corrupted but not lost (James 3:9). Part of that image involves the ability to reason, which is central to interpretation. It is apparent that the ability to understand what an ancient author meant (whether biblical or nonbiblical is not important at this point) has not been lost. We can understand the writings of other people. We can also understand the meaning the biblical writers sought to share. Sin may cause us not to want to accept or believe what they say, but this involves significance and not understanding. Furthermore, the result of sin on the reasoning process of humans affects both Christians and non-Christians. There is nothing in Scripture that tells us that the regenerating work of the Spirit transforms the mental abilities of people. What it does affect is our value systems, the significance we attribute to the meaning of biblical texts.

If we recognize that anyone with normal intelligence can obtain a correct mental grasp of the meaning of Scripture, then is the ability of all humans to understand the meaning a work of the Spirit? To understand the illumination of the Spirit in this manner, however, would be simply to equate it with human intelligence. This reduces the illumination of the Spirit to the ability of humans to reason and still does not resolve the issue, for it does not explain what the Spirit provides for the believer that the unbeliever does not possess.

A Concluding Illustration

The role of the Spirit in biblical interpretation can perhaps best be described by means of this imaginary situation. At the annual lectureship on biblical studies at the Interpretive School of Theology, Ludwig Kopfwissen of Wissenheim University delivers an address entitled "Paul's Doctrine of Justification by Faith." In this one-hour lecture Kopfwissen describes, more clearly than anyone else has ever done before, what Paul meant by his doctrine of justification by faith. He also carefully and brilliantly describes the implications of this doctrine in the life of the Christian church both past and present. If the apostle Paul were present, he might even say, "Thank you, Professor Kopfwissen. No one has ever explained what I meant as clearly and as well." After he is warmly applauded, however, the professor adds, "Aber Sie wissen doch, dass es alles nur Humbug ist!—But you know, of course, that this is all nonsense!"

After the address someone happens to see the wife of Professor Kopfwissen, who is a committed Christian, and asks her, "Frau Professor, what do you think Paul meant by his doctrine of justification by faith?" To this she replies, "You must understand that my training is not in theology but in chemistry, but I guess"—and at this point tears begin to form in her eyes—"I guess Paul meant that God has done everything for us!"

Who understands Paul's teaching better? The professor or his wife? The issue, of course, depends upon what is meant by "understands." If, as defined in chapter 2, it means a correct mental grasp of Paul's meaning, it is clear that Professor Ludwig Kopfwissen understands Paul better. He has a far greater grasp of the principle willed by the apostle. But, as in 1 Corinthians 2:14, it is folly to him, because he has not been convicted and convinced by the Spirit of its truth. He cannot appreciate it, because such conviction comes from the Spirit. On the other hand, Frau Kopfwissen appreciates the meaning of Paul's teaching. She, too, understands, although not nearly as completely, what Paul meant, but through the Spirit she accepts this as the wisdom of God.

What, then, are the implications of this for the study of the Bible? There are several. For one, the role of the Spirit in interpretation is not an excuse for laziness. If we do not know the meaning of a biblical word, all the prayer in the world cannot substitute for a Bible dictionary. For understanding the biblical text, meditation is no replacement for looking up how the author uses such terms elsewhere in his writings. The goal of acquiring a correct mental grasp of the author's meaning is not achieved by personal piety. To pray that the Spirit would help us understand the meaning of a text because we do not want to spend time studying the text or using the tools that have been made available to us (such as commentaries, lexicons, concordances, and dictionaries) may border on blasphemy, for it seeks to use the Spirit for our own ends. The Holy Spirit brings to the believer a blessed assurance of the truthfulness of the biblical teachings, but he cannot be manipulated to cover for laziness in the study of the Word of God.

On the other hand, to pray that the Spirit would help us recognize the truth of the text (its significance) or to show which of the implications apply particularly to us and our situation (divine guidance with respect to personal relevance) is both highly appropriate and devout. For what does it profit to study the Bible and even understand its meaning perfectly, if we do not submit to its teaching and obey its implications for our lives?

Questions

1. How would you respond at a Bible study or in a Sunday school class when two people say, "The Holy Spirit has shown me that the text means . . . ," and these two allegedly Spirit-given interpretations are contradictory?
2. Can a person understand the "four spiritual laws" and not be a Christian?
3. Can a person understand the meaning of John 3:16 and not be a Christian? Can a person understand the truthfulness of John 3:16 and not be a Christian? (Note that the significance one attributes to a text may be positive or negative.)
4. Do you know a person who understands the meaning of John 3:16 but is not a Christian?
5. What advantage does a Christian have over a non-Christian in the study of the Bible?

6. Explain what Paul meant in 1 Corinthians 2:14 in your own words.

7. Besides conviction, what else does the Spirit do in conversion?

Exercise in Definition

Which of the terms used in chapter 2 best describes each of the following statements? For answers, see appendix 2.

1. "If Paul meant what you say, no one would have understood him, for no one in his day would have interpreted his words in that manner."
2. "You have been interpreting this passage as a historical narrative, but it is not a historical narrative but a prophecy."
3. "The reason why Luke wrote this Gospel was to assure Theophilus that Jesus had indeed risen from the dead."
4. "Now I get it!"
5. "I wonder if Moses would have thought that cheating on one's income taxes is stealing."
6. "When Jesus said these words, no doubt his audience would have thought that he was making a christological claim."
7. "Among other things, this word can mean sincere trust or only mental assent."
8. "I find it difficult to accept what Isaiah means here."
9. "I do not really think that it is important to understand what Paul meant."
10. "I think that it is far more important to understand what Paul means today."
11. "I do not think that the passage means what you are suggesting, because the present imperative found in the text cannot be interpreted in this manner."
12. "From Matthew 16:18 we learn that Jesus only began to teach his disciples concerning his coming death after Peter had confessed at Caesarea Philippi that he was the Christ."
13. "Paul's command probably would also include the following nuances."
14. "I think that the commandment not to take the name of the Lord our God in vain means that I should not say 'Oh, God!' anymore."
15. "Another way of expressing what Paul is saying is that the cross of Christ has removed every legal charge that God had against the Galatians."

4

Different Games in the Same Book

Different Forms of Scripture

Within the Bible, as within literature in general, there exist two main kinds of language: referential language and commissive language. When we use referential language, the main goal is to pass on information. This form of language seeks to describe. It tends to be nonemotional in nature and to pass on facts. In our society such language is becoming more and more important, for it is the language of science. Physicists, chemists, biologists, engineers, computer technicians, and medical doctors use this form of language when communicating with one another. It is also the language of philosophers, automobile mechanics, dentists, and tire salesmen. It is the advice we receive in hardware stores, lumber yards, cooking recipes, and word processing seminars.

On the other hand, commissive language, or "perlocutionary utterances" in speech-act theory, has as its main goal evoking decisions, conveying emotions, eliciting feelings, arousing sentiment, and affecting change. It is the language of poets, people in love, college football coaches, lieutenants leading men in battle, motivational speakers, and speakers at high school graduations. Whereas referential language appeals to the mind, commissive language appeals to the heart. The former is more cognitive in its aim, the latter more emotive. The difference can be seen most easily when we compare different kinds of literature. We read an automobile manual in a different way than we read a love letter. The description of a "0.016-inch gap" between the electrodes of a spark plug is interpreted literally, as meaning that we should leave a 0.016-inch gap between the ground point and the center electrode of each spark plug. The description of missing a sweetheart so much that our heart aches, that we cannot sleep, that our heart stops beating, is interpreted quite differently. Automobile repair manuals are meant to be taken literally and are referential in nature. Love letters are not. They are to be interpreted figuratively, metaphorically, for they are commissive in nature. If we interpret repair manuals figuratively and love letters literally, disaster, or at least a lack of communication, will result.

One should not conclude that referential language cannot convey emotions or that commissive language cannot convey information. A physician may use referential language to convey a diagnosis. The description "inoperable melanoma of the pancreas" is primarily referential in nature, but the meaning it conveys, incurable cancer, is nevertheless extremely emotive. Some information will elicit feelings by its very nature. We can read the most sterile, objective description of the history of the Auschwitz death camp, and, despite the referential nature of the account, it will affect our feelings and emotions. Similarly, a love letter, despite its commissive nature, nevertheless conveys information: it reveals the love of the letter writer for the reader. As a result the terms "referential" and "commissive" are not exclusive in nature. They reflect rather the primary purpose of the language being used.

The descriptions "referential" and "commissive" extend not only to different kinds of literary forms but also to the very words used within those forms. Note how various expressions used in the abortion debates are frequently intended to convey not just information but emotions: fetus vs. unborn baby; pro-choice vs. pro-life; abort vs. murder; control of reproductive organs vs. killing one's baby. Compare also the following terms: escort, call girl, lady of the night, prostitute, whore. Or the following: the biblical account, the biblical story, the biblical myth, what took place. Smart advertisers, preachers, and propagandists are well aware of how the choice of the right word can affect people. In this respect, the terms "pro-life" and "pro-choice" must be labeled quite successful. They are stirring and emotive terms.

Playing by the Rules: Meaning and Literary Forms

It is obvious that our choice of words may at times be motivated less by a desire to inform and enlighten than by a desire to arouse and affect the emotions and will of the reader. Speech-act theory, which argues that verbal utterances seek not only to say things but also to do things, strongly emphasizes this. The biblical writers were well aware of this aspect of language, of course, and consciously chose to use words and literary forms that would best convey their meaning. At times they sought primarily to convey certain information (Luke 1:1–4). They then used those referential forms and terms that were best suited to convey this information. When they sought to convey the divine laws, they would use certain legal forms, such as are found in Exodus, Leviticus, Numbers, and Deuteronomy. At times the best form available to share certain information was that of a letter or epistle. Thus we find in the Bible various letters such as those of Paul, Peter, and John. At other times the narrative form was used to share information that was primarily historical in nature. Much of the Bible is made up of such material (Genesis through Esther, Matthew through Acts). Even in the prophetic literature, we find narrative in Jeremiah 26–29, 32–45, 52; Haggai 1–2; cf. also Daniel 1–6.

Other forms of literature tend to be more commissive in nature. In such a category we would certainly place the Psalms and the Song of Solomon. It should also be noted that within the narrative materials we find poetry (Exod. 15; Judg. 5; 1 Sam. 2; Jesus's use of poetry in the Gospels) and emotive sayings as well (see the discussion of Jesus's use of exaggeration in chapter 13 below). Some biblical literature tends to contain elements of both kinds of language. Proverbs and prophecy are examples of this.

It is clear that there are various kinds of literary forms in the Bible. Each of these forms, or "genres," possesses its own rules of interpretation. In using these literary forms, the authors consciously submitted themselves to the rules governing these forms in order to share their meaning with their readers. They assumed that their readers would interpret their words according to the rules governing that literary form, which provides "well-worn grooves of expectation" (James L. Bailey, "Genre Analysis," in *Hearing the New Testament: Strategies for Interpretation*, ed. Joel B. Green, 2nd ed. [Grand Rapids: Eerdmans, 2010], 141). If we are not aware of the rules under which the biblical author wrote, misinterpretation almost certainly will take place. Think for a moment of a European soccer fan attending American football and basketball games for the first time. In football the offensive and defensive players can use their hands to push their opponents. In basketball and soccer they cannot. In basketball players cannot kick the ball, but they can hold it with their hands. In soccer the reverse is true. In football everyone can hold the ball with their hands but only one person can kick it. In soccer everyone can kick the ball but only one person can hold it. Unless we understand the rules under which the game is played, what is taking place is bound to be misinterpreted.

The Rules of the Game

~~Soccer player holding the ball~~	Football player holding the ball	Basketball player holding the ball
Soccer player throwing the ball from out of bounds	~~Football player throwing the ball from out of bounds~~	Basketball player throwing the ball from out of bounds
Soccer player kicking the ball	Football player kicking the ball	~~Basketball player kicking the ball~~

In a similar way, different "game rules" are involved in the interpretation of the different kinds of biblical literature. The expression "literary criticism" is often used to describe the investigation of the present form of biblical texts in light of the rules governing their various genres. (Unfortunately, "literary criticism" is also used to describe source criticism, the investigation of the alleged sources used in the writing of the present form of a text.) In playing his "game," each biblical author sought to convey his meaning under the rules covering the particular literary form he used. Unless we know those rules, we will almost certainly misinterpret his meaning. If we interpret a parable (Luke 16:19–31) as if it were narrative, or if we interpret poetry (Judg. 5) as if it were narrative, we will err. Similarly, if we interpret a narrative such as the resurrection of Jesus (Matt. 28:1–10) as a parable, we will also err (cf. 1 Cor. 15:12–19).

A good example of the importance of this occurred in my own life as a young Christian. I did not like reading the Beatitudes. Whenever I read them I became depressed, for they always made me feel guilty and wonder whether I was truly a Christian. This was because I misunderstood their literary form. I read them as being conditions of membership for entrance into the kingdom of God. As a result when I read, "Blessed are the poor in spirit, for theirs is the kingdom of heaven. . . . Blessed are the meek, for they shall inherit the earth" (Matt. 5:3, 5), I felt condemned, because I knew that I was not as poor in spirit or meek as I should be. There was too much pride and arrogance in my life. Furthermore, I was not one who could turn the other cheek easily (Matt. 5:39). Similarly, when I read, "Blessed are those who hunger and thirst for righteousness, for they shall be satisfied" (Matt. 5:6), I realized that I did not long for God's righteousness as much as I should. (Who does?) The result was again feelings of guilt and depression.

As time went on, however, I began to wonder if my guess as to the literary form of the Beatitudes, and as a result my understanding of the rules governing their interpretation, was correct. Should the Beatitudes be interpreted as conditions of membership for entrance into the kingdom of God? Or should they instead be interpreted as blessings pronounced upon those who already are citizens of the kingdom? In other words, are the Beatitudes to be understood as entrance requirements for salvation or as ascriptions of praise and congratulations to those who already possess salvation? It became evident that rather than being entrance requirements, the Beatitudes are meant to be understood as blessings pronounced upon those who already are members of the kingdom. This is evident for several reasons. For one, the audience to whom these Beatitudes were delivered was the disciples (Matt. 5:1–2; Luke 6:20). Thus, they cannot be conditions for becoming disciples in that they were addressed to those who already were disciples. Second, the closest analogies to the Beatitudes are the words of comfort addressed to God's people in such places as Isaiah 29:19; 49:13; and especially 61:1–2. Third, the grammatical form of the Beatitudes is not conditional in nature. There is no "*If* you become poor in spirit, you will inherit the kingdom of heaven." Rather the grammatical form is that of a pronouncement. Finally, the fact that Matthew 5:3 and 10 both end with "for theirs is the kingdom of heaven" and form an inclusio indicates that the evangelist understood everything in Matthew 5:3–10 as dealing with the same basic theme. As a result they must be interpreted as blessings pronounced upon God's people, those who are "persecuted for righteousness' sake" (Matt. 5:10) or may be persecuted because of their faith in the future.

In my earliest attempts to understand the Beatitudes, I was playing under the wrong game rules. I misinterpreted the particular literary form with which I was dealing. Thus, a correct understanding of the meaning was impossible. And it would have remained impossible unless I changed my expectation of the kind of game (literary form) that I was playing. I was using soccer rules when I was really playing basketball; I was using the rules for interpreting entrance requirements into the kingdom instead of the rules for interpreting pronouncements of blessings on those who had already entered the kingdom. Yet this did not make a correct interpretation hopeless. It was always possible to start over and change to another generic expectation, from soccer to basketball, from entrance requirements to pronouncements of blessing. When I approached the Beatitudes with a new and correct expectation appropriate to this literary form, understanding was possible, for I now shared the same rules of interpretation associated with this literary genre as Jesus and Matthew.

Today I find encouragement and strength from these congratulatory words of blessing. Thus, when I was asked if there was a passage of Scripture I wanted read at my father's funeral, one of the passages I chose was the Beatitudes. When the pastor then read, "Blessed are those who mourn, for they shall be comforted" (Matt. 5:4), I was able to understand that these were divine words of blessing and comfort addressed by God to us who mourned the death of our beloved Christian father and husband. God was promising us that there was coming a day of great comfort when "mourning and crying and pain will be no more" (Rev. 21:4 NRSV), a day of joyous reunion (1 Thess. 4:14). (There is also a sense in which the Beatitudes challenge me "to become what I am"—that is, to become in my daily living what I am in Christ—but this is secondary to their primary purpose of providing encouragement and comfort from their pronouncements of blessing.)

In the following chapters we will look at the rules governing various literary forms found in the Bible. Since we want to understand what the author meant when he wrote (i.e., the principle he willed to convey), we need to know the rules he followed when he used a particular literary genre. Knowing that the writers of Scripture willingly submitted themselves to the generic expectations governing these literary forms, we will be better able to understand what they meant if we know these rules. Thus, in the following chapters we will look at the norms of language involved in biblical narrative, covenants and laws, poetry, psalms, proverbs, prophecy, idioms, parables, hyperbole, and epistles and letters.

There are many other literary forms in the Bible that we could discuss. The selection of the forms chosen is somewhat arbitrary, but they represent those most frequently found in the Bible. Some genres have not been discussed because the rules that apply to them are similar to other genres that are discussed. Thus such literary forms as similes and metaphors are not discussed separately because the rules for interpreting them are described in the chapter on parables. Similarly, we have not treated the Gospels as a separate literary genre, because they can be included in the larger category of biblical narrative. We likewise have not dealt with the rules for interpreting apocalyptic literature, because they are essentially the same as in the interpretation of prophecy. Because of limitations of space, we shall not discuss such forms as riddles, satire, visions, midrash, household codes, genealogies, the supposed "we" travel narrative form (which we now know never existed), or theophanies.

Questions

1. Have you ever misinterpreted something because you were interpreting it by the wrong set of rules? For example, what is "traveling" in college basketball? In professional basketball? I once saw a friend strike out in slow-pitch softball because he thought the rules were the same as in fast-pitch softball. He thought you received three strikes, as in fast-pitch softball, whereas in our game of slow-pitch you received only two!
2. Why does the difference between referential and commissive language not require a change in the definition of "meaning" given in chapter 2?
3. Does an incorrect understanding of the literary form of a text mean that we will never be able to grasp the meaning of that text?

Exercise in Definition

Which of the terms used in chapter 2 best describes each of the following statements? For answers, see appendix 3.

1. "Sometimes I wonder if what Mark meant in Mark 10:21 was that we, too, should sell all that we have and give it to the poor."
2. "From this passage we discover that the practice of hospitality was very important in biblical times."
3. "In the interpretation of the Bible a concordance is a useful tool for discovering _____."
4. "When I read a commentary on this passage, it finally made sense."
5. "This event in Acts took place during a time of great political unrest in the first century."

6–7. "Explanation seeks to help a person with respect to _____;
exhortation seeks to help a person with respect to _____."

8. "Although I can grasp what Paul means by these words, I cannot explain them to you."

9. "The form of this verb means that this sentence is either a statement in the present tense or a continuing command."

10. "It is expected that at this point in his letter Paul would give a thanksgiving or prayer."

11. "Jesus meant by this prayer _____."

12. "In writing down this prayer in his Gospel, Luke meant _____."

13. "By writing down this prayer in his Gospel, Luke means for us to _____."

14. "As a Jew and Pharisee, Paul must have thought that the death of the Messiah was absurd."

15. "Should the following story be interpreted as a myth or as a historical narrative?"

PART 2

The Specific Rules for the Individual Games

5

The Game of Stories

Biblical Narrative

The first and most frequently found literary form in the Bible is narrative. Within the Judeo-Christian tradition this genre of literature possesses unique importance. Many people first encounter the Bible by means of its stories. These stories, whether of Joseph, Moses, Samson, David, Isaiah, Jesus, Paul, or someone else, all involve biblical narrative. Vast sections of the Bible use this form. Over 40 percent of the OT and nearly 60 percent of the NT consist of narrative. This involves books such as Genesis, Exodus, Joshua through Esther, Matthew through Acts, and large portions of Numbers, Deuteronomy, and the Prophets.

A great deal of effort has been spent on investigating this literary form and how to interpret it. Discouraged by the questionable results of the source-critical investigation of biblical narrative, which seeks to discover the hypothetical sources lying behind the present text, and frustrated by the very different results of various historical-critical attempts to discover "what really took place," a new approach has come to the forefront of narrative studies that focuses its attention on the final canonical form of these narratives. This is a most welcome advance over past interests that focused their attention on the different subject matters found in these narratives rather than on the meaning of the narratives conveyed by their final form.

Unfortunately, technical and confusing terminology has been introduced into the discussion that the uninitiated find perplexing and difficult. Readers tend to be overwhelmed when encountering concepts such as

the real author (the actual, historical person who wrote the work);

the implied author (the author whom the reader can reconstruct from reading the work);

the narrator, sometimes defined as an overt or covert narrator (the person who in the work relates the story but who may be unreliable and thus not the implied author);

the omniscient and omnipresent narrator (the person who in the work relates the story and is present everywhere and knows everything, such as what people are thinking);

the story world (the world created by the author in the work but which may not be real);

point of view (the perspective that the author/narrator brings to the story, that is, the meaning of the author);

the intended reader (the reader whom the author had in mind when he wrote);

the real reader (the present person reading the account);

the ideal reader (a reader who possesses sufficient information to interpret the account correctly); and

the implied reader (the reader whom the implied author assumed would read his text).

Other terms coined that refer to the story itself include

scene (the individual frames that comprise the narrative whole);

plot (the plan and sequence of the story from beginning to end, which is usually seen as consisting of conflict, complications, and resolution);

characterization (how characters are described and portrayed);

setting (the physical and social background and time in which the narrative is placed); and

dialogue (the focus of the conversation between usually two individuals).

It should be noted that most of the terminology and methodology used in the study of biblical narrative has been obtained from the study of fictional narrative. There are significant differences, however, between the

writing and interpretation of fictional narrative and of biblical narrative.
The historical and traditional nature of the subject matter found in biblical
narrative places far greater restraints on the writers of biblical narrative
than on the writers of fiction. It also places greater restraints on the readers
of biblical narrative than on the readers of fictional narrative. Questions
that interpreters of fiction may ask are ludicrous with respect to biblical
narrative, as the following examples make clear:

> Why did the author of this Gospel choose to have his hero die by means
>   of crucifixion?
> Why did he choose to give him the name "Jesus"?
> Why did he pick the city of Jerusalem as the place to culminate his story?
> Why did he not choose Rome or Corinth?
> Why did he choose to have a disciple betray Jesus?
> Where did he come up with the idea of ending his story with a resur-
>   rection from the dead?

History and tradition did not permit the Gospel writers any choice in
such matters!

In our discussion of biblical narrative we shall simplify the terminology associated with the investigation of this kind of literature. We shall
refer to the author and make no distinction between the real author and
the implied author. Such a distinction is unnecessary as long as we realize
that our knowledge and understanding of the author are imperfect and
come from the text itself. An example of this is found in the four Gospels.
All the Gospels are anonymous and make no overt claims as to authorship. The present ascriptions, "The Gospel according to Matthew," "The
Gospel according to Mark," and so on, date from the middle of the second
century. The titles "According to Matthew," "According to Mark," and
so on, are earlier and may date from the turn of the first century. These
ascriptions stem from tradition, not from any specific claim made in the
Gospels themselves. Whereas good historical evidence can be offered in
support of the traditional authorship of these Gospels, when we refer to
Matthew, Mark, Luke, and John in our discussion, we simply mean the
authors of the first, second, third, and fourth canonical Gospels and what
we can know about them from these Gospels. Furthermore, since we assume that the narrator of the biblical accounts is reliable and espouses the
same viewpoint as the author, we shall make no distinction between them
but shall treat these terms as synonymous.

The expression "story world" seems more appropriate in dealing with narratives that use the genre of myth. As we shall see, biblical narrative assumes a this-worldly framework of time and space, and therefore this expression is an unnecessary intrusion of issues of significance into the search for a text's meaning. (The use of "story world" with respect to a work such as Dwight Eisenhower's *Crusade in Europe* seems misleading, and to those unfamiliar with the technical meaning of this term in literary criticism it may suggest a fictional world as the scene of what is described.) As for "point of view," since the point of view in the story is that of the author/narrator, the expression is essentially a synonym for the meaning the author/narrator gave to the events he was reporting. Since the writer believed that he spoke for God, his point of view and God's point of view are the same. Likewise, the writer's point of view in the Gospels is the same as Jesus's point of view. Being God's spokesman, the writer was not limited in place and time. He could thus express God's point of view and possessed a literary omnipresence (Gen. 3:1–24; Job 1:6–12; 2:1–6) and omniscience (Gen. 6:6, 8; 29:20; 38:15; 2 Sam. 11:27; Luke 2:19, 38; John 2:23; 4:1; Acts 24:26) in writing his account.

The Genre of Biblical Narrative: Myth or History?

During the first three millennia in which biblical narratives existed, interpreters all thought that they were historical accounts. Even those who applied an allegorical method of interpretation to these accounts acknowledged that the events were also literally true. Despite the presence of the miraculous in such accounts, the events they portray were interpreted as having occurred in the real world of time and space. Interpreters believed that if one had been present at the time when these events took place, they would have witnessed them occurring just as described in the biblical narrative. In other words, interpreters of biblical narrative all assumed that this literary form was historical in nature. The closest analogy to this material would be reports of other historical events.

With the coming of the Enlightenment in the seventeenth and eighteenth centuries, however, skepticism arose with regard to the supernatural. At first this skepticism was applied to pagan mythology and various church traditions, but it was not long before it was applied to the Bible. In England the deists began to question various kinds of biblical narratives containing miracles. Did an ax head really float (2 Kings 6:6)? Did the sun really stand still (Josh. 10:12–14)? It was not long before the historicity of all the miracles of the Bible began to be questioned.

As skepticism increased toward the biblical narratives that spoke of miraculous events, the issue arose as to how such narratives could be "meaningful" if they were not historically true. Previous to the Enlightenment the meaning of a text was sought by investigating the willed meaning of the author. This was accessible because the author intentionally conformed to the semantic limitations of the language governing the literary form he used. With respect to biblical narrative, a literal, grammatical exegesis provided the meaning of the text. The historical subject matter being discussed was assumed to correspond with the description given by the author. Yet what was to be done when someone no longer believed that the miracles found in the biblical stories really occurred? It is interesting to note that for the most part the question was never raised as to whether these accounts were meaningful and possessed significance. Despite their supposedly fictional nature, accounts of miracles were assumed to be meaningful. They had to be meaningful. This was a given. The close ties to the Christian church maintained by many who denied the possibility of miracles did not permit them to conclude that, since the meaning of the story involved a miracle, this meaning had no significance even though the story was untrue. Thus, in order to preserve the meaningfulness of the biblical narratives, meaning was redefined and sought elsewhere than in the communicative intention of the author. The meaning of the miracle stories in the Bible had to be found somewhere other than in what the author consciously willed to convey in his text.

Three alternatives presented themselves. The first was to seek the meaning in the event portrayed in the text. This was the approach of rationalism. Rationalists in the eighteenth and nineteenth centuries saw the meaning as contained in the actual event reported in the text, not in the Bible's portrayal of that event. The event was actually quite different from its portrayal in the Bible. The literal description, which was miraculous, was not what actually took place. Meaning was consequently to be sought not in the account but in the event. The account was only a witness to and interpretation of the divine revelation found in the event itself. The present narratives unfortunately are fictionalized portrayals of the events overlaid with myths (miracles) by the traditions and biblical writers. Nevertheless, a real, nonsupernatural event lay behind this account, and discovering it was the goal of rationalism. One should therefore seek to reconstruct the actual event in order to find what really happened. In so doing it was assumed that something meaningful would be discovered in this event. Thus, what actually took place in the feeding of the five thousand was not a miraculous multiplication of loaves and fishes. Rather, it all started when a little boy was willing to share his few loaves and fishes. This caused others, who had brought more food than they needed, to share their food, and the result was that all the people were fed. Thus, the meaning of the biblical text was to be found in the reconstructed and "demiraculized" event.

Whereas the reconstruction just given resulted in a meaning or point (i.e., if people will only share what they have, there will be more than enough to go around), most rationalistic reconstructions left the interpreter with little or nothing to preach or teach. Orthodox Christianity found meaningfulness and divine revelation in such events and their interpretation as the exodus, the giving of the law on Mount Sinai, the birth of Jesus, and Jesus's death and resurrection, but these were all supernatural, miraculous events. What is the value of a misinterpreted event such as the sun shining through the clouds and illuminating Jesus and two men on a mountain? Where is there any meaningfulness in Jesus walking along the shore and being mistaken as walking on the sea?

The influence of rationalism was so great that even those who believed in the historical veracity of the text shifted their attention away from the author's willed meaning and focused their attention on the subject matter of the event. Thus, what the author willed to teach by the event was lost sight of, and the event was seen as containing meaning in and of itself. The biblical stories as a result were treated independently of the literary context and interpretation that their authors gave them. (Think of how often the preaching and teaching of Gospel narratives by evangelical Christians focuses not on the intent of the evangelists in telling these account—that is, on their "meaning"—but rather on their subject matter. The focus in such instances is the same as for rationalists: meaning is sought in the event or subject matter rather than in the inscripturation of that event by the evangelists. Of course, the difference is huge. Evangelicals believe that the biblical accounts are true and accurate descriptions of what took place; rationalists believe they are false and inaccurate, but for both, meaning is sought in the event and not in the inspired interpretation of the evangelists.)

A second major attempt to find meaningfulness in the miracle stories of the Bible, while denying their facticity, was the theory of accommodation. According to this view, the authors of the biblical narratives knew that the events they were telling did not occur in the manner reported. They, like those proposing this theory, knew that no such miracles had occurred. But the authors realized that they were living among and seeking to minister to readers who believed in miracles and the presence of the supernatural in life. Thus, they shaped the principles and truths they sought to teach in the form of miracle stories. It should be noted that, according to the accommodationists, the meaning of these stories is what the authors willed to teach by them. However, the meaning was to be found in the willed meaning of authors who consciously created myths that their readers would think were true for the purpose of teaching ideal truths and principles.

In comparing the rationalist and the accommodationist approaches we find an interesting paradox. The rationalists, on the one hand, thought little of the intellectual ability of the biblical narrators, who badly misinterpreted what actually took place. The accommodationists, however, preserved the intellectual ability of the writers, for the writers were intelligent enough to know that these events were not true. Furthermore, they were brilliant in using the mythical mind-set of their readers to teach various religious principles. On the other hand, the rationalists protected the integrity of the biblical writers. They might not have been very smart, but they were honest! The accommodationists, while protecting the authors' intelligence, sacrificed their integrity. The biblical writers were quite dishonest, for they purposely misled their readers into thinking that what they were reporting was actually true. The view of the accommodationists also possessed a serious flaw in that they were never able to demonstrate that the biblical writers did not believe the historicity of what they were reporting. On the contrary, one thing that seemed reasonably clear to supernaturalists and nonsupernaturalists alike was that the biblical authors truly believed the facticity of what they were reporting. Consequently, the approach of the accommodationists to interpreting the miracle accounts in the Bible never gained a serious following.

The third major attempt to find meaning in miraculous biblical narratives was the mythical approach. Those who favored this view accepted the integrity of the authors and acknowledged that the biblical writers truly believed in the events they were reporting. They also referred to the authors' meaning by appealing to their inner subconsciousness that gave rise to the miracle stories (myths) that they reported. These biblical myths were essentially religious ideas dressed in historical clothing. The goal of their approach was to strip away the mythical dress of these miracle stories and discover their underlying meaning. This in turn was seen as the truth that was working in the subconsciousness of the authors as they wrote these myths. (This "subconsciousness" should not be confused with the "unconscious meaning" of an author's meaning discussed in chapter 2, for an unconscious meaning is a legitimate implication originating out of the consciously willed meaning of the author.) In the nineteenth century these subconscious meanings at work in the author tended to be understood as nineteenth-century liberal truths and values. In the twentieth century they tended to be twentieth-century existentialistic truths and calls for decision.

The main problem with the mythical approach to biblical narrative is that it confuses historical issues and literary genre. If we leave aside the question of the facticity of the miracle stories in the Bible, the whole question of whether these stories are myths becomes extremely easy to answer. The biblical narratives are not myths. They do not possess a mythical literary form. The stories in the Bible are best described as "realistic narrative" in that they are straightforward and use the language of ordinary events. The biblical stories take for granted the world as we tend to experience it. Mythical monsters and places are not found in them. Real events are described involving real persons, in real places, at real times. The biblical narratives assume that what is depicted in them had in fact actually taken place. There is no difference between biblical narrative and history with respect to literary genre. To call the biblical stories myths is an incorrect genre description and confuses a historical judgment such as "Miracles do not happen, so that the biblical narratives are untrue" with a literary one such as "Biblical narratives use the literary form of myth." To assess a biblical narrative as mythical, therefore, has nothing to do with the literary form of the narrative and how we can ascertain what the author meant. It is rather a judgment concerning the facticity of the narrative, and this affects significance, not meaning. It is essentially a historical judgment based on an incorrect judgment of their literary form rather than on the results of open historical investigation.

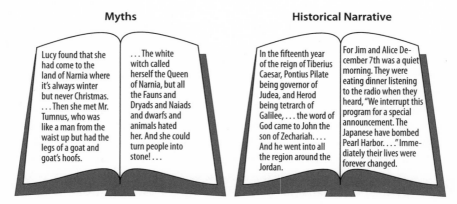

Myths   **Historical Narrative**

Lucy found that she had come to the land of Narnia where it's always winter but never Christmas. . . . Then she met Mr. Tumnus, who was like a man from the waist up but had the legs of a goat and goat's hoofs.

. . . The white witch called herself the Queen of Narnia, but all the Fauns and Dryads and Naiads and dwarfs and animals hated her. And she could turn people into stone! . . .

In the fifteenth year of the reign of Tiberius Caesar, Pontius Pilate being governor of Judea, and Herod being tetrarch of Galilee, . . . the word of God came to John the son of Zechariah. . . . And he went into all the region around the Jordan.

For Jim and Alice December 7th was a quiet morning. They were eating dinner listening to the radio when they heard, "We interrupt this program for a special announcement. The Japanese have bombed Pearl Harbor. . . ." Immediately their lives were forever changed.

In the process of seeking to make the biblical narratives meaningful, the rationalists, the accommodationists, and the mythicists were all seeking to find relevance in this form of biblical material. Yet the preoccupation with the facticity of the subject matter caused them to lose sight of where meaning is to be found. The meaning of a biblical narrative is to be found in what the author willed to teach his reader by recalling this account. It is not found in some hypothetical subconsciousness of the biblical authors. Nor is it found in the event itself; it is not identical with its subject matter. Thus the goal of the biblical exegete in interpreting historical narrative involves not the divine revelation contained in the event (a legitimate goal of systematic theology) but rather the divine revelation contained in the biblical authors' interpretation of that event. This can be seen rather clearly if we seek to complete the following sentence: "I, Mark, have told you how one day Jesus was crossing the Sea of Galilee with his disciples when a great storm arose . . . because _____." We cannot fill in the blank by simply retelling the subject matter of Mark 4:35–41. Meaning is not simply retelling what happened in history in AD 30. The meaning of Mark 4:35–41 involves what Mark sought to teach his readers by retelling this story.

Principles for Interpreting Biblical Narrative

The purpose of biblical narrative is not merely to tell what took place in the past. Rather, it is to relate these past events to biblical faith. Thus, the meaning of such texts involves not primarily what happened but rather the interpretation of what happened. Unlike legal materials or letters, however, the meaning of a narrative is taught implicitly rather than explicitly. The writers of the biblical narratives seldom say, "Now the point I am trying to make by this story is . . ." The meaning of a narrative is thus more elusive for the reader. To facilitate the interpretation of biblical narrative, investigation of the following is especially useful.

Context

Since a biblical narrative is always part of a larger narrative, the author assumes that his readers will seek to discover the meaning of a particular narrative in light of the overall meaning of the book. This is a good example of what is known as the hermeneutical circle. The reader, seeking to understand the part (the particular narrative), does so in light of an understanding of the whole (the entire book). In turn, the resulting understanding of the part makes clearer the understanding of the whole. It is common sense to realize that we must interpret a chapter in a book in light of the rest of the book, and of course we interpret the whole book in light of its individual chapters. This whole process is both helpful and frustrating. It is frustrating in that it ultimately requires the reader to possess an understanding of the entire work to interpret correctly the particular narrative he or she is reading. It is helpful, however, because the author provides by his entire work a useful context for the reader to interpret each narrative.

Sometimes the immediate context provides a clue to how the author intends his readers to interpret the narrative. An example is found in Mark 1:2–8. In this passage Mark tells the story of Jesus's baptism by John the Baptist. Frequently this passage is read (and taught) as follows:

As it is written in Isaiah the prophet,

> Behold, I send *my messenger* before <u>your</u> face,
>   *who* will prepare <u>your way</u>,
> *the voice of one crying in the wilderness:*
>   'Prepare the way of <u>the Lord</u>,
>   make <u>his paths</u> straight.'"

John appeared, baptizing in the wilderness and proclaiming a baptism of repentance for the forgiveness of sins. And all the country of Judea and all Jerusalem were going out *to him* and were being baptized *by him* in the river Jordan, confessing their sins. Now *John* was clothed with camel's hair and wore a leather belt around *his* waist and ate locusts and wild honey. And *he* preached, saying, "After *me* comes <u>he who is mightier than I</u>, the strap of whose sandals <u>I am not worthy</u> to stoop down and untie. *I have baptized you with water*, but <u>he will baptize you with the Holy Spirit</u>." (Mark 1:2–8, italics and underlining added)

In the above passage, the italicized words tend to receive the emphasis when read. If the passage is preached or taught, the speaker may spend time on such things as John's godly parents, his miraculous birth, when and where he ministered, or how he died. A speaker who has done some research about John the Baptist may share information about John found in the works of Josephus, talk about the relationship of John's and Jewish proselyte baptism, or discuss John's possible relationship to the Qumran community, which also had Isaiah 40:3 as its theme verse.

Yet Mark provides a context by which he wants his readers to interpret this narrative. His immediate contextual hint is found in Mark 1:1: "The beginning of the gospel of Jesus Christ, the Son of God." Although there is a textual problem concerning whether the expression "the Son of God" was originally part of the verse, this context indicates that the meaning of the following passage does not lie in the history of John the Baptist. In Mark's understanding, Mark 1:2–8 is a narrative about Jesus, not John.

This narrative is told by Mark in order to help his readers know that Jesus is the Christ, the Son of God. John the Baptist has no importance in and of himself for Mark. He is valuable only because he helps Mark tell who Jesus is. Thus the emphasis in reading this passage should be not on the italicized words but on the underlined words. This narrative enables Mark to show that Jesus of Nazareth is the Promised One, the Christ, the Son of God. John is the person the OT promised would one day come to prepare for the Messiah and Lord. Jesus is that One! (Note that "the LORD" in Isaiah 40:3, for whom John was to prepare, is in Hebrew *YHWH*, the God of Israel.) From the context that Mark provides in 1:1, we know what his meaning of the present narrative is.

This is confirmed when we take into consideration the context of the entire book. The Gospel according to Mark is a Gospel about Jesus. From beginning to end Jesus is the focus of attention. There is no narrative in the book that does not in some way center on him. He is the main content, the focus, and the object of the entire Gospel. Thus, as we read Mark 1:2–8 we need to ask the question, Why did Mark in telling us about Jesus include this story? The larger context of the entire work also seeks to have us read this narrative in light of what it teaches about Jesus of Nazareth.

Introductions and Conclusions

Another way in which an author gives clues as to how he wants his readers to interpret a narrative is through his introduction and conclusion to the narrative. Deuteronomy ends with a conclusion that summarizes the books of Exodus through Deuteronomy:

> And Joshua the son of Nun was full of the spirit of wisdom, for Moses had laid his hands on him. So the people of Israel obeyed him and did as the LORD had commanded Moses. And there has not arisen a prophet since in Israel like Moses, whom the LORD knew face to face, none like him for all the signs and the wonders that the LORD sent him to do in the land of Egypt, to Pharaoh and to all his servants and to all his land, and for all the mighty power and all the great deeds of terror that Moses did in the sight of all Israel. (34:9–12)

With this summary the author concludes the Pentateuch and introduces the book of Joshua. Similarly, in Exodus 3:6–12 the author begins with an introduction that reveals what is to take place in Exodus through Deuteronomy. The introduction to the book of Joshua gives readers the theme of this book in the opening verses: "After the death of Moses the servant of the

LORD, the LORD said to Joshua son of Nun, Moses' assistant, 'Moses my servant is dead. Now therefore arise, go over this Jordan, you and all this people, into the land that I am giving to them, to the people of Israel'" (1:1–2). Clearly we are to interpret this book recognizing that it is about the divinely ordained successor to Moses whom God would use to lead the children of Israel into the promised land.

In Judges the author likewise introduces readers to the theme of his work in the opening verses: "After the death of Joshua, the people of Israel inquired of the LORD, 'Who shall go up first for us against the Canaanites, to fight against them?' The LORD said, 'Judah shall go up; behold, I have given the land into his hand'" (1:1–2). The author reveals to us that this book is about a period in which there was a leadership crisis in Israel. No leader existed to succeed Joshua. And the author drives this point home in the concluding summary of the work when he points out that "in those days there was no king in Israel. Everyone did what was right in his own eyes" (21:25; cf. 17:6; Deut. 12:8). The future role of the tribe of Judah is also pointed out in 1:1–2, for when Israel received its king, he would come from Judah.

The Gospel writers also assist their readers in reading their individual narratives by the contextual clues given in their introductions and conclusions:

> Now Jesus did many other signs in the presence of the disciples, which are not written in this book; but these are written so that you may believe that Jesus is the Christ, the Son of God, and that by believing you may have life in his name. (John 20:30–31)

> The book of the genealogy of Jesus Christ, the son of David, the Son of Abraham. . . . Now after Jesus was born in Bethlehem of Judea in the days of Herod the king. . . . Then Jesus came from Galilee. . . . Then Jesus was led by the Spirit. (Matt. 1:1; 2:1; 3:13; 4:1)

> Inasmuch as many have undertaken to compile a narrative of the things that have been accomplished among us, just as those who from the beginning were eyewitnesses and ministers of the word have delivered them to us, it seemed good to me also, having followed all things closely for some time past, to write an orderly account for you, most excellent Theophilus, that you may have certainty concerning the things you have been taught. (Luke 1:1–4)

Each Gospel writer seeks through his various narratives to tell his readers about Jesus. As a result, most narratives in the Gospels should be interpreted as dealing with the identity and mission of Jesus.

Yet there is also a larger context within which the biblical narratives are written. The writers of the historical narratives in 1 and 2 Samuel, 1 and 2 Kings, and 1 and 2 Chronicles build upon the content of the Pentateuch, Joshua, and Judges. They accept as normative what has happened and is taught in these books, and they expect their readers to be acquainted with them and to accept them as normative as well. In a similar way the NT writers build on the teachings of the OT (Matt. 1:1; Mark 1:2–3; Rom. 1:2; 4:1–3; 9:1–5; Heb. 1:1–2; James 1:1; etc.).

Authorial Comments

On numerous occasions the authors of the biblical narratives intrude into accounts and give clues to their readers for interpreting these narratives. A familiar example of this is found in the expression that a king did "what was right in the eyes of the LORD" (1 Kings 14:8; 15:5, 11; 22:43; 2 Kings 10:30; 12:2; 14:3; 15:3, 34; 18:3; 22:2; 2 Chron. 14:2; 20:32; 24:2; 25:2; 26:4; 27:2; 29:2; 31:20; 34:2. What is right in God's eyes is explained in Exod. 15:26; Deut. 6:17–18; 13:18). Frequently the writer also describes why a king did right in the Lord's eyes and thus shares his value system with his readers. The authors of these books also reveal who did "evil in the eyes of the LORD" (1 Kings 11:6, 33; 14:8; 15:26, 34; 16:19, 25; 21:25; 22:52; 2 Kings 3:2; 8:18, 27; 13:2, 11; 15:9, 18, 24, 28; 16:2; 21:2, 15–16, 20; 23:32, 37; 24:9, 19; 2 Chron. 12:14; 22:4; 28:1; 33:2, 9; 36:5, 9, 12) and what this evil was.

Throughout the biblical narratives we find various insertions by the narrator/author that are intended to help the reader. In his Gospel, Mark frequently inserts such comments when foreign words appear in his account (5:41 ["Taking her by the hand he said to her, 'Talitha cumi,' which means, 'Little girl, I say to you, arise'"]; 7:11, 34; 15:22, 34) or to help his readers better understand the incident he is reporting (12:12 ["And they were seeking to arrest him but feared the people, for they perceived that he had told the parable against them. So they left him and went away"], 18, 42; 14:1–2, 56; 15:7, 16, 42; cf. Gen. 13:6; 14:2; Judg. 13:16; 1 Sam. 9:9; 2 Sam. 13:18; 19:32). The latter he frequently introduces in the Greek text with a "for" (1:16 ["Passing alongside the Sea of Galilee, he saw Simon and Andrew the brother of Simon casting a net into the sea, for they were fishermen"], 22; 2:15; 3:10, 21; 5:8, 28, 42; 6:14, 17, 18, 20, 31, 48, 50, 52; 7:3–4; 9:6, 31–32, 34; 10:22; 11:13, 18, 32; 14:2, 40, 56; 15:10; 16:4, 8). At times the Gospel writer also inserts an important theological comment in order to assist his readers in seeing the theological importance of the incident. In 7:19,

Mark adds, "(Thus he declared all foods clean.)" This enables the reader to understand that one of the implications of this incident is that it was no longer necessary to keep Jewish food regulations as to kosher or unkosher. Another such insertion is found in Mark 8:35, where the evangelist adds the term "gospel" to the saying (cf. the parallel sayings in Matt. 16:25 and Luke 9:24). Thus he indicates that to lose one's life for Christ is to lose one's life for the sake of the gospel. Elsewhere Mark appeals directly to his readers to pay attention to what they are reading (13:14) and mentions persons that only his early readers would know (15:21).

Authorial Summaries

Another way in which a narrator provides clues to help his readers know the meaning of his narrative is by inserting summary statements within the text. After the account of the creation in Genesis 1:1–30, the narrator summarizes God's work: "And God saw everything that he had made, and behold, it was very good" (v. 31). Such summaries are also found in the Gospels. After the opening description of Jesus's coming on the scene, Mark gives a summary that provides the reader with both a time frame and a theme for the ministry of Jesus: "Now after John was arrested, Jesus came into Galilee, proclaiming the gospel of God, and saying 'The time is fulfilled, and the kingdom of God at hand; repent and believe in the gospel'" (Mark 1:14–15). The themes of the coming of the kingdom of God (4:11, 26, 30; 9:1, 47; 10:14–15, 23–25; 11:10; 12:34; 14:25; 15:43) and the preaching of the gospel (1:4, 7, 38, 39, 45; 3:14; 5:20; 6:12; 7:36; 13:10; 14:9) are constant emphases in the narratives following 1:14–15. Later, Mark provides another summary to help his readers understand that Jesus's death was both necessary and in accordance with the divine plan: "And he [Jesus] began to teach them that the Son of Man must suffer many things and be rejected by the elders and the chief priests and the scribes and be killed, and after three days rise again. And he said this plainly" (8:31–32). The importance of this theme for Mark is seen in the fact that this summary is repeated time and time again (9:30–31; 10:32–34, 45). Through his summaries Luke likewise points out the divine necessity of the various gospel events he records, especially the death of Jesus (9:22; 13:33; 17:25; 18:31–33; 22:37; 24:7, 26–27, 46; Acts 17:3).

In Acts as well, Luke uses summaries to assist his reader in understanding this work. He uses many summaries to emphasize the numerical growth of the early church (2:41, 47; 4:4; 5:14; 6:1, 7; 9:31; 11:21, 24; 12:24; 14:1, 21; 16:4–5; 19:20). In light of the advice of Gamaliel (5:35–39), "a teacher of the law held in honor by all the people" (5:34), this numerical growth indicates for the readers of Acts that the Christian message and movement "is of God" (5:38–39). Luke uses the largest three summaries in Acts (2:42–47; 4:32–35; 5:12–16) to describe various positive characteristics of the life of the early church. These include prayer, the sharing of economic resources, the presence of apostolic signs and wonders, the presence of the apostolic teaching (cf. 2:42 with Luke 1:1–2), a favorable reputation among the people, and more.

Repetition

Another way an author shares his meaning with the reader is by repeating key themes. The author of Judges, for example, reveals his purpose in writing by means of the constant repetition of two main themes. One involves Israel's cyclical experience of rebellion, retribution, repentance, and restoration (see 3:7–9 for a succinct summary of this). When Israel does "evil in the sight of the LORD" (2:11–12; 3:7, 12; 4:1; 6:1a; 10:6; 13:1a), the LORD delivers them over to their enemies (2:14; 3:8, 12; 4:2; 6:1b; 10:7–9; 13:1b). When Israel cries in repentance to the LORD (3:9a, 15a; 4:3; 6:6–7; 10:10–16), the LORD then delivers them (3:9b, 15b; 4:4–24; 6:11–25; 11:1–33). Clearly, the author of Judges seeks to teach his readers that sin leads to judgment but that repentance leads to salvation.

An additional example of repetition by which the author of Judges helps his readers understand his work is found in the constantly repeated phrase "In those days there was no king in Israel" (17:6; 18:1; 19:1; 21:25). The author points out that the result of this is that chaos and anarchy reigned in Israel. At times God raised a deliverer or judge to rescue various tribes from their enemies, but the result of lacking a divinely ordained line of kings is that "everyone did what was right in his own eyes" (17:6; 21:25). The author ends his work (21:25) with these words and thus prepares his readers for the coming of God's gift of the monarchy. Note also how the biblical writers reveal God's sovereign rule over events by repeating the phrase "thus fulfilling the word of the LORD that he had spoken" or something similar (1 Kings 2:27; 8:15, 24; 12:15; 15:29; 16:12, 34; 2 Kings 1:17; 23:16; 24:2; 2 Chron. 6:4, 15; 36:20–21).

We find a similar kind of repetition of key themes in the Gospel according to Luke. Luke continually emphasizes the importance of the Holy Spirit in the life and ministry of Jesus. The Spirit is involved in the birth of John the Baptist (1:15) and the conception of Jesus (1:35). Before his birth the Spirit bears witness to Jesus (1:41–45). At his baptism Jesus is anointed by the Spirit in a powerful way ("in bodily form, like a dove," 3:22). "Full of the Holy Spirit" he is then led by the Spirit into the wilderness (4:1). When he returns "in the power of the Spirit" to Nazareth (4:14), he announces in his first sermon, "The Spirit of the Lord is upon me" (4:18). Clearly, by this repetition Luke wants his readers to understand the importance of the Spirit in the life and ministry of Jesus, and this prepares for the importance of the Spirit for the life and ministry of the church in Luke's second work, Acts.

Proportion

Another helpful tool for interpreting biblical narrative involves the amount of space that an author devotes to certain aspects of a story. We will refer to this again in the investigation of story parables as "who/what gets the most space" (see p. 172). This can be seen in two narratives found in Mark 5. Mark spends an unusual amount of space describing a demon-possessed man in 5:2–5, 9.

> And when Jesus had stepped out of the boat, immediately there met him out of the tombs a man with an unclean spirit. He lived among the tombs. And no one could bind him anymore, not even with a chain, for he had often been bound with shackles and chains, but he wrenched the chains apart, and he broke the shackles in pieces. No one had the strength to subdue him. Night and day among the tombs and on the mountains he was always crying out and cutting himself with stones. . . . And Jesus asked him, "What is your name?" He replied, "My name is Legion, for we are many."

The second is found in 5:25–26.

> And there was a woman who had had a discharge of blood for twelve years, and who had suffered much under many physicians, and had spent all that she had, and was no better but rather grew worse.

In both these stories the author has heightened the tragic and hopeless condition of the man and woman and the inability of those who sought to help. Jesus's ability to heal these two people indicates his great might and power. The greater the problem and hopelessness of the man and woman, the greater must be Jesus, the Son of God, who takes not twelve years to heal the woman but an instant and brings immediate relief to the demon-possessed man whose healed condition (sitting, clothed, and in his right mind [5:15]) is contrasted with his previous bondage.

Authoritative Speakers

Another way in which an author helps his readers understand the meaning of his narrative is by placing key dialogues in the mouths of various speakers. The reader knows, because of who is speaking, whether what is being said represents the mind of the narrator. For instance, when God or Jesus speaks, the reader knows that the author wants what is being said to be accepted as true. Similarly, when faithful servants of God, such as a patriarch, prophet, or apostle, speak, this too can be relied upon as being true and authoritative unless the narrator reveals otherwise. At times various characters are portrayed positively by the narrator, and the reader thus recognizes that what they say or do is to be accepted as being in accordance with the will of God. For example, Luke goes out of his way to describe Joseph of Arimathea as "a good and righteous man . . . looking for the kingdom of God" (Luke 23:50–51). Because he was a member of the Council, which had plotted against Jesus, Luke also adds that Joseph "had not consented to their decision and action" (23:51). Thus we can accept his action in burying Jesus as being good and noble. When Luke describes Zechariah and Elizabeth as being childless (Luke 1:7), to prevent this from being misinterpreted as a sign of judgment upon them (cf. Lev. 20:20–21 and Jer. 22:30) or as one of shame (cf. Gen. 29:32–30:2; 1 Sam. 1:5–6, 11; Luke 1:24–25) he points out that "they were both righteous before God, walking blamelessly in all the commandments and statues of the Lord" (Luke 1:6). Thus, we can rely on them as positive examples of piety except, as Luke points out, for Zechariah's momentary lack of faith (Luke 1:11–20).

Throughout the Bible the narrators help their readers understand how to interpret their words. This is often done through the use of positive characters (1 Sam. 29:9; 2 Sam. 14:17, 20; 19:27; 1 Kings 18:13; Job 1:1), but it is also done through evil characters (Gen. 13:13; 1 Sam. 2:12; 25:3; 2 Sam. 20:1; 1 Kings 12:8). The latter provide counsel and actions that are to be avoided. Even if an author does not provide an editorial description of these characters, we are able to judge whether he approves or disapproves of them according to whether they exemplify the character and plan of God revealed in the rest of the Bible. Even apart from any editorial comment, the reader knows whether they are to be viewed positively or negatively due to the teachings found in the earlier canonical writings. Similarly, unless they inform their readers otherwise, the authors assume that the actions, teachings, and behavior of the characters in the Gospels and Acts are to be interpreted positively or negatively in light of the teachings found in the OT.

Mark gives his readers an important interpretive clue in 1:34, "And he [Jesus] would not permit the demons to speak, *because they knew him*" (italics added). This assists his readers in understanding that the various confessions of the demons ("I know who you are—the Holy One of God" [1:24]; "What have you to do with me, Jesus, Son of the Most High God?" [5:7]) and the Markan summary of the demons' confession ("And whenever the unclean spirits saw him, they fell down before him and cried out, 'You are the Son of God.' And he strictly ordered them not to make him known" [3:11–12]) are to be believed as accurate confessions of who Jesus is, because the demons are reliable spokesmen reflecting the Markan point of view that Jesus is "the Christ, the Son of God" (1:1).

Dialogue or Direct Discourse

Within a narrative account, as in story parables (see p. 171), one way in which a narrator focuses the attention of his readers is through the use of dialogue. When indirect discourse (conversation reported indirectly) turns to direct discourse (conversation denoted by quotation marks), this is a clue that careful attention should be paid to what is being said. Thus, in the story of Jesus's stilling the storm, the key to understanding the narrative comes in the words uttered by the disciples: "Who then is this, that even the wind and the sea obey him?" (Mark 4:41). What Mark seeks to share with his readers as he recounts this tradition is that Jesus is the Christ, the Son of God. He is Master of nature itself, and even the dangers and threats of nature cannot overwhelm those who are his children.

Within various accounts we come across dialogues between God and his servants, and within those dialogues the major theme of the narratives becomes clear. It is in the divine theophany in Exodus 3, in which God directly speaks to Moses, that the author provides the clue for understanding both this narrative and the entire book. This narrative and book is about the One who said to Moses, "I am the God of your father, the God of Abraham, the God of Isaac, and the God of Jacob. . . . I have surely seen the affliction of my people who are in Egypt. . . . I have come down to deliver them out of the hand of the Egyptians and to bring them up out of that land to a good and broad land, a land flowing with milk and honey" (vv. 6–8). Within this narrative the direct discourse tells us that Moses will be used of God to lead the people of Israel out of their bondage to the Pharaoh of Egypt and ultimately into the land of Canaan. Similarly, in the opening discourse of Joshua 1:2–9, where the LORD speaks to Joshua, the author sets the tone for not just the following narrative but the entire book.

Conclusion

The interpretation of biblical narrative presents some unique problems. This is especially true for those who deny the historicity of the events recorded in them. If, however, the meaning of a biblical narrative is determined by the communicative intent of the author, then the historicity or lack of historicity of the event recorded in it does not in any way change the meaning of the account. The account means what the author willed to say by the account, whether the event described in it is true or untrue. Thus both critical and evangelical scholars can work together in seeking to understand the meaning of biblical narratives. To be sure, the significance attributed to that meaning will be radically different. Paul understood this. The interpretation that Paul gave to the death and resurrection of Jesus will always remain the same, regardless of whether Jesus rose from the dead or not. But if Christ did not rise from the dead, the interpretation Paul gave to it is foolish. It is a falsehood, and faith in this fictional story is futile (1 Cor. 15:12–19). Christianity stands or falls on the facticity of the biblical narratives. It cannot seek meaning in some mythical subconsciousness of the authors that gave birth to these fictions. Even less can it seek meaning in a reconstruction of "what really happened." The meaning of a biblical narrative is what the author meant to teach by the event recorded in it. Since that meaning depended in their minds on the facticity of what they were reporting, the meaning must be rejected if we do not believe these events occurred. It cannot, however, be changed into something else.

As for discovering that meaning, we have observed several principles that will assist us. The literary context that the author has given is most valuable. This context involves not just the verses that precede and follow the passage but the entire work within which the author has placed it. We must interpret a particular narrative in light of the theme and purpose of the entire book in which it is found. This requires study, but that study will be rewarded with a clearer understanding of how this particular narrative (the part) fits into the entire book (the whole). At other times authors assist their readers in interpreting the narrative by inserting various comments into the account. These may provide historical or cultural information needed to help understand the narrative. At times an author may provide a summary of some sort, and this can appear not just at the end of the narrative but at the beginning or in the middle as well. Through repetition an author also helps the reader understand what he sought to teach. Another way of assisting the reader is by using authoritative speakers who represent the point he is making. Likewise, by his use of dialogue an author helps his readers focus on the importance of what is being said. Keeping all this in mind, we can understand the meaning of a biblical narrative as long as we do not confuse this meaning with its subject matter. We will be assisted in this if, as we investigate such narratives, we seek to fill in the following paradigm: "I [the biblical author] have written that . . . [the biblical narrative] because _____."

Questions

1. What are some indications that a biblical author gives to readers that what follows is a parable? A historical narrative? A fable?
2. What is the main difference between a historical-like narrative, such as Shakespeare's *Julius Caesar* or Margaret Mitchell's *Gone with the Wind*, and a historical narrative, such as Winston Churchill's *The Second World War* or Cornelius Ryan's *The Longest Day*?
3. When reading a book, to which parts should we pay particular attention in order to understand the author's purpose? What about a biblical book?
4. Why did/do many interpreters of biblical narrative reject the definition of "meaning" given in chapter 2?
5. Can you define what is meant by "context" in this chapter?
6. How would you interpret a work beginning, "Once upon a time . . ."? How would you interpret a work beginning, "It was early on the morning of June 6, 1944. A small ship landed secretly on the shores of Normandy when . . ."? Would you look for the meaning differently? What would be different? Would you treat the significance differently? The subject matter?

6

The Game of Rules

Covenants and Laws

In this chapter we shall look at two related literary forms found in the Bible. These are found in the opening narrative of the Bible (Genesis) and throughout the OT and NT. They form the basis of humanity's relationship with God. These two forms, covenant and law, are closely related, for the laws of the Bible are based on a covenantal relationship between God and the believer.

Covenant

The importance of the covenant in the Bible is not always recognized. We read of the covenants God made with Adam/Eve and Noah. It is the Abrahamic covenant, however, that is the most important. This covenant (Gen. 12, 15, 17) is renewed with Isaac (Gen. 26:1–5) and Jacob (Gen. 28:10–17; 35:9–15), remembered (Exod. 2:23–25) and renewed (Exod. 19:1–9; Deut. 7:6–11) during the exodus from Egypt, renewed with Joshua (Josh. 24:14–27, esp. vv. 25–27), and referred to time and time again in the OT (e.g., with respect to David [2 Sam. 7:8–16; 23:5]; by Solomon [1 Kings 8:9, 23]; and by the biblical narrator [2 Kings 13:23]). Jeremiah 31:31–34 refers to a coming new covenant, which finds its fulfillment in Jesus (Luke 22:20; 1 Cor. 11:25). And it is this new covenant, the fulfillment of the covenant initiated with Abraham, that is the hope of the believer (Acts 3:25; Gal. 3:6–9, 15–18, 29).

A great deal has been learned in the past century concerning the covenant form. This is due to the discovery of numerous covenants in the literature of the ancient Near East, especially in the Hittite literature. There were two main kinds of covenants. The difference between them depends on the relationship of the people involved. If the relationship involves equals (Gen. 14:13; 21:27–32; 26:28–31; 31:44–50; 1 Sam. 18:3; 1 Kings 5:12), this results in a parity covenant. In such a covenant both parties mutually agree as equals to obey similar stipulations. The other form is called a suzerainty covenant. This is not a treaty among equals, for an ancient suzerain was a feudal lord. In a suzerainty covenant the lord unilaterally establishes the terms and conditions for his subjects. The subjects in turn can only accept or reject the covenant and its terms. This kind of covenant contains such things as

- *Preamble*: In the preamble the author of the covenant identifies himself.
- *Historical prologue*: This describes the previous relationship of the two parties and emphasizes the gracious character of the suzerain in his past dealings with the lesser party. It provides justification for the stipulations that follow.
- *Stipulations*: This describes the obligations and responsibilities of the lesser party and involves such things as the prohibition of establishing relationships and treaties with other nations (e.g., "You shall have no other gods before me," Exod. 20:3), support for the suzerain, the obligation to hate the suzerain's enemies, and various prohibitions and commands. These stipulations are not conditions for entering the covenant but for remaining true to it. The prime stipulation involves loyalty to the suzerain.
- *Provision for continual reading*: This was meant to insure familiarity with the covenant by the people and their descendants.
- *List of witnesses*: Frequently the suzerain would appeal to the gods (cf. "heaven and earth," Deut. 30:19) to bear witness to the establishment of the covenant.
- *Blessings and curses*: These are contingent on the subjects' obedience or disobedience.
- *Ratification ceremony*: This generally included a sacrifice and oath and was frequently followed by a common meal.

Not all of these elements are always present. The most important are the preamble, the historical prologue, the stipulations, and the blessings and curses.

Biblical Covenant	Declarations of Covenants, Conditions, and Restrictions
Preamble	
—	
—	
Historical prologue	Witnessed
—	
—	Definitions
Stipulations	1. Party A
—	2. Party B
—	Duties of party A
Provision for continual reading	1. Security
—	2. Landscaping
—	3. Collection and garbage
List of witnesses	
—	
—	Duties of party B
Blessings and cursings	1. Maintenance and repair
—	2. Minimum landscape plan
—	3. Mailboxes
Ratification ceremony	
—	
—	

Within the OT no divine covenant follows the order listed above exactly or contains all these elements, but it is evident that the OT covenants are patterned along similar lines. The Abrahamic covenant and the various versions of this covenant are clearly not parity covenants: they are not covenants among equals. On the contrary, the conditions of the covenant are made unilaterally. It is the LORD God of Israel who establishes these covenants and determines their conditions. The covenant he establishes with the people of Israel, however, is gracious. It is not earned or merited but due entirely to the mercy and grace of God. Even the blessings are not earned or merited, for they are offered as rewards for obedience, not as pay that is owed.

When we compare the OT covenants with the form of the suzerainty covenant, we find some remarkable parallels:

Genesis 12:1–3

Preamble: "Now the LORD said to Abram . . ." (12:1a).

Stipulations: "Go from your country and your kindred and your father's house to the land that I will show you" (12:1b).

Blessings: "I will make of you a great nation, and I will bless you . . ." (12:2).

Genesis 17:1–14

Preamble: "I am God Almighty" (17:1).

Stipulations: "This is my covenant. . . . Every male among you shall be circumcised . . ." (17:10–14).

Blessings: "I [will] make my covenant between me and you, and [will] multiply you greatly" (17:2). "You shall be the father of a multitude of nations" (17:4–8; cf. 17:15–16).

Exodus 19–24

Preamble: "I am the LORD your God . . ." (20:2).

Historical prologue: "Thus you shall say to the house of Jacob, and tell the people of Israel: 'You yourselves have seen what I did to the Egyptians, and how I bore you on eagles' wings and brought you to myself'" (19:3–4). "I am the LORD your God, who brought you out of the land of Egypt, out of the house of slavery" (20:2).

Stipulations: "Now therefore, if you will indeed obey my voice and keep my covenant . . ." (19:5). "You shall have no other gods before me . . ." (20:3–17).

Provision for continual reading: "Then he took the Book of the Covenant and read it in the hearing of the people" (24:7).

List of witnesses: "All the people answered together . . ." (19:8; cf. 24:3, 7).

Oath: "'All that the LORD has spoken we will do'" (19:8). "Moses came and told the people all the words of the LORD and all the rules. And all the people answered with one voice and said, "All the words that the LORD has spoken we will do'" (24:3).

Deuteronomy

Preamble: "These are the words that Moses spoke to all Israel . . ." (1:1–5).

Historical prologue: (1:6–4:49).

Stipulations: (5:1–26:19, comprising general [5:1–11:32] and specific [12:1–26:19] commands).

Blessings and curses: (27:1–30:20).

List of witnesses: "I call heaven and earth to witness against you this day . . ." (30:19; cf. 4:26; 31:19; 32:1).

Provision for continual reading: (27:1–14; 31:9–13).

Joshua 24:1–33

Preamble: "And Joshua said to all the people, 'Thus says the LORD, the God of Israel . . .'" (24:2a).

Historical prologue: "Long ago, your fathers lived beyond the Euphrates . . . and they served other gods. Then I took your father Abraham from beyond the River and led him . . ." (24:2b–13).

Stipulations: "Now therefore fear the LORD and serve him . . ." (24:14–21).

List of witnesses: "'You are witnesses against yourselves that you have chosen the LORD, to serve him.' And they said, 'We are witnesses'" (24:22).

Provision for continual reading: "And Joshua wrote these words in the Book of the Law of God" (24:26).

Oath: "And the people said to Joshua, 'The LORD our God we will serve, and his voice we will obey'" (24:24).

The parallels between the examples given above and ancient suzerain treaties are quite impressive. As they recorded these covenants, the writers of Scripture expected their readers to recognize them as suzerain treaties and to understand their various elements. Knowing this treaty form and what is involved enables us to interpret the biblical examples better. We shall mention two principles involved in interpreting such treaty forms.

One is that we must always keep in mind the unilateral and gracious nature of the biblical covenants. These covenants are not treaties established among equals. On the contrary, they originated in the graciousness of a most superior party—God himself. Thus, we must remember at the start that they should not be interpreted as a means of placing God in our debt or under obligation to us. The sovereign LORD may willingly obligate himself to us, but this has nothing to do with our worthiness or merit. The covenant originated in grace and is based on grace alone.

The second is that the stipulations found in a covenant are not to be understood as requirements in order to initiate a positive relationship with God. On the contrary, they presume an already-existing covenantal relationship. The Ten Commandments of Exodus 20:2–17 are not directed to people outside a covenantal relationship, revealing how they may enter into such a relationship. They are given to God's people, who have already been redeemed from bondage (Exod. 20:1), and describe how that relationship can be maintained so that God's people may continue to experience his blessing. The intimate association between the covenant God made with Israel and the stipulations or laws associated with that covenant can be seen in the numerous references made to the ark of the covenant and the fact that within the ark were contained the Ten Commandments (Exod. 25:16, 21; 40:20; 1 Kings 8:9).

Law and Commandments

In the Bible a large section, the books of Genesis through Deuteronomy, is called the "Law." The "Law" can also refer to the entire OT (cf. John 10:34; 12:34; 15:25; 1 Cor. 14:21, which refer to the "Law" but quote another part of the OT). Usually, however, the Law is associated with Exodus 20–Deuteronomy 33. Within this section we find material other than laws. However, since there are over six hundred commandments or laws found in Genesis–Deuteronomy, these five books are usually referred to as "the Law." (Genesis does not contain any of this legal material but is part of the Law, because it serves as the introduction to Exodus–Deuteronomy and because, according to tradition, Moses wrote all of these books. In actuality, however, these five books, also called the Pentateuch, consist mostly of narrative.)

When we compare the laws found in this section of the OT with ancient Near Eastern laws, we can observe at times a striking similarity. For instance, the laws concerning false witness (Exod. 23:1–3; Deut. 19:16–21; cf. Hammurabi Laws 1–4), kidnapping (Exod. 21:16; cf. Hammurabi Laws 14), animals left to the safekeeping of others (Exod. 22:10–13; cf. Hammurabi Laws 265–67), animals borrowed from others (Exod. 22:14–15; cf. Hittite Laws 74–76), and an ox goring another ox (Exod. 21:35–36; cf. Eshnunna Laws 53–55; Hammurabi Laws 250–52) are alike in both content and wording with laws and regulations in other societies of the ancient Near East. Note the following example:

> If a seignior [a man of rank] has destroyed the eye of the son of a man [of similar rank], they shall destroy his eye. (Hammurabi Laws 196–201; *Ancient Near Eastern Texts Relating to the Old Testament*, ed. J. B. Pritchard, trans. and annotated by W. F. Albright et al., 2nd ed. [Princeton: Princeton University Press, 1955], 175)

> If anyone injures his neighbor, as he has done it shall be done to him, fracture for fracture, eye for eye, tooth for tooth; whatever injury he has given a person shall be given to him. (Lev. 24:19–20)

The laws of the Bible can be classified according to form into two types: casuistic law and apodictic law. The former is a case-by-case law, which usually goes something like this: "*If* A takes place, *then* B will be the consequences." Casuistic law usually involves secular or civil matters. Apodictic law, however, is declarative and categorical. It tends to consist of prohibitions, commands, and instructions. These laws are often unqualified, understood to be divine commands, and tend to be more "religious" in nature. Most laws in the ancient Near East tend to be casuistic. This is also true with respect to the OT.

The laws of the Bible are not exhaustive in nature. They serve as principles that govern behavior by means of the implications they contain. Thus the command "You shall not commit adultery" (Exod. 20:14) has numerous implications concerning lust (cf. Matt. 5:27–30) and pornography even though these things are not explicitly mentioned in the command itself. A useful analogy between the laws contained in the OT and their various implications is how the Constitution of the United States relates to the various laws passed by Congress. The articles of the Constitution contain implications that these laws bring out. (The analogy is not a perfect one, however, because some laws passed by Congress may violate the Constitution. Others may not be contained within the principles of the Constitution but do not violate them.) The laws of the OT were understood by their authors as involving principles that went beyond the specific meaning found in the law itself, even as the authors of the Constitution understood their work as containing numerous unstated implications.

Another distinction frequently made between various laws involves not so much their form as their content. These are frequently divided into three classifications: ethical laws (such as the Ten Commandments or Ten "Words" [Exod. 20:1; 34:27–28; Deut. 4:13; 10:4]), cultic laws (such as the ritual laws involving sacrifices, qualifications for priestly duty, and prohibition of unclean foods), and civil laws (penalties for crimes, inheritance regulations, etc.). Some have objected to this threefold division because the OT does not explicitly make such a distinction and at times these classifications appear to overlap. Were the laws regulating disease and cleansing (Lev. 13–15) cultic or civil? Were they both? Because they involve priests and sacrifice, it is not easy to determine.

The distinction among the ethical, cultic, and civil dimensions of the law is nevertheless both useful and grounded in the NT distinction. Jesus saw a distinction between the cultic and ethical dimensions of the law when he said, "There is nothing outside a person that by going into him can defile him, but the things that come out of a person are what defile him" (Mark 7:15; cf. also vv. 18–23). Mark also understood the distinction when he added the comment "Thus he declared all foods clean" (Mark 7:19). Luke and Paul likewise witness to this distinction in Acts 10; 15; Galatians 2:11–21; 1 Corinthians 6:12–20; 8; 10:23–11:1; and above all, Romans 14.

When the NT refers to the laws of the OT, it understands the cultic and civil laws as being no longer binding. The OT foresaw that a time would come when a new covenant would be established. At that time some of the stipulations involved in the old covenant would come to an end. In the new covenant all foods are cleansed (Mark 7:19; cf. Acts 10:9–16), the sacrificial system and its priesthood have become superfluous through the once-for-all sacrifice of Jesus and his eternal priesthood on our behalf (Heb. 7–8; 10:1–10), and circumcision is no longer required (Gal. 5:2–6). The civil laws of the OT are also no longer binding, since the OT theocratic nation of Israel no longer exists, and the NT covenant people is not defined as a body of people associated with a particular race and territory. The principles of such laws, however, may still reflect divine guidelines that an organized society would do well to follow. Such principles, which limit revenge and seek reciprocity between crime and punishment ("eye for eye, tooth for tooth, hand for hand, foot for foot, burn for burn, wound for wound, stripe for stripe," Exod. 21:24–25) and see a difference in actions according to whether they are intentional or accidental (Num. 35:6–34), provide good counsel for any society to follow.

As to the ethical dimension of the OT laws, there is no reason to think that they would change drastically, for they reflect the character of God. The NT writers understand them as still binding. Certainly Matthew understands them in this way when he quotes Jesus, "Do not think that I have come to abolish the Law or the Prophets; I have not come to abolish them but to fulfill them. . . . Therefore whoever relaxes one of the least of these commandments and teaches others to do the same will be called least in the kingdom of heaven, but whoever does them and teaches them will be called great in the kingdom of heaven" (Matt. 5:17, 19). Matthew then proceeds to show that the greater righteousness that Jesus demands involves not merely an external keeping of the specific commands of the law. The Pharisees and teachers of the law did that. In Matthew 5:21–48 the higher righteousness Jesus demands involves keeping the entire principle found in these commands and their various implications. Jesus's summary of the whole law as encapsulated in the two commands to love God and one's neighbor (Mark 12:28–34) also indicates that the ethical teachings of the law are still to be kept. The fact that Paul (Gal. 5:14; Rom. 13:9) and James (James 2:8) quote Jesus's summary of the law indicate that they thought similarly. It is best therefore to assume that these OT laws are still binding for the believer unless specifically abrogated in the NT.

When interpreting the laws of the Bible, it is important to remember several things. First of all, we must remember that they are associated with a gracious covenant. The attempt to keep the commandments perfectly will always fail and can never lead to salvation. Due to our fallen nature and sin, we do not (Rom. 3:1–20) and cannot keep the commandments perfectly (Rom. 7:7–25; cf. Matt. 6:12; 1 John 1:5–10). Furthermore, the attempt to keep the commandments cannot save, because to be saved one must be a beneficiary of this gracious covenant. It is only after a covenantal relationship is already established, based on God's grace, that the stipulations of the law are given. We must never forget how covenant and law are related. It is after God establishes a covenant of grace with his people that he gives the stipulations of the law. The exodus (Exod. 14; 20:2) preceded the giving of the law on Mount Sinai (Exod. 20:3–17). The order cannot be reversed: salvation precedes obedience. Obedience is the *result* of salvation, not its cause!

Yet after a person has entered into this covenant and become God's servant, he or she needs to and desires to serve God. The new nature and heartfelt gratitude of the believer demand this. The debates about lordship salvation and "Once saved, always saved?" have all too often lost sight of the fact that salvation takes place within a covenantal relationship. That covenant brings with it numerous benefits. One of them is regeneration. The regenerated heart will seek to serve God. What serving God involves is described in the laws and stipulations he has given in his covenant. How that service is then rendered is by obedience to those laws. It would be a strange "faith" indeed that did not result in a regenerated heart and life and was unconcerned or antagonistic toward God's laws. However else the Bible might describe such a "faith," it would not describe it as saving faith. It is more like the faith that James says the demons possess (James 2:19).

Another principle for interpreting the laws of the Bible is to note that their specific meaning does not exhaust everything contained in that meaning. The laws of the Bible contain principles that have numerous implications. Even if the law is worded as a specific command or prohibition rather than a general principle, its meaning is not exhausted by obeying the specific law. Thus, even laws that seem out of date and no longer applicable may carry useful and appropriate implications for today. If a command such as "eye for eye, tooth for tooth" does not seem to be applicable today, it is only because the interpreter is not aware of the principle and the various implications contained in that statement. Its principle, that punishment should fit the crime, will always be relevant.

Similarly, the casuistic law found in Exodus 21:28–29 has important implications for today: "When an ox gores a man or a woman to death, the ox shall be stoned, and its flesh shall not be eaten, but the owner of the ox shall not be liable. But if the ox has been accustomed to gore in the past, and its owner has been warned but has not kept it in, and it kills a man or woman, the ox shall be stoned, and its owner also shall be put to death." In practice this penalty does not seem to have been literally carried out in Israel, but a severe financial penalty was administered. Today, too, we need to make a distinction between harm or death brought about by accident or by careless negligence.

One additional principle for interpreting the laws of the Bible can be mentioned. The law reveals our sin and depravity. Even in our best moments we fail to keep the laws of God perfectly. Thus, we must recognize that we need forgiveness and grace. One purpose of the law is to show us our need of God's grace (Rom. 7:7–25). If we stand outside a covenantal relationship with God, it intends to drive us to repentance and to seek God's saving grace. If we stand within that covenantal relationship, it shows us that time and time again we fail to keep the divine stipulations of the covenant and that we must confess our sins (1 John 1:9) and pray, "Forgive us our debts" (Matt. 6:12). (Cf. how the OT sacrifices graciously provided for such circumstances in Lev. 4:1–6:7 and 7:1–10.) We enter into a covenantal relationship with God on the basis of grace alone, and that relationship is maintained on the basis of grace as well.

Questions

1. What is a covenant? Do you belong to any covenant, such as a community covenant of homeowners or an organization that has a covenant?
2. How is the covenant God made with the children of Israel like a human covenant? How is it unlike a human covenant?
3. How are covenant and law related? Can a person enter into a covenant with God and not accept the rules and laws associated with it?
4. Can a person stand in a covenantal relationship with God (i.e., be "saved") and continually and willfully live a life of sin and disobedience? How would you support your answer to this question?

7

The Game of Rhythm

Poetry

One of the literary forms frequently found in the Bible is poetry. What distinguishes biblical poetry from prose is not so much any one single feature as a combination of them. Clearly the most important feature is parallelism, or rhythmic balance between different lines. Another feature is terseness. In poetry the lines of sentences tend to be much shorter in comparison to the lines found in prose. The lines also tend to be of equal length, whereas in prose there is great variety in the size of sentences. Poetry also tends to be disinclined to use conjunctions and particles. (In a recent study it was pointed out that Hebrew prose tends to use the sign of the direct object [*'et*], the relative pronoun [*'asher*], and the definite article [*ha*] six to eight times more than Hebrew poetry.) On the other hand, poetry is far more inclined to use figurative language, that is, nonliteral figures of speech that can be simple (metaphor, analogy, hyperbole, personification, etc.) or extended (similitude, parable, riddle, idioms, etc.).

Poetry is not clearly distinguished from prose in older translations of the Bible such as the KJV, but in modern translations such as the RSV, NEB, NIV, REB, NRSV, NLT, and ESV, the poetic sections of the Bible are clearly seen. If we skim through the more historical books of the OT, from Genesis to 2 Chronicles, we find that most of the material in these books appears as solid paragraphs, as prose. On the other hand, if we skim through Job,

Psalms, Proverbs, Isaiah, and the other prophets, we find that much, if not most, of the material in these books appears in broken lines, as poetry. The solid blocks of black text typify the prose sections of Scripture; the poetic sections contain much more white space, and the black text is quite broken. Yet even in the prose sections of the Bible, we find major sections of poetry (see Gen. 3:14–19; 4:23–24; 49; Exod. 15; Num. 6:24–26; 21:27–30; 23:7–10, 18–24; 24; Deut. 32–33; Judg. 5; 1 Sam. 2:1–10; 15:22–23; 2 Sam. 1:19–27; 22; 23:1–7; 2 Kings 19:21–28; 1 Chron. 16:8–36; 2 Chron. 6:41–42).

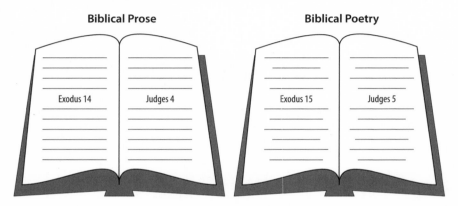

Biblical Prose   Exodus 14   Judges 4   **Biblical Poetry**   Exodus 15   Judges 5

Poetry Compared to Prose

The use of poetry in ancient times, as in our own, indicates that the writer is less concerned with precise description or scientific accuracy than with evoking emotions and creating certain impressions. Poetry is clearly commissive rather than referential in nature (see pp. 68–69). Physicians do not use poetry to describe their patients' medical problems, but lovers do when they seek to express their love for each other. The biblical poets and songwriters frequently used this form in their praise and adoration of God. When they did so, however, they anticipated that their readers would interpret what they wrote according to the rules governing such poetry. We are fortunate that in the Bible we have at least two places where prose and poetic accounts of the same event appear side by side. By comparing them we can see that they function in different ways, although in each instance they still convey what the author meant by the verbal symbols he placed in these different literary genres.

One example in which prose and poetic accounts of the same event are found side by side is Exodus 14–15. It is obvious that chapter 14 is prose because of its solid black paragraphs and that chapter 15 is poetry because of the unevenness of its paragraphs and the amount of white space. The writer also makes this clear by his introduction: "Then Moses and the people of Israel *sang this song* to the LORD, saying . . ." (15:1). Thus, whereas we have in chapter 14 a description of the LORD's victory over the army of Pharaoh in the form of prose, in chapter 15 that victory is described in poetry.

We find in the poetic version of this victory several descriptions that cannot be taken literally:

> I will sing to the LORD, for he has triumphed gloriously;
>   the horse and his rider he has thrown into the sea. (v. 1)

> Pharaoh's chariots and his host he cast into the sea,
>   and his chosen officers were sunk in the Red Sea. (v. 4)

> In the greatness of your majesty you overthrow your adversaries;
>   you send out your fury; it consumes them like stubble. (v. 7)

> At the blast of your nostrils the water piled up;
>   the floods stood up in a heap;
>   the deeps congealed in the heart of the sea. (v. 8)

> You stretched out your right hand;
>   the earth swallowed them. (v. 12)

> Sing to the LORD, for he has triumphed gloriously;
>   the horse and his rider he has thrown into the sea. (v. 21)

It is clear that in the verses above we have a highly metaphorical description of how God delivered his people from the army of Pharaoh. In verses 1, 4, and 21 God is depicted as a mighty warrior who picks up in his hands the forces of Pharaoh and throws them into the Red Sea. Yet in chapter 14 the forces of Pharaoh are described as having followed the people of Israel into the Red Sea, so that when the waters returned to their normal position, the Egyptians drowned. We also find in verse 7 a rather awkward description of God's destruction of the Egyptian forces. They are "consumed . . . like stubble." But Pharaoh's forces were not burned: they drowned. This, however, poses no problem for the writer, because the expression "consumed . . . like stubble" is a common metaphor for judgment and destruction (cf. Isa. 5:24; 47:14; Joel 2:5; Obad. 18; Nah. 1:10), and God brought judgment and destruction that day upon Pharaoh's army. (For an example within poetry itself of literal and picturesque descriptions of the same event standing side by side, compare 2 Sam. 22:1–4 with 22:7–20, and Ps. 18:1–3 with 18:6–15.)

Another example in which prose and poetic accounts of the same event stand side by side is found Judges 4 and 5. In the fourth chapter of Judges the author describes in prose the defeat of the Canaanite commander Sisera by the Israelite tribes of Naphtali and Zebulun. The forces of Israel are led by the prophetess Deborah and the reluctant Barak. The battle is described in the straightforward manner of a historical narrative in verses 12–16, as is the death of Sisera in verses 17–22. A historical summary concludes the account in verses 23–24. The account in chapter 5, however, is obviously quite different. The solid black prose of chapter 4 is replaced with the broken, uneven white space of chapter 5. This indicates that chapter 5 consists of poetry. The writer even tells us this in verse 1 when he states, "Then *sang* Deborah and Barak the son of Abinoam on that day."

When we compare the poetic description of the battle in chapter 5 with that of chapter 4, we notice several differences. We read, for example, in 5:4–5:

> LORD, when you went out from Seir,
>   when you marched from the region of Edom,
> the earth trembled
>   and the heavens dropped,
>   yes, the clouds dropped water.
> The mountains quaked before the LORD,
>   even Sinai before the LORD, the God of Israel.

Here, in contrast to chapter 4, we read that when God led his people into battle, "the earth trembled" and "the mountains quaked" (cf. Nah. 1:5). In the past some commentaries interpreted this literally and referred to earthquakes having been involved in the defeat of Sisera and his army. But it is interesting to note that no reference to earthquakes is found in the prose description of the battle in chapter 4. In poetry and song, how can the author describe to his readers that the people were led in battle by the LORD? It is by saying that when God led his people against Sisera, "the earth trembled" before them. "The mountains quaked" in fear when God led the people of Israel into battle. This is how the poet has described the victory God gave his people over their enemies. We should not interpret this literalistically, however, for this is the language of poetry. As poetry it seeks to elicit an emotive response of awe and joy rather than to impart information about the technicalities of the battle.

We also find in 5:19–20 the following description:

> The kings came, they fought;
>   then fought the kings of Canaan,
> at Taanach, by the waters of Megiddo;
>   they got no spoils of silver.
> From heaven the stars fought,
>   from their courses they fought against Sisera.

Again it is interesting to note that in the past, before the poetic nature of much of the OT was recognized, commentaries often interpreted "From heaven the stars fought" as indicating that God sent meteor showers upon the Canaanite army, as in Joshua 10:11, and helped defeat them in this manner. (Note that Josh. 10:11 is not poetic in form.) We have no hint, however, of any astronomical phenomena in the prose description of the battle in chapter 4. This only appears in the poetic song celebrating this victory in chapter 5 and should cause us to question whether the author wanted his readers to interpret this literally. It appears more likely that he was seeking to describe in song what happened when Israel went into battle. God was with them, giving courage to his people and instilling fear in their enemies. The poet describes this by stating that the stars of heaven (and, of course, the *God* of the stars of heaven) fought on behalf of the people of Israel.

A final illustration of the poetic nature of chapter 5 can be seen by comparing the description of the death of Sisera in 5:24–30 with that in 4:17–22. In the earlier account the author portrays Sisera as fleeing on foot (4:17), explains why he trusted Jael (4:17), how Jael greeted Sisera (4:18), how Sisera was thirsty (4:19), and that Sisera was asleep from exhaustion when Jael drove a tent peg through his temple (4:21). Nothing of this is "sung" about in chapter 5. On the contrary, the synonymous parallelism (see pp. 117–19) found in verses 26 and 27 is not concerned with a careful explanation of what happened. It seeks rather to sing about the defeat of Israel's dreaded enemy:

> She struck Sisera;
>   she crushed his head;
>   she shattered and pierced his temple.
> Between her feet
>   he sank, he fell, he lay still;

between her feet
   he sank, he fell;
where he sank,
   there he fell—dead. (Judg. 5:26c–27)

For other poetic "songs," compare Deuteronomy 31:30–32:43; 1 Samuel 2:1–10; 2 Samuel 1:17–27; 2 Kings 19:21–28; and Luke 1:46–55.

In Colossians 1:15–20 we have an example of NT poetry that is somewhat confusing. For some reason the poetic character of this passage is not delineated in most English translations (the New American Bible and the New Jerusalem Bible are exceptions), but it is in the Nestle-Aland edition of the Greek New Testament. The poetic parallelism is seen most clearly as follows:

A	*He is the* image *of the* invisible God, *the firstborn* of all creation. (1:15)	A′	And *he is the* head *of the* body, the church. He is the beginning, *the firstborn* from the dead, that in everything he might be preeminent. (1:18)
B	*For by* [in] *him* all things were created, in heaven and on earth, visible and invisible, whether thrones or dominions or rulers or authorities— (1:16a–b)	B′	*For in him* all the fullness of God was pleased to dwell, (1:19)
C	*all things* were created *through him* and *for him.* And he is before all things, and in him all things hold together. (1:16c–17)	C′	and *through him* to reconcile *to himself all things*, whether on earth or in heaven, making peace by the blood of his cross. (1:20)

The parallelism of the above is clearer in the Greek text than in translation.

The difficulty in interpreting this passage is due to 1:20. At first glance this verse appears to teach universalism, that in the end "all things" will be saved (reconciled). The problem evangelical Christians have with this verse and this interpretation is not that they do not want to be universalists. On the contrary, we all have friends and relatives who are not believers, and no Christian wants to think that these friends and relatives will perish eternally. Thus, I would always vote a "universalist ballot" in this respect. The problem is that the fate of unbelieving people will not be decided by how Christians vote! Heaven is not a democracy. God does not act by majority vote. The fate of unbelieving people is determined by the will and character of God, and God has revealed elsewhere in numerous places that when people die without having repented and having put their faith in Jesus Christ, the result is eternal separation from God. The basic problem with this passage is that it appears to conflict with what Paul and the Scriptures clearly teach elsewhere (e.g., Rom. 2:6–10; 1 Thess. 5:9; and 2 Thess. 1:9).

There have been a number of ways in which this conflict has been explained. One of the most common is to understand the universal reconciliation of 1:20 in terms of Colossians 2:15 and Philippians 2:10–11. A serious hostility exists between God and "all things," and the reconciliation that takes place involves a reluctant submission to God's lordship by those opposed to him. It is the kind of peace that comes about by God crushing Satan (Rom. 16:20). Thus, the reconciliation of all things that takes place does not involve a serene and blissful peace in which animosity and opposition come to an end and all experience the blessings of the kingdom of God. Rather, it is a reconciliation in which all enemies and opposition come under the rule of God and must acknowledge his lordship. In his rule and lordship, however, God judges and condemns the unrighteous to eternal judgment.

Perhaps a better way of interpreting 1:20, however, is to take into consideration the poetic nature of this passage. It is interesting to note that the words *all* and *all things* are used eight times in the Greek text. This is not surprising in light of the fact that in the Jewish and Greek literature of Paul's day, the term "all" appears with unusual frequency in statements describing God's role in creation. The poetic nature of the passage and the use of "all" in literary statements dealing with creation should caution us against demanding a literal interpretation of this term. Poetic license might require its use in this passage even if the author did not want the term to be interpreted literally. We should also note the poetic balance between the following:

A *all things (ta panta)* were created
   B *through him (di' autou)* and
      C *for him (eis auton*; 1:16d)
   B′ and *through him (di' autou)* to reconcile
      C′ *to himself (eis auton)*
A′ *all things (ta panta*; 1:20a)

In light of this poetic parallelism, we need to be careful not to press the language too literally. Colossians 1:15–20 is best understood as a joyous, poetic statement (it may even be a song) that celebrates the creative and redemptive work of Jesus as the Redeemer and Lord of all creation. We should not demand of it a literal, scientific accuracy any more than we require this of the great Christmas hymn when we sing

Hail the heav'n-born Prince of Peace!
Hail the Sun of Righteousness!
Light and life *to all* He *brings* [not "offers" but "brings"]
Ris'n with healing in His wings. ("Hark! the Herald Angels Sing,"
    by Charles Wesley)

The meaning of Colossians 1:15–20 is what Paul meant when he wrote it. But in writing this, he accepted its poetic nature. Thus, his use of "all" should not be pushed (see the ninth and tenth rules for detecting exaggeration, pp. 186–87). What Paul meant to reveal in this poem is that Jesus Christ is divine, that he is the one who is to inherit the rule of the world (he is the "firstborn"), that he is the one through whom the world was created, that he existed before all things, that he is the ruler of the church and its redeemer, and that it is through his sacrificial death that God has brought about reconciliation with the church. To press this literary form and require that each of these statements be interpreted literally in each instance, however, is to violate the norms of language involving poetry under which the apostle worked.

Another Pauline passage where this must be kept in mind is Romans 5:12–19:

Therefore, as one trespass led to condemnation for all men,
so one act of righteousness leads to justification and life for all
    men.
For as by the one man's disobedience the many were made sinners,
so by the one man's obedience the many will be made righteous.
    (vv. 18–19; cf. also 1 Cor. 15:22)

Specific Forms of Poetry

When we think of what makes a poem, two things usually come to mind. A poem possesses rhyme and rhythm. Both are found in the following nursery rhyme:

Mary had a little lamb.
Its fleece was white as snow,
and everywhere that Mary went
the lamb was sure to go.

Rhyme is present in the words *snow* and *go*. Rhythm, however, is even more essential for poetry than rhyme, and we should note that the second and fourth lines of this nursery rhyme have a similar rhythm of six beats. In a similar way, what is essential to biblical poetry is parallelism. (For examples of rhyme in poetry, see Isa. 5:7 and 33:22 in the Hebrew text.) This means that the lines of Hebrew poetry have a similar cadence or rhythm. The original term used to describe this parallelism was *parallelismus membrorum*. (Robert Lowth coined this term to describe Hebrew poetry in 1753, and his work was written in Latin.) This rhythmic parallelism can occur in different forms. (The appropriateness of the following designations is debated, but they are traditional and none of the alternative designations has won universal approval.)

Synonymous Parallelism

In this kind of parallelism the second and following lines repeat the sense of the first line but usually with some variation. It may strengthen or develop that thought. Sometimes the same thought is essentially repeated as in the following:

> Ask, and it will be given to you;
> > seek, and you will find;
> > > knock, and it will be opened to you.
> For everyone who asks receives,
> > and the one who seeks finds,
> > > and to the one who knocks it will be opened. (Matt. 7:7–8)

In this example we have three parallel lines that for all intents and purposes repeat the same thought. To ask, to seek, and to knock are simply different ways of saying the same thing. They are synonyms for praying. They do not denote different kinds or intensities of prayer. Similarly, to be given, to find, to have something opened, and to receive are just different ways of saying God will answer one's prayers. (The use of passive verbs allowed the devout Jew to avoid using God's name [YHWH, or LORD] and thus avoid the danger of using the sacred name in vain.)

> . . . hallowed be your name.
> Your kingdom come,
> your will be done,
> > on earth as it is in heaven. (Matt. 6:9c–10)

In this second example, which comes from the Lord's Prayer, we again have a threefold repetition of the same essential thought. When God answers any of the three lines, the same event will take place. Jesus will return, and history as we know it will come to its conclusion. Only then will God's name be hallowed on earth as it is in heaven, his kingdom come on earth as it is in heaven, and his will be done on earth as it is in heaven. Thus, these three petitions in the Lord's Prayer repeat the same longing that the early church expressed when it prayed "Our Lord come [*Marana tha*]!" (1 Cor. 16:22; cf. Rev. 22:20).

> Love your enemies,
> do good to those who hate you,
> bless those who curse you,
> pray for those who abuse you. (Luke 6:27b–28)

In this example we again have a repetition of similar thoughts. In the first line, we have the more general teaching, "Love your enemies," whereas in the following three lines we have specific examples of how that love is to be manifested. We have another example of this in Mark 3:4, when Jesus asks,

> Is it lawful on the Sabbath
> to do good or to do harm,
> to save life or to kill?

From the first general thought (do good vs. do harm) we proceed to a more specific application (to save life vs. to kill).

In synonymous parallelism the number of lines can vary. There must be at least two (which is the most common; see Isa. 54:1a–b [Gal. 4:27a–b]; Mark 3:24–25; 8:18; Rom. 11:33), but there are also examples of three (Ps. 100:1–2; Isa. 51:11c–e; Jer. 9:23; Hos. 5:1a–c; Amos 8:10; Mic. 1:7a–c; Mark 9:43–48; Luke 12:53; 23:29; 1 Cor. 13:1–3) and even four parallel lines (Jer. 2:8; 4:23–26; 5:17; Mark 13:24–25; Matt. 10:35–36; Luke 6:29–30, 37–38; 17:27). If we know that a saying involves synonymous parallelism, then we are able to deduce a helpful interpretive principle from this. Each line in such examples must be asserting the same or a related truth. Thus, if in the Lord's Prayer we are uncertain about what it means to pray for God's name to be hallowed, we are assisted by realizing that this request is similar to praying that God send his kingdom. From the rest of the Gospels we know what the latter means. The kingdom of God, which has already arrived in part in the coming of Jesus and the Spirit, still awaits its glorious consummation. To pray for the consummation of the kingdom means to pray for God to bring history to a close and to establish his glorious reign upon the earth. Thus we know, because of the synonymous parallelism, that the other two "thou petitions"—for the name of God to be hallowed and his will to be done on earth as it is in heaven—must deal with a similar thought. These three petitions pray for something far beyond what God can do in our hearts, in the life of a Christian, in the life of a church, and even in the life of Christendom as a whole. It looks forward to that great day when every knee will bow and every tongue confess that Jesus Christ is Lord to the glory of God the Father (Phil. 2:10–11). Thus, by knowing the literary form we are able to interpret the more obscure petition in the parallelism by the clearer one.

Similarly, if we want to know what it means to love our enemies, we can find insight and help from the parallel lines of Luke 6:27–28. By knowing that these four lines are an example of synonymous parallelism, we are able to understand the less-clear statements by the more-clear. To love our enemies primarily means to do loving acts. The four parallel lines do not speak of emotions. They speak of the Christian doing loving acts of kindness toward his or her enemies. This is why Jesus can command his followers to love their enemies. He appeals not to the emotions of his followers but to their wills, which he can command to do loving acts of kindness.

Antithetical Parallelism

In this form of poetry, the second line contrasts with the first. Instead of providing a synonymous parallel or a specific example of the general content found in the first line, it provides an antithetical statement. This is the most common form of parallelism in the Bible. In Jesus's teachings alone we have over 130 examples. In Proverbs there are entire chapters (10–15) that are devoted to this literary form. Here are some examples:

> A wise son makes a glad father,
> but a foolish son is a sorrow to his mother. (Prov. 10:1)

> Better is a dinner of herbs where love is
> than a fattened ox and hatred with it. (Prov. 15:17)

> So, every healthy tree bears good fruit,
> but the diseased tree bears bad fruit.
> A healthy tree cannot bear bad fruit,
> nor can a diseased tree bear good fruit. (Matt. 7:17–18)

So everyone who acknowledges me before men, I also will acknowledge before my Father who is in heaven,
but whoever denies me before men, I also will deny before my Father who is in heaven. (Matt. 10:32–33)

One who is faithful in a very little is also faithful in much,
and one who is dishonest in a very little is also dishonest in much.
(Luke 16:10)

Whereas in synonymous parallelism we frequently find examples that are three or four lines long, because of its very nature antithetical parallelism is usually limited to two lines. This is seen in the above examples, although in the third example we have an instance in which the first two and the last two lines are also an example of antithetical parallelism.

In interpreting this literary form we should note again that if we understand any of the two statements making up the example, this will help us understand the other. It should also be remembered that in interpreting antithetical parallelism we are dealing with poetry and not prose. We need to allow for the possibility of poetic license. Thus, if what we find seems to conflict at first glance with what the same author or another biblical writer says elsewhere, we should take note of the poetic nature of the passage.

Step or Climactic Parallelism

In this form of parallelism, sometimes also called staircase parallelism, the second line picks up the thought of the first line. However, instead of repeating that thought or giving an example as in synonymous parallelism, it advances the thought an additional step. As a result, although the two thoughts are related, the second raises the first to a higher level and brings it to a climax. This form does not occur as frequently in the Bible, but some examples are as follows:

	and whoever receives me receives him who sent me. (Matt. 10:40)
Whoever receives you receives me,	

	I have not come to abolish them but to fulfill them. (Matt. 5:17)
Do not think that I have come to abolish the Law or the Prophets;	

In the first example we can see a clear advance of the first statement by the second. The one who receives a disciple is in fact receiving Jesus, and in turn the one who receives Jesus receives God himself. The second example reveals that, far from coming in order to do away with the OT (the Law and the Prophets), Jesus came not just to keep them but to bring them to their fulfillment. For Matthew this involves Jesus's fulfillment of the prophetic promises not only by his ministry and sacrificial death, but by his revealing some of the unstated implications of the OT teachings. Thus, what follows in Matthew 5:21–48 reveals not a rejection of the law by Jesus but rather his understanding of some of its implications. Other examples of this literary form are found in Matthew 5:22; 6:22; 10:34; Mark 2:27–28; 9:37; and Luke 10:16.

Chiastic Parallelism

Another form of poetic parallelism involves a particular structure called a chiasmus. In a chiasmus we have an inverting of parallel statements, in the form *ABB′A′*. The first statement consists of two parts (*A* and *B*). The second consists of two parts as well, but they are in reverse order (*B′* and *A′*). This is best seen by way of some examples:

A Whoever *exalts* himself

   B will be *humbled*,

   B′ and whoever *humbles* himself

A′ will be *exalted*. (Matt. 23:12)

A For whoever would *save* his life

   B will *lose* it,

   B′ but whoever *loses* his life for my sake and the gospel's

A′ will *save* it. (Mark 8:35)

In Matthew 6:24 we find a triple chiasmus:

A No one can serve two masters,

   B for either he will *hate* the one

      C and *love* the other,

      C′ or he will be *devoted* to the one

   B′ and *despise* the other.

A′ You cannot serve both God and money.

It is apparent that the verses above are not only examples of chiastic parallelism but of antithetical parallelism as well. Other examples of this kind of parallelism are as follows:

Isaiah 22:22: open/shut/shut/open

Isaiah 29:17: Lebanon/fruitful field/fruitful field/forest

Jeremiah 2:19 (in Hebrew): will punish/your wickedness/your backsliding/will rebuke

Matthew 7:6: dogs/pigs/trample [pigs do this]/turn to attack you [dogs do this]

Mark 2:22: wine/old wineskins/wineskins burst/wine is destroyed

Mark 2:27: Sabbath/man/man/Sabbath

Mark 9:43: hand/cut it off/crippled/two hands

Mark 10:31: first/last/last/first

Examples of larger structures appear in Romans 2:7–10 (A = v. 7; B = v. 8; B′ = v. 9; A′ = v. 10) and Philippians 2:6–11 (A = v. 6; B = v. 7; B′ = v. 8; A′ = vv. 9–11).

Another poetic form that is sometimes mentioned is synthetic parallelism. This is the most ambiguous and vague of the poetic forms, and there is confusion in defining it and understanding exactly how it functions. Thus we have not dealt with it.

From what we have examined in this chapter, however, it is evident that by knowing the literary form of biblical poetry, we are better able to understand how the various parts relate to one another and thus to understand what the biblical writers were seeking to convey when they expressed their meaning using this literary form.

Conclusion

The amount of poetry found in the Bible and in the teachings of Jesus is impressive. In the Gospels alone we find over 220 examples of various forms of poetic parallelism in the teachings of Jesus. Clearly, the world of the biblical writers was one in which people sought to express their thoughts using emotive and picturesque language. This is clearly seen in the poetry of the Bible, for the metaphorical nature of this material is impressive, and we cannot read it without feeling the heartbeat of the authors. It is clear that the writers felt deeply about what they were saying in this form of literature. They were not interested in merely conveying information, although their poetry certainly does this. They were seeking to elicit an emotion and/or decision and to impress their readers with the importance of what they were saying (cf. 2 Sam. 1:23).

Another reason poetry appears in such abundance in the Bible is that the poets' audiences were oral societies. How could a speaker assist hearers in retaining the divine message he was delivering? He could not expect his audience to take notes or to record his words on an iPod. As a result, he placed his message in easy-to-remember forms. The rhythmic nature of poetry assists greatly in memory. For example, if I were asked to write out the first verse of the great hymn "The Church's One Foundation," I would have no trouble remembering the first line: "The church's one foundation is Jesus Christ her Lord." After this, however, I would have difficulty until I began to hum the tune and sing the hymn to myself. In this manner, the remaining lines would become clear: "She is his new creation by water and the word. . . ." Likewise, it is easier to remember the rhythmic content of Matthew 7:7–8 than a similar amount of material from Romans 3:21–31.

In our attempt to understand the meaning of this biblical material, we need to remember such things as the nature of poetry (its use of picturesque and nonliteral language) in contrast to prose and the particular form of the poetry (whether it is synonymous, antithetical, step, or chiastic parallelism). To interpret poetry as if it were prose can only lead to misunderstanding. Whether we are interpreting prose or poetry, of course, we are still seeking to understand the communicative intention of the author in writing these words. However, the rules governing the one literary form are different from the rules governing the other.

Questions

1. What is poetic license? Why is this necessary in poetry?
2. Read Proverbs 3–7. Do you find figurative language? Which do you find more of, synonymous or antithetical parallelism?
3. Where else might we find poetry in the Bible?
4. What is the value of knowing if a passage is an example of synonymous or antithetical parallelism?

8

The Game of Songs

Psalms

The largest poetic section of the Bible is the book of Psalms. Psalms, the largest book of the Bible, consists of 150 individual psalms arranged in five "books" (1–41; 42–72; 73–89; 90–106; 107–150). Each book ends with a doxology (41:13; 72:18–19; 89:52; 106:48; 150). Psalms 1 and 2 serve as introductions to the entire book of Psalms, and Psalm 150 serves as a doxology for the book of Psalms as a whole. The name *Psalms* comes from the Greek word *psalmos* that translates the Hebrew *mizmor*, which appears in the titles of fifty-seven psalms, and refers to a song accompanied by music. The psalms and their present arrangement were compiled over an extended period of time. This is clear from the editorial comment found in 72:20, "The prayers of David, the son of Jesse, are ended." Compare also Psalm 137, which speaks of the fall of Jerusalem in 587 BC and the Babylonian exile, and Psalm 107, which speaks of the return from exile. The largest number of psalms are attributed to David (seventy-three); twelve are attributed to Asaph, eleven to the Sons of Korah, two to Solomon, and one to Moses. Some of the psalms are even repeated in part or as a whole (Ps. 14 = Ps. 53; Ps. 40:13–17 = Ps. 70; Ps. 57:7–11 = Ps. 108:1–5; Ps. 60:5–12 = Ps. 108:6–13). Some other places "psalms" or songs can be found in the OT are Exodus 15:1–18; Deuteronomy 32:1–43; 1 Samuel 2:1–10; 2 Samuel 22:2–51; Isaiah 12:4–6; Jonah 2:2–10; and Habakkuk 3:2–19.

We have dealt with the rhythmic nature of the psalms in chapter 7, on poetry. Here we shall deal with the forms of the individual psalms themselves rather than the kinds of poetry found within them. These forms are not rigid, and some of the classifications are somewhat arbitrary. Certain psalms can be classified in more than one way. Various psalms of Zion (Pss. 46, 48, 76, 84, 87, 122, and 134) can also be classified as hymns, and certain community laments (Pss. 14 and 137) are psalms of Zion as well. Some psalms do not seem to fit any major classification; others are hybrids.

Psalms of Lament

Laments make up the largest category of psalms. They consist of both individual lament psalms (Pss. 3–7, 9–10[?], 13, 17, 22, 25–28, 31, 35, 36[?], 38–39, 41–43, 51–52, 54–59, 61–64, 69–71, 77, 86, 88, 102, 109, 120 [?], 130, 140–43) and community lament psalms (Pss. 12, 14, 44, 53, 58, 60, 74, 79–80, 83, 85, 90, 94, 106[?], 108[?], 123, 126, 129[?], 137). The exact number is uncertain because the classification of some psalms is debated. Although not all of the following elements are contained in each, we frequently find the following:

> *Address to God*: "O LORD" (13:1); "O God" (74:1); "to the LORD" (142:1). Sometimes the reason why an appeal is made to this God is included, as in "O LORD my God, in you do I take refuge" (7:1); "Give ear, O Shepherd of Israel, you who lead Joseph like a flock! You who are enthroned upon the cherubim" (80:1); "O LORD, God of my salvation" (88:1; cf. also 5:2; 70:1, 79:9).

> *Lament or description of need*: "How long, O LORD? Will you forget me forever? How long will you hide your face from me? How long must I take counsel in my soul and have sorrow in my heart all the day? How long shall my enemy be exalted over me?" (13:1–2; these verses are a fourfold example of synonymous parallelism); "Why do you cast us off forever? Why does your anger smoke against the sheep of your pasture?" (74:1–11; verse 1, quoted here, consists of a twofold example of synonymous parallelism); "I cry out day and night before you. Let my prayer come before you; incline your ear to my cry!" (88:1b–12); "With my voice I cry out to the LORD; with my voice I plead for mercy to the LORD" (142:1–4). At times within the lament, there is found a protest or claim of innocence by the psalmist (7:3–5, 8–9; 17:3–5; 26:1–3; etc.).

Petition or prayer for help: "Consider and answer me, O LORD my God" (13:3–4); "Remember this, O LORD, how the enemy scoffs, and a foolish people reviles your name" (74:18–23); "But I, O LORD, cry to you; in the morning my prayer comes before you" (88:13–18); "I cry to you, O LORD; I say, 'You are my refuge, my portion in the land of the living.' . . . Attend to my cry" (142:5, 6). Usually the petition involves help and rescue in the present life, but in 49:15 and 73:24 the divine salvation involves the life to come.

Confession of confidence: "But I have trusted in your steadfast love; my heart shall rejoice in your salvation" (13:5); "Yet God my King is from of old; working salvation in the midst of the earth. You divided the sea by your might" (74:12–17); "I say, 'You are my refuge, my portion in the land of the living'" (142:5b–c, 7c–d). Such a confession of confidence is missing from Psalm 88.

Vow or confession of praise: "Salvation belongs to the LORD; your blessing be on your people!" (3:8); "I will give to the LORD the thanks due to his righteousness, and I will sing praise to the name of the LORD, the Most High" (7:17); "I will sing to the LORD, because he has dealt bountifully with me" (13:6); "Bring me out of prison, that I may give thanks to your name! The righteous will surround me, for you will deal bountifully with me" (142:7). Such a vow or confession of praise is missing from Psalms 74 and 88.

The honest and candid relationship of the psalmist and his God found in the lament psalms has brought encouragement and comfort to believers for three thousand years. In his pain and doubt the psalmist cries out to God and pours out his heart. He does not seek in his prayer to be "religiously correct" but instead bares his soul and his complaint,

> My God, my God, why have you forsaken me?
>   Why are you so far from saving me, from the words of my
>   groaning?
> O my God, I cry by day, but you do not answer,
>   and by night, but I find no rest. (22:1–2)

A millennium later, Jesus of Nazareth felt that the psalmist's words described his own feeling as well (Mark 15:34). Yet all of this takes place in a confident trust that God would not forsake them and would hear their cry (Ps. 22:24). Throughout the centuries the honesty of the lament psalms have been a gracious gift bringing comfort and solace to millions who as they "walk through the valley of the shadow of death" (23:4) find hope and assurance that God's "goodness and mercy shall follow [them] all the days of [their] life and [that they] shall dwell in the house of the LORD forever" (23:6).

Psalms of Praise and Thanksgiving

These psalms are the opposite of the lament psalms. Although some scholars have sought to make these into two different kinds of psalms (praise psalms and thanksgiving psalms), they are probably best seen as one and the same. Both thanksgiving and praise go together. There is no thanksgiving without praise and no praise without thanksgiving. As in the psalms of lament, we have individual (18, 30, 32–34, 40, 66, 75, 81, 92, 106, 108, 111, 113, 116, 138, 145–50) and group (65, 67, 105, 107, 114, 117, 124, 136) praise and thanksgiving psalms. At times it is difficult to know whether a psalm is better classified as an individual or a group praise psalm (cf. 145–50). This form of psalm generally contains the following:

> *Introductory praise*: Frequently they begin with the call, "Praise the LORD! [*Hallelujah*]" (106:1; 111:1; 112:1; 113:1; 135:1; 146:1; 147:1; 148:1; 149:1; 150:1). Other introductory expressions include "We give thanks to you, O God; we give thanks, for your name is near" (75:1) and "I give you thanks, O LORD, with my whole heart" (138:1). Sometimes the introductory call of praise is directed to a person or group: "Bless the LORD, O my soul, and all that is within me, bless his holy name!" (103:1; cf. 34:1; 67:3; 104:1; 134:1; 145:1–2; 146:1b–2); "Let Israel be glad in his Maker; let the children of Zion rejoice in their King!" (149:2); "My soul makes its boast in the LORD; let the humble hear and be glad" (34:2); "Shout for joy to God, all the earth; sing the glory of his name" (66:1). There may even be present a call to a particular mode of praise: "Let them praise his name with dancing, making melody to him with tambourine and lyre!" (149:3; cf. 33:2–3; 81:2–3; 92:3; 108:2; 147:7; 150:3–5).
>
> *Description of what God has done*: This may involve God's deliverance from persecution, illness, or forgiveness of sins: "who forgives all your iniquity, who heals all your diseases, who redeems your life from the pit" (103:3–19); "On the day I called, you answered me; my strength of soul you increased" (138:3–7); "Put not your trust in princes. . . . Blessed is he whose help is the God of Jacob . . . who executes justice

for the oppressed" (146:3–9); "For the LORD takes pleasure in his people; he adorns the humble with salvation" (149:4–9).

Concluding word or call to praise: Some psalms of praise and thanksgiving conclude with "Praise the LORD! [*Hallelujah*]" (104:35; 116:19; 117:2), and some both begin and end this way (106:1, 48; 113:1, 9; 135:1, 21; 146:1, 10; 148:1, 14; 149:1, 9; 150:1, 6; cf. 8:1, 9; 103:1, 22; 104:1, 35; 118:1, 29). Others conclude as follows: "O LORD my God, I will give thanks to you forever!" (30:12); "Be glad in the LORD, and rejoice, O righteous, and shout for joy, all you upright in heart!" (32:11); "Blessed be God, because he has not rejected my prayer or removed his steadfast love from me!" (66:20).

Other Types of Psalms

Several other kinds of psalms, whose classification is due less to form than to content, can also be mentioned.

Psalms of Zion: These do not possess a specific form, but their content centers on Jerusalem and the temple. Some examples of this are Psalms 46, 48, 50(?), 76, 84, 87, 100, 122, 134–35; cf. 14.

Entrance psalms: These are ritual psalms involved in entering into Jerusalem and the temple and include Psalms 15, 24, 100, 118; cf. 92.

Royal psalms: These are frequently associated with the messianic hope because the pattern of the good king in these psalms ultimately describes the anointed king who is to come, the Messiah (Pss. 2, 18, 20–21, 45, 72, 89, 91[?], 101, 110, 132, 144).

Hymns to God: It is not easy to distinguish these from psalms of praise and thanksgiving and from psalms of Zion, but these tend to focus primarily upon God's kingly rule over creation. Often included in this category are Psalms 8, 19, 29, 47, 68, 93, 95–99, 103–4.

Wisdom psalms: These include Psalms 1, 15, 19, 37, 49, 73, 112, 119, 127–28, 133; cf. 78, 82, 90.

Trust psalms: This classification is somewhat arbitrary, but the theme of trust and confidence is found in Psalms 11, 16, 23, 62, 91, 121, 125, 131.

Penitential psalms: We have treated this form of psalm under the general category of psalms of lament. The lament psalms that are frequently classified as "penitential" are Psalms 6, 32, 38, 51, 102, 106(?), 130, 143.

Imprecatory psalms: These psalms are referred to in chapter 11, on idioms (Pss. 35, 58, 69, 83, 109, 137; see pp. 155–56).

Conclusion

Although knowledge of these forms is useful for classifying the psalms, the primary value lies in the area of interpretation. An example of this can be seen in Psalm 13. At the end of this lament psalm the confession of confidence and the vow of praise found in verses 5–6 look entirely out of place. There is no logical connection between these two verses and what has preceded. Yet they are not some later scribal addition to the psalm to make it more acceptable. On the contrary, they are normal elements in a lament psalm. They are vital parts in this literary form. Rather than appearing out of place, they should be expected by the reader. The psalmist in his lament is addressing his God. When he does so, he always has the goodness and mercy of God in mind. Thus, he laments in hope, with the expectation that what God has promised in his covenant he will do on his behalf. We must always read such laments in light of the fact that they are not made in despair but in faith. The psalmist addresses God not in order to curse or condemn him but to remind him of his oath and covenant, in the hope that in doing so God would deliver him.

The faith manifested in a psalm of lament involves the essence of a person's relationship with God. The parallel between the form of such psalms and the order of worship found in many Christian churches should be noted:

Psalm of Lament	Church Service
Address to God	Invocation / Call to worship
Lament or description of need	Prayer of confession
Petition or prayer for help	Prayer of confession
Confession of confidence	Lord's Prayer / Assurance of forgiveness
Vow or confession of praise	Doxology / Concluding hymn

A thanksgiving or praise psalm reveals that the cause for such praise and thanksgiving always rests on what God has done in the past and the gracious covenant he has established. It is not based on philosophical truths or abstract attributes of God. Even God's future acts are based on what he has done in the past. This may involve those actions he has done on the part of the individual (some scholars refer to such thanksgiving psalms as declarative praise psalms) or what he has done for the redeemed community (these are sometimes called descriptive praise psalms). Thus, we must remember that such psalms arise from the covenantal relationship the psalmist and his hearers/readers possess with God. There are some psalms that refer to God's greatness in creation (8:3–8; 19:1–6; 104). Yet even if the psalmist refers to this or God's providence over creation (65:6–13), he is referring not to the God of the nations but to the God of Abraham, Isaac, and Jacob. It is the God who has chosen Israel who is being praised.

Questions

1. Why are lament psalms not psalms of despair? Have you ever poured out your heart to God in the way the psalmist does in his lament psalms?
2. What might be some implications of the psalms of Zion and entrance psalms for Christians today?
3. Do you have anything like the penitential psalms in your church services?
4. What does the psalmist focus on in his praise and thanksgiving psalms? What do we focus on? What is the common element? What are some of the specific differences?

9

The Game of Wisdom

Proverbs

Wisdom literature is a broad designation of a literary form found in all cultures. It covers a wide range of genres including proverbs (see below), sayings (1 Kings 20:11), beatitudes (Prov. 8:32, 34), riddles (Prov. 1:6), allegories (Ezek. 17:2–10), questions (Prov. 20:9), admonitions (Prov. 4:23; 16:3), prohibitions (Prov. 4:10–19), instructions (often parental; Prov. 2:1–7:27), dialogues (Prov. 30:1–6), didactic narratives (Job 1–2; Prov. 7:6–27), numerical sayings (Prov. 30:18–31), rhetorical questions (Prov. 30:4), poems (Prov. 1:20–33; 31:10–31), parables (Luke 6:39; 12:16–20), teachings (Prov. 21:19), psalms (Ps. 1), comparative sayings (Prov. 10:26; 19:12), "better than" sayings (Prov. 28:6), and others. These various forms of Wisdom literature often overlap, in that sayings, beatitudes, admonitions, prohibitions, instructions, and so on, are frequently found in a passage of another form, so that the various forms of Wisdom literature are not mutually exclusive.

One of the most common forms of Wisdom literature is the proverb. Related terms are "maxim," which refers to a proverb giving advice on behavior; "axiom," which refers to a proverb whose truth is assumed as self-evident and not needing proof; and "aphorism," which is the broadest term of all and refers to a concise statement of a principle or truth. A proverb is a pithy saying that expresses a general truth that has become common property and whose authorship is generally unknown. Proverbs are found throughout the

Bible. Best known are those found in the book called Proverbs, but major parts of the books of Job, Psalms, Ecclesiastes, and James consist of proverbs. The proverb was a popular form of Jesus's teachings, and examples are found throughout the Gospels (e.g., Matt. 6:21, 22, 34; 7:12; 26:52c; Mark 3:24; Luke 16:10). They are also found scattered throughout the rest of the Bible (e.g., Ps. 49:16–20; Isa. 5:21; Jer. 23:28b; 31:29).

One of the best known proverbs is found in Proverbs 22:6: "Train up a child in the way he should go; even when he is old he will not depart from it." I heard of a pastor who told his congregation after reading this verse, "I know that my children will follow the Lord, because I am training them up in the way they should go." As a father I am thankful to God that my three children are committed Christians. Yet it would be the height of folly and arrogance to claim that they are committed Christians because their father trained them perfectly in the way they should go. On the contrary, it is because of God's grace that they have followed the Lord. And all too often, this has been despite the inconsistencies and failures of their father. Furthermore, such a public statement by the pastor placed his children under a terrible burden. If they do choose to serve the Lord, this is now to be credited to their father's godliness. Only if they choose not to serve the Lord can they manifest their own individuality! More important still, however, is the fact that this reveals an incorrect understanding of what a proverb is and how it should be interpreted.

Is a proverb to be interpreted as a universal law? Is it like the law of the Medes and the Persians, which could never be overruled (Dan. 6:8; cf. Esther 8:8)? Is it to be interpreted absolutely, like the laws of thermodynamics, which describe what must always take place? It is apparent when reading proverbs that many of them seem to be less than absolute in their applicability:

- "But whoever listens to me [wisdom] will dwell secure and will be at ease, without dread of disaster" (Prov. 1:33; cf. also 2:7–8). Do not some believers experience suffering and even martyrdom because of their faithfulness to God?
- "Honor the LORD with your wealth and with the firstfruits of all your produce; then your barns will be filled with plenty, and your vats will be bursting with wine" (Prov. 3:9–10). Does "tithing" ensure farmers of being wealthy and successful? Note how in Proverbs 15:16–17; 19:22; and 28:6 the writer knows that faithfulness does not always result in prosperity (cf. also Tobit 4:21, from the OT Apocrypha).

- "The LORD does not let the righteous go hungry, but he thwarts the craving of the wicked. A slack hand causes poverty, but the hand of the diligent makes rich" (Prov. 10:3–4). Is all poverty due to laziness?
- "Disaster pursues sinners, but the righteous are rewarded with good" (Prov. 13:21). Is prosperity a measure of piety? Are there no pious poor? Are all rich people devout? (cf. Luke 6:20).
- "A servant who deals wisely will rule over a son who acts shamefully and will share the inheritance as one of the brothers" (Prov. 17:2). How often do "servants" share the inheritance equally with the children?
- "Whoever oppresses the poor to increase his own wealth, or gives to the rich, will only come to poverty" (Prov. 22:16). Do not some people become quite wealthy by their oppression of the poor?
- "For all who take the sword will perish by the sword" (Matt. 26:52; cf. Prov. 15:1; Matt. 6:21; Luke 16:10; etc.). Some mercenaries seem to do quite well with the sword!

It is clear that these proverbs cannot be considered absolute laws, because they have exceptions. They tend to focus on one aspect of a situation rather than all the possibilities. They are nevertheless true in general. In June 1945, would many people in Germany have disagreed with the general truth of Matthew 26:52?

Proverbs are not laws. They are not even promises. They are generalizations learned from careful observation and a wise analysis of life. Such observation is not limited to the Bible but is found throughout ancient Sumerian, Akkadian, Egyptian, and Greek literature, as well as in most present-day cultures. Yet the biblical proverbs are not simply secular pronouncements of wisdom but have an added dimension to them. They have been formulated not simply by observing life, but by observing life in the light of divine revelation. Although they lack a concern for salvation history and the major events of Israel's history, they posit the God of Israel (Prov. 1:7; 2:6) as the center of creation (Prov. 8:22–31). The sacred name of the God of Israel, LORD (YHWH), is used almost ninety times in the book of Proverbs. Thus, the biblical proverbs reveal not just the best of human wisdom but wisdom that is filtered through the revelation of Scripture and recorded under the direction of the Spirit.

A proverb is a short, pithy saying that expresses a wise, general truth concerning life. A biblical proverb is a short, pithy saying that expresses a wise, general truth concerning life from a divine perspective. Because of the general nature of proverbs, exceptions are possible. The existence of such exceptions in no way refutes the truth of the proverb, for what a proverb says is true in the majority of instances. Thus, the fact that godly parents who train their children in the way they should go at times have ungodly children does not refute this proverb. In the majority of instances the result is indeed children who desire to follow in the faith of their parents.

The Making of a Biblical Proverb

We cannot understand the book of Job without realizing that this piece of Wisdom literature wrestles with this very problem. Job is a devout man whose world has fallen apart. His "comforters" are well versed in the proverbs found in the Wisdom literature of their time. Their error is that they assume that these proverbs are absolute laws without exceptions. As a result, they believe that the tragedies Job has experienced must be due to his ungodliness. Note how they throw various proverbs at him. After his wealth, his children, and health have been taken from him, they say:

Remember: who that was innocent ever perished? Or where were the upright cut off? As I have seen, those who plow iniquity and sow trouble reap the same. (4:7–8)

But he saves the needy from the sword of their mouth and from the hand of the mighty. (5:15)

Does God pervert justice? Or does the Almighty pervert the right? If your children have sinned against him, he has delivered them into the hand of their transgression. If you will seek God and plead with the Almighty for mercy, if you are pure and upright, surely then he will rouse himself for you and restore your rightful habitation. (8:3–6; cf. 11:13–20; 18:5–21; etc.)

In the case of Job, however, these proverbs do not apply. He is an exception. His misfortunes are not due to his sin. Thus, he cannot repent of any specific sin that caused them. He is an exception to such proverbs as "When a man's ways please the LORD, he makes even his enemies to be at peace with him" (Prov. 16:7; cf. 10:9, 15, 29; 11:6; 12:7, 21; 13:21; etc.).

Conclusion

In interpreting this form of literature, we must be aware of the fact that a proverb functions as a general truth. The presence of exceptions does not refute the truth of a proverb. Of course, some proverbs, such as those dealing with the character of God, can be universal in scope (cf. Prov. 6:16–19; 11:1; 12:22: "Lying lips are an abomination to the LORD; but those who act faithfully are his delight"). A proverb, however, need not be universal, as long as it involves observations of what generally happens in life. These wise and memorable observations, often found in poetic form, provide inspired principles upon which believers can and should build their lives. The authors of the biblical proverbs wanted their readers to interpret them as general truths and to understand the principles they sought to convey through them. They also expected their readers to interpret them in light of their immediate context (the whole verse [cf. Prov. 26:4 and 5], section, chapter, and book in which they are found), the larger context of the Scriptures in general, the presence of parallelism (synonymous, antithetical, step, chiasmic), and the cultural world of the original readers.

Thus, even if Proverbs 22:6 cannot be absolutized into a universal law, it nevertheless reveals a great truth that should encourage Christians to rear their children in the "fear and admonition" of the Lord. The fact that such children more often than not follow in the footsteps of their parents should motivate us to do so with great dedication. In my own experience I have not ceased being impressed when I encounter second- and third-generation pastors, missionaries, and dedicated laypeople who witness to the truth of this proverb. Of course, there are exceptions. The writer of Proverbs was no doubt aware of Eli's sons, who did not follow in the paths of their devout father, and of people who did not follow in the ways of their godly parents (cf. the kings of Judah who were good and did right in the eyes of the LORD in 2 Chronicles 14ff. and how some were followed by evil sons). Nevertheless, at times these exceptions, like the prodigal son, come to their senses (Luke 15:17; cf. the case of Manasseh in 2 Chron. 33:12) and return home to the faith of their parents.

Questions

1. Can you find a biblical proverb, one not given in this chapter, that as a general rule is true but has exceptions?
2. Can you think of some present-day proverbs that we willingly accept even though there are exceptions?
3. Can you make up a proverb?
4. What kind of poetry is found in Proverbs 10–17? (See chapter 7, above.)

10

The Game of Prediction

Prophecy

For many people prophecy is a synonym for prediction. As a result, the prophetic books of the Bible are frequently thought of simply as long lists of predictions concerning future events. Yet when we read the prophetic literature, it is evident that a great portion, if not the greatest portion, of these books consists of narrative and proclamation. This aspect of prophecy is also evident from the fact that within the Hebrew OT canon, the books of Joshua through 2 Kings, which consist primarily of narrative, are called the Former Prophets. This reveals that a prophet was understood as a *forth*teller of the divine message, not just a *fore*teller of future events. His ministry was often more concerned with proclamation than with prediction. (Note that under "prophecy" in the Oxford English Dictionary, the first possible meaning listed is "The action or practice of revealing or expressing the will or thought of God," and only the second meaning given is "The action of foretelling or predicting.")

In this chapter, however, we shall look at the predictive dimension of prophecy. Such prophecy is found throughout the Bible, from Genesis (cf. 3:15; 12:2–3; 27:39–40; 49:1–28) to, of course, Revelation. Major sections of the Gospels are devoted to prophetic prediction (Matt. 24–25; Mark 13; Luke 13:28–35; 21:5–36; and so on). Frequently a distinction is made between prophecy and apocalyptic. The former is usually associated with this-worldly events, such as the judgment of sin in history and the call to repentance in order to escape that judgment. The latter, on the other hand, focuses on other-worldly events (such as the final judgment of sin), sees the world's sinfulness as ultimately beyond resolution in this world, and thus looks forward to the creation of new heavens and a new earth. Such a distinction, however, is overly simplistic, for as we shall see, prophecy frequently uses cosmic terminology in its depiction of this-worldly future events. It should also be noted that the Apocalypse (Rev. 1:1), or book of Revelation, refers to itself as a book of prophecy (Rev. 1:3; 22:7, 18–19). In this chapter we shall not distinguish between prophecy and apocalyptic, for the imagery used is similar. What is different is the referent: "normal" events, such as the destruction of Jerusalem (Jer. 4:1–6:30), the defeat of Egypt by Babylon (Ezek. 30–32), and the overthrow of the Babylonian empire (Isa. 13:1–27), as opposed to the arrival of the kingdom of God (Luke 3:4–6 [cf. Isa. 40:3–5]; Acts 2:16–21 [cf. Joel 2:28–32]) and its ultimate consummation (Mark 13:24–27; Rev. 21).

In this chapter we shall not deal with various subtypes of prophecy such as prophecies of disaster, pronouncements of doom and woe, prophetic dirges, pronouncements of salvation and deliverance, prophecies against foreign nations, prophetic dirges, hymns, liturgies, disputations, and lawsuits. We shall also not discuss the sources of the prophet's messages (e.g., dreams [Num. 12:6], ecstatic visions [Isa. 1:1; 2:1; 6:1; Amos 1:1; Mic. 1:1; Nah. 1:1], direct encounters in which God speaks to the prophet [Jer. 1:7–2:3; Hosea 1:2–3:5], and the "word of the LORD" coming to the prophet [Jer. 7:1; 46:1f.; Ezek. 20:2]). Instead we shall focus in this chapter on some general guidelines for interpreting the prophetic message.

Within this literary genre we encounter certain assumptions (game rules) the prophetic authors shared with their readers. The prophets expected that their readers would interpret their prophecies according to the rules associated with this literary form. Unfortunately, some of these rules are not clear to us today, and this causes serious difficulties in interpreting this kind of literature.

Judgment Prophecies

One of the rules of prophetic literature, and one that most readers of the Bible are unaware of, involves prophecies of judgment. An example of this is found in Jonah 3:4, where the prophet proclaims to the city of Nineveh, "Yet forty days, and Nineveh shall be overthrown!" When the city hears this message, the people, "from the greatest of them to the least of them" (v. 5), put on sackcloth as a sign of mourning and anguish, and the king himself decrees a time of mourning and repentance. We then read, "When God saw what they did, how they turned from their evil way, God relented of the disaster that he had said he would do to them, and he did not do it" (3:10). But what about Jonah's prophecy? Does the lack of divine judgment on Nineveh make Jonah a false prophet?

Not at all, for Jonah, and both the hearers and readers of this prophecy, knew something about judgment prophecies of which most modern-day readers are unaware. This rule concerning judgment prophecies—shared by Jonah, the Ninevites, and the original readers of this book—is found in Jeremiah 18:7–10:

> If at any time I [the LORD] declare concerning a nation or a kingdom, that I will pluck up and break down and destroy it, and if that nation, concerning which I have spoken, turns from its evil, I will relent of the disaster that I intended to do to it. And if at any time I declare concerning a nation or a kingdom that I will build and plant it, and if it does evil in my sight, not listening to my voice, then I will relent of the good that I had intended to do to it. (Cf. 17:24–27; 22:4–5; 26:3–5; Ezek. 33:13–16.)

Another example of this rule is found in Micah 3:12, where the prophet states,

> Therefore because of you
>   Zion shall be plowed as a field;
> Jerusalem shall become a heap of ruins,
>   and the mountain of the house a wooded height.

In Jeremiah 26:16–19 this prophecy is quoted and its lack of fulfillment noted. Micah was not considered a false prophet, however. The prophecy was not fulfilled because the king and the people had feared the Lord and sought his favor (26:19). Thus, God relented of the judgment that had been prophesied. Still another example of a judgment prophecy that was averted is found in 1 Kings 21:20–29.

The rule shared by Jonah and his hearers (and the biblical author and readers) is that judgment prophecies are conditional. Jonah knew this. This was why he fled from the LORD. If Jonah had been commissioned to preach a prophecy of judgment upon Nineveh that was irreversible, he would gladly have gone to Nineveh. He would have run to Nineveh to preach such a message! Oh, how wonderful it would have been for him to preach to the people of Nineveh that God's judgment was about to fall upon them and that there was no way of escape! How joyously he would have proclaimed such a message of damnation and destruction on this evil kingdom.

But Jonah knew that if he proclaimed this prophecy, there was a possibility that the Ninevites would repent and be spared of the divine judgment. This possibility is what Jonah feared and dreaded. Jonah wanted these brutal Nazis of his day to be damned. He wanted them destroyed, and he knew that any judgment prophecy always presumed that such judgment could be avoided if the people repented. This is evident from what we read in Jonah 4:1–2:

> But it displeased Jonah exceedingly [that Nineveh had repented and escaped divine judgment], and he was angry. And he prayed to the LORD and said, "O LORD, is not this what I said when I was yet in my country? That is why I made haste to flee to Tarshish; for I knew that you are a gracious God and merciful, slow to anger and abounding in steadfast love, and relenting from disaster."

One of the rules that the prophetic writers shared with their readers is that judgment prophecies always assume that if the hearers repent, the judgment will not take place. This was part of the generic expectation involving the literary genre of judgment prophecies.

The Language of Prophecy

Another aspect of prophecy the interpreter must consider involves the vocabulary used by the prophetic writers. Much of the terminology found in prophecy makes use of customary imagery used in this genre. For instance, in the judgment prophecy found in Isaiah 13:9–11 we read

> Behold, the day of the LORD comes,
>   cruel, with wrath and fierce anger,
> to make the land a desolation
>   and to destroy its sinners from it.
> For the stars of the heavens and their constellations
>   will not give their light;
> the sun will be dark at its rising,
>   and the moon will not shed its light.
> I will punish the world for its evil,
>   and the wicked for their iniquity;

> I will put an end to the pomp of the arrogant,
>   and lay low the pompous pride of the ruthless.

Because of the cosmic imagery found in this prophecy, many interpreters assume that it is referring to the end of history. Yet it is clear from the context in Isaiah 13:1 ("The oracle concerning Babylon which Isaiah the son of Amoz saw") and 13:19 that the prophecy concerns the Babylonian empire of the sixth century BC. (Cf. also the reference to Babylon's sixth-century enemies, the Medes, in 13:17–18.) The Babylonian kingdom that destroyed Jerusalem and the Solomonic temple and sent the elite of Judean society into exile would experience divine judgment.

> And Babylon, the glory of kingdoms,
>   the splendor and pomp of the Chaldeans,
> will be like Sodom and Gomorrah
>   when God overthrew them. (13:19)

Yet this judgment is described in cosmic terminology. Such terminology, however, was part of the imagery and symbolism available to the prophets when they sought to describe God's intervention in history and his sovereign rule over the kingdoms of this world (cf. Dan. 2:21; 4:17, 25, 34–35; 5:21). Such imagery was not meant to be interpreted literalistically. The sun was not actually going to be darkened; the moon would not stop giving its light; the stars would not stop supplying their light. What the author willed to communicate by this imagery, that God was going to bring judgment upon Babylon, was to be understood literally but not literalistically. And that willed meaning, God's judgment upon Babylon, did take place. This prophecy was fulfilled with the rise and rule of the Persian Empire over the territories once ruled by Babylon, and the later readers of this prophecy knew that this prophecy had indeed been fulfilled. Babylon had been judged as the prophecy proclaimed, and the cosmic imagery indicates that this was God's doing. The imagery itself, however, was understood by the prophet and his audience as part of the stock terminology used in this kind of literature to describe God's intervention into history.

Similar imagery is used by Jeremiah in his description of the coming destruction of Jerusalem (4:3–6, 10–12, 14, 16, 23–28, 31; 5:1ff.):

> I looked on the earth, and behold, it was without form and void;
>   and to the heavens, and they had no light.
> I looked on the mountains, and behold, they were quaking,
>   and all the hills moved to and fro.

> I looked, and behold, there was no man,
>   and all the birds of the air had fled.
> I looked, and behold, the fruitful land was a desert,
>   and all its cities were laid in ruins before the Lord, before his
>   fierce anger.

For thus says the Lord, "The whole land shall be a desolation; yet I will not make a full end.

> "For this the earth shall mourn,
>   and the heavens above be dark;
> for I have spoken; I have purposed;
>   I have not relented, nor will I turn back." (Jer. 4:23–28)

Similar imagery is also used in the lament of Ezekiel 32:5–8 to describe the destruction of the pharaoh of Egypt and his army.

> I will strew your flesh upon the mountains
>   and fill the valleys with your carcass.
> I will drench the land even to the mountains with your flowing
>   blood,
>   and the ravines will be full of you.
> When I blot you out, I will cover the heavens
>   and make their stars dark;
> I will cover the sun with a cloud,
>   and the moon shall not give its light.
> All the bright lights of heaven will I make dark over you,
>   and put darkness on your land," declares the Lord God. (cf.
>   32:1–2, 11–21)

In Acts 2:14–21, Peter and Luke interpreted the events of Pentecost in a similar way as they saw in it the fulfillment of the prophetic message of Joel:

But Peter, standing with the eleven, lifted up his voice and addressed them: "Men of Judah and all who dwell in Jerusalem, let this be known to you, and give ear to my words. For these people are not drunk, as you suppose, since it is only the third hour of the day. But this is what was uttered through the prophet Joel:

> "'And in the last days it shall be, God declares,
>   that I will pour out my Spirit on all flesh,

and your sons and your daughters shall prophesy,
    and your young men shall see visions,
    and your old men shall dream dreams;
even on my male servants and female servants
    in those days I will pour out my Spirit, and they shall prophesy.
And I will show wonders in the heavens above
    and signs on the earth below,
    blood, and fire, and vapor of smoke;
the sun shall be turned to darkness
    and the moon to blood,
    before the day of the Lord comes, the great and magnificent day.
And it shall come to pass that everyone who calls upon the name of
    the Lord shall be saved.'"

These cosmic signs did not literally take place at Pentecost, even though what the author willed to convey by those signs did. God did enter into history and bring about the fulfillment of the prophecy of Joel. In fulfillment of his promises God gave to the church the gift of the new covenant. The long-awaited kingdom had arrived and brought with it its firstfruits, for the Spirit came upon every believer, as Joel had foretold. The conventional cosmic imagery used in this prophecy of Joel was understood by both Peter and Luke as being fulfilled in the events of Pentecost.

There have been attempts to deny that the prophecy of Joel 2:28–32 was fulfilled at Pentecost. Usually this is due to a misunderstanding of the figurative nature of this cosmic terminology. Some have suggested that Luke and Peter believed that Pentecost was "kind of like" what Joel prophesied but not its actual fulfillment. Its actual fulfillment still lies in the future, when these cosmic signs will be literalistically fulfilled. Such a manipulative interpretation of this passage of Acts, however, is impossible in light of Peter's words in Acts 2:16: "this [2:2–4] is what was uttered through the prophet Joel." Furthermore, such interpretative gymnastics are unnecessary when we are willing to accept what the author meant by the use of such terminology. We need only note other passages to see how widespread the use of such cosmic terminology is in the Bible (Isa. 24:23; 34:1–5; Jer. 4:28; 13:16; 15:9; Ezek. 32:7–8; Joel 2:10, 31; 3:15; Amos 8:9; Hab. 3:11; Matt. 24:29; Mark 13:24–25; Luke 21:25; Rev. 6:12). Attempts to see Mark 15:33; Matthew 27:45; and Luke 23:44–45 as the fulfillment of this prophecy also err. They do not explain the signs of Acts 2:19 and most of 2:20. Second, and more important, Peter and Luke associate the fulfillment of these signs with what was happening then and there on the day of Pentecost, not on Good Friday.

The Figurative Nature of Prophetic Language

A clear example of a nonliteral prophecy is found in Isaiah 11:6–9 and 35:8–10. In describing the peace and security of the messianic age the author writes in 11:6–9:

> The wolf shall dwell with the lamb,
>   and the leopard shall lie down with the young goat,
> and the calf and the lion and the fattened calf together;
>   and a little child shall lead them.
> The cow and the bear shall graze;
>   their young shall lie down together;
>   and the lion shall eat straw like the ox.
> The nursing child shall play over the hole of the cobra,
>   and the weaned child shall put his hand on the adder's den.
> They shall not hurt or destroy
>   in all my holy mountain;
> for the earth shall be full of the knowledge of the LORD
>   as the waters cover the sea.

Yet later in 35:8–10 he writes:

> And a highway shall be there,
>   and it shall be called the Way of Holiness;
> the unclean shall not pass over it.
>   It shall belong to those who walk on the way;
>   even if they are fools, they shall not go astray.
> No lion shall be there,
>   nor shall any ravenous beast come up on it;
> they shall not be found there,
>   but the redeemed shall walk there.
> And the ransomed of the LORD shall return
>   and come to Zion with singing;
> everlasting joy shall be upon their heads;
>   they shall obtain gladness and joy,
>   and sorrow and sighing shall flee away.

In reading these two passages it is evident that we have a problem if we interpret the imagery literalistically. In the first passage, wild beasts are present in the messianic age, living peaceably with the rest of creation; in the second, wild beasts are not present. Yet there is no contradiction in the mind of the author. The author of Isaiah 35 knew what was written in

Isaiah 11. In his mind the two statements did not contradict each other. On the contrary, the willed meaning of these two figurative scenes is identical. In the messianic kingdom there is peace and security. The metaphorical language in which this is described may be different (wild animals living peaceably or no wild animals being present), but what the author sought to convey by this imagery is the same. There will be no more war, no more fighting, no more hostility. There will be peace. Even nature will be at peace with itself. We must not confuse the metaphorical nature of the language the prophet uses with the meaning he wills to convey by that language. The context he provides by having both passages in his work helps his readers understand the meaning of each passage. It should not therefore surprise us that in Isaiah 65:25 the prophet once again uses the imagery of 11:6–9 to describe the messianic age and states:

> The wolf and the lamb shall graze together;
>> the lion shall eat straw like the ox,
>> and dust shall be the serpent's food.
> They shall not hurt or destroy
>> in all my holy mountain.

The poetic nature of these three sayings and of prophecy in general reinforces the figurative nature of this genre.

Another example of the figurative nature of prophetic language is found in Luke 3:4–6:

> The voice of one crying in the wilderness:
> "Prepare the way of the Lord,
>> make his paths straight.
> Every valley shall be filled,
>> and every mountain and hill shall be made low,
> and the crooked shall become straight,
>> and the rough places shall become level ways,
> and all flesh shall see the salvation of God."

This summary of the message of John the Baptist, which comes from Isaiah 40:3–5, is found in each of the Gospels (Mark 1:3; Matt. 3:3; John 1:23). Only Luke, however, adds Isaiah 40:4, which refers to the valleys being filled in, the mountains and hills being made low, the crooked roads becoming straight, and the rough places being made smooth. If these statements are to be interpreted literalistically, this would result in major geographical and topographical changes on this planet. But Luke makes no mention of such physical changes accompanying the ministry of John the Baptist. This imagery, furthermore, is found throughout the Bible (cf. Isa. 42:16; 45:2; 49:11; Zech. 4:7) and in the intertestamental literature:

> For God has ordered that every high mountain and the everlasting
>   hills be made low
>   and the valleys filled up, to make level ground,
>   so that Israel may walk safely in the glory of God. (Baruch 5:7
>   NRSV)

> And the high mountains shall be shaken,
> And the high hills shall be made low,
> And shall melt like wax before the flame. (Enoch 1:6 [Charles
>   translation])

It is clear that Luke understood this imagery figuratively, as referring to the humbling of the proud and the exaltation of the repentant through the preaching of John the Baptist (cf. Luke 14:11 and 18:14, where the verb "made low" means "to humble").

Still another example of the figurative nature of prophetic terminology is found in the description of the new Jerusalem in Revelation 21. The walls of the city are described as 144 cubits (note the symbolism: 144 = 12 × 12; cf. also 7:4–8; 21:12), or over two hundred feet, thick (21:17). The thickness of these walls is meant to indicate the safety and security of the new Jerusalem. Who could break through walls so strong and thick? Yet at the same time, we also read that the gates of the city are never shut (21:25). What good are such massive walls if the gates are left open? And since the gates of a city were the weakest part of a city's defense system, why would someone want twelve gates (21:12)? Once again the prophet has used different metaphors, which at first glance look contradictory, to describe the security and safety of the new Jerusalem. Thick walls reveal safety, but so do the gates (and their number) being open all the time. The meaning of this figurative language is clear. The believer will not need to worry, for there is peace and security in the new Jerusalem. For other examples of figurative terminology in prophecy, compare Isaiah 3:24–4:1; 34:1–17; Jeremiah 4:23–31; 15:8–9; Nahum 1:4–5; Habakkuk 1:6–9; and Mark 13:14–16. Compare also how Ezekiel describes the coming destruction of Jerusalem and subsequent exile of 587 BC ("And because of all your abominations I will do with you what I have never yet done, and the like of which I will never do again" [5:9]) and how Daniel represents it ("For under the whole heaven there has not been done anything like what has been done against Jerusalem" [9:12]). How does one reconcile this with the greater destruction of Jerusalem and the temple by the Romans in AD 70, if one interprets these two passages literalistically?

The Making of a Biblical Prophecy

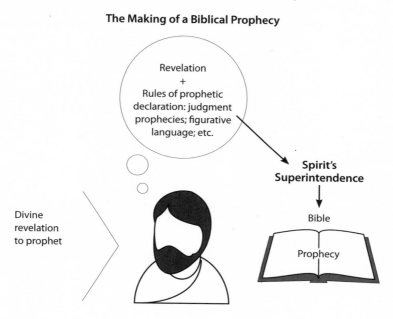

The *Sensus Plenior*, or "Fuller Meaning," of the Text

There are times when a prophetic text appears to have a fulfillment other than what the prophet himself expected. (The following are frequently given as examples: Matt. 1:22–23; 2:15, 17–18; John 12:15; 1 Cor. 9:9; 10:3–4.) Is it possible that a prophecy may have a fuller meaning or "deeper sense" than the prophet envisioned? According to this view, whereas the prophet willed to convey one truth, God had a different truth he willed to convey by the same vocabulary and grammar. This involves not an implication flowing out of the prophet's willed meaning but a different meaning independent of and unconnected with the author's communicative intention. If we assume, for the sake of argument, that this does in fact occur, this fuller meaning, or *sensus plenior*, can never be known until after the fact. The willed meaning of the prophet is accessible to the reader because of the context the author has provided. We know the prophet's vocabulary, style, grammar, and the ground rules for interpreting prophecy. This and the literary context he provides enable us to understand what he willed to convey by his prophecy. But what about the alleged fuller meaning of God? How can we know this? The literary context does not help, for we have no access to God's vocabulary, style, and grammar, but only the prophet's.

Two other difficulties are connected with such a view. The first involves how we today can discover a fuller, divine meaning in a text of which the divinely inspired author was ignorant. It seems somewhat arrogant to assume that our knowledge is sufficiently greater than that of the inspired prophets that we can know something about their words of which they were totally unaware. Two errors seem to be at work here. The one demeans divine inspiration; the second elevates human reason to the extent that the present-day interpreter's reasoning is superior to the divine meaning given to the prophet. (We cannot help but think here of those who claim to possess such a fuller understanding of the return of the Son of God that they can predict the time of his coming, when the Son of God himself claimed that he did not know this [Mark 13:32].)

The other difficulty with this view is that proof of such a fuller meaning can only be demonstrated by events after the "fuller meaning" of the prophecy has taken place. Before the fulfillment of this deeper meaning, no one understood the *sensus plenior*. An interpreter cannot ascertain in a prophetic text some hidden meaning that the biblical author was unaware of and did not intend. From a pragmatic point of view, since we can only perceive such a deeper fulfillment after the fact, seeking such deeper meanings beforehand is of little value. At its best it is purely speculative, for we cannot know with certainty such a future, deeper meaning from the prophecy itself.

Rather than appealing to a fuller sense distinct and different from that of the biblical author's, it may be wiser to see if the supposed *sensus plenior* is in reality an implication of the author's conscious meaning. Thus, in 1 Corinthians 9:9 when Paul quotes Deuteronomy 25:4 ("You shall not muzzle an ox when it is treading out the grain") as a justification for ministers of the gospel being supported for their work, this is not a fuller meaning of the text unrelated to what the author sought to convey. Rather, it is a legitimate implication of the willed principle contained in Deuteronomy 25:4. As a principle, if animals should be allowed to share in the benefits of their work, how much more should the "animal" created in the image of God and proclaiming the Word of God be allowed to share in the benefits of that work. Thus, what Paul is saying is not a fuller and different meaning from what the writer of Deuteronomy meant. On the contrary, although this specific implication was unknown to the

OT author, it is part of his conscious and willed principle. Perhaps such prophecies as Matthew 1:22–23 and 2:15 are best understood as revealing implications of the original prophecies in Isaiah 7:14 and Hosea 11:1. Whereas in Isaiah's day the prophet meant that a maiden would give birth to a son who was named "Immanuel" and that this would serve as a sign to King Ahaz of the nation's deliverance from the Assyrian threat, that willed meaning also allows for a virgin one day to give birth to a son who would be "Immanuel," and this also would serve as a sign. Similarly, whereas God showed his covenantal faithfulness by leading his "son," the children of Israel, back from Egypt to the promised land in Moses's day, how much more would he, according to Matthew's understanding of Hosea 11:1 in 2:15, lead his only "Son," Jesus, back from Egypt to the promised land.

Conclusion

As a young Christian I was taught to approach the prophecies of the Bible as if they were photographic portraits of future events. They were to be understood as divine camera shots of what was to take place one day. As time progressed, however, I became aware of the figurative language used by the prophets. As a result, I suggest a different, perhaps better analogy.

There is considerable difference between the art of the fifteenth and sixteenth centuries and that of the nineteenth and twentieth centuries. Fifteenth- and sixteenth-century art is realistic in nature and seeks to reproduce objects in a way similar to how a photographer does today. A scene in the paintings of that day shows the buttons people have on their clothing clearly, even if they are standing in the distance. Everything is painted in exact detail. A magnifying glass held over small sections of the painting reveals amazing detail. It almost seems that the painter had microscopic brushes in order to paint with such precision. On the other hand, at the end of the nineteenth and the beginning of the twentieth centuries, artists tended to be more impressionistic than realistic in their paintings. Viewed from close up, such paintings often appear to be only globs of paint. You have to stand back and observe the overall painting in order to understand what the artist is seeking to convey. I would suggest that the ancient prophets "painted" their prophetic message more along the lines of such nineteenth- and twentieth- century Impressionists as Monet and Renoir than in the manner of the Flemish and Italian schools of the fifteenth and sixteenth centuries. The prophets do not provide us with a telescope that allows us to see future events with microscopic precision.

They do not even provide us with a clear glass window through which we can see the future. Instead they provide us with a stained-glass window whose hues and colors emphasize God's omnipotence, omniscience, and sovereignty over the future that promises bliss and glory for those who "do justice . . . love kindness, and . . . walk humbly with [their] God" (Mic. 6:8) but sorrow and judgment for those who practice evil.

When interpreting prophetic literature, we must remember that meaning is determined by the author. The author in turn sought to share that divinely revealed meaning by means of this particular literary form. In doing so he submitted himself to the rules governing this form of literature, which were known to him and his readers/hearers. If we want to understand his willed meaning, we must know those rules and interpret his work within the historical and literary context he provides. If we tear his prophecy out of this context and neglect those rules, we will never understand his willed meaning contained in such literature. Instead, we will treat his prophetic message as predictive inkblots into which we will pour our own meanings. As a result, the prophetic message will no longer be a word from God's inspired prophet but rather a word from a confused and uninspired interpreter. We shall then be "teaching as doctrines the precepts of men" (Mark 7:7 RSV).

When we interpret various prophecies within their historical contexts, it is evident that what was a future prediction then (when the prophet wrote) may no longer be a future prediction now (when we read the prophecy). Most OT prophetic predictions have already found their fulfillment in such events as the fall of Jerusalem (Jeremiah; Ezekiel); the judgment of nations such as Samaria (Hosea; Amos; Micah), Babylon (Isa. 13–14; 21; 47; Jer. 50–51; Daniel), Edom (Jer. 49:7–22; Ezek. 25:12–14; Obadiah), Moab (Isa. 15–16; Ezek. 25:8–11), Damascus (Isa. 17; Jer. 49:23–27), Ethiopia (Isa. 18), Egypt (Isa. 19; Jer. 46; Ezek. 29–32), Tyre (Isa. 23; Ezek. 26–28), Nineveh (Nahum; Zeph. 2), and Philistia (Jer. 47; Ezek. 25:15–17; Zeph. 2); the return of the Jews from Babylonian exile (Isa. 40–66; Jer. 30–33; Ezek. 40–48; Mic. 4–5; Haggai; Zechariah); the birth, ministry, death, and resurrection of Jesus Christ (Isa. 4; 7; 9; 11; 40; 53; Jer. 23; 33; Mic. 5; Zech. 3); and the coming of the Spirit at Pentecost (Jer. 31; Joel 2). There are others, however, that still await fulfillment, such as the coming of a great tribulation (2 Thess. 2); the appearance of the man of lawlessness, or antichrist (2 Thess. 2:3–10; 1 John 2:18; 4:3); the glorious appearing of the Son of Man (Matt. 24; Mark 13; 1 Thess. 4; 2 Thess. 2); and the final judgment (Matt. 25; Rev. 20). By seeking to understand the willed meaning of the author for the situation in which he wrote, we will be able to avoid interpreting certain prophecies that have already been fulfilled, such as the return of the Jews from Babylonian exile, as having had a present-day fulfillment or as still awaiting a future fulfillment.

Questions

1. Unlike Jonah's prophecy against Nineveh, there are judgment prophecies in the Bible that did take place, and the prophet knew that they would. Does this refute what we have said about judgment prophecies in this chapter?
2. Read Mark 13:12–27. Is any of the terminology used in this portion of Scripture figurative or hyperbolic? Is any of it literal? On what basis does one decide this?
3. What is the difference between *fore*telling and *forth*telling?
4. Are most of the OT prophecies in Isaiah, Jeremiah, and Ezekiel already fulfilled or still to be fulfilled? How do we decide this?

11

The Game of Jargon

Idioms

One of the most difficult forms of literature to interpret is the idiom. The reason is that with idioms, what the author meant by these words often bears little or no relationship to the literal meaning of the individual words. An idiom is a set phrase whose meaning does not derive from the normal meanings of the individual elements making up the phrase. In fact, frequently its meaning is quite different from and even contrary to the normal use of these words. We can only know if a combination of words is an idiom by finding this same combination in different places and noting from the context that its meaning is different from the normal meaning conveyed by these words. We will then begin to recognize that these words belong together as a set phrase peculiar to itself and must be interpreted as such.

I still remember upon my return from sabbatical study overseas when a friend told me about a new restaurant and said, "Bob, you ought to go there. The food is really bad." I was totally confused by what he said. That same week I heard another person say, "It's really bad" about something I knew he liked. Then I heard someone on television say the same thing, and she, too, was clearly using the expression in a positive sense. It began to dawn on me that during my time overseas the phrase "It is really bad" had become an idiom whose meaning was radically different from the literal meaning of those words. What people meant by this idiom was "It is really *good*."

Numerous examples of such idioms exist in the English language. We have all had people say to us, "Have a good day." Yet despite the fact that the wording of this expression is an imperative, we have never interpreted this as a command from our friends that we must have a good day. We have recognized that this is an idiom for saying good-bye. Similarly, the expression "God bless you" is not a command addressed to God demanding that he bless. Rather, it is either a prayer, such as "I pray that God may be gracious to you and bless you" or, more likely, like "Gesundheit," something we say after a person sneezes, even if we do not know why we say it. "How are you?" frequently functions not as a question regarding our health and well-being but simply as a greeting. Idioms illustrate how the meaning of a phrase is determined not by what the individual words mean but by what the author willed by the expression as a whole. Expressions such as "to pay through the nose" and "to put one's foot in one's mouth" have nothing to do with one's nose or foot but are idioms for paying too much for something and saying something foolish. Some other common idioms include "raining cats and dogs," "cock-and-bull story," "dark horse," "flash in the pan," "up a blind alley," "kick the bucket," "not playing with a full deck," and "breaking the ice."

Love-Hate Imagery

In the Bible we encounter numerous idioms. In using these expressions the authors recognized that they were idioms and expected that their readers would interpret them as such. One of the most troubling of the biblical idioms is found in Malachi 1:2–3:

> "I have loved you [Jacob]," says the LORD. But you say, "How have you loved us?" "Is not Esau Jacob's brother?" declares the LORD. "Yet I have loved Jacob but Esau I have hated. I have laid waste his hill country and left his heritage to jackals of the desert."

As he refers to God's election, Paul quotes this passage in Romans 9:13 in support and writes, "As it is written, 'Jacob I loved, but Esau I hated.'" The troublesome nature of these verses is immediately apparent. How can a God who loves the world (John 3:16) and desires all people to be saved (1 Tim. 2:4; 2 Pet. 3:9) hate Esau? If we ignore the idiomatic nature of these words and interpret them literalistically as meaning God "hated" Esau—that is, he intensely detested and willed harm on the people of Edom—we then have the following conundrum: God loves the world (John 3:16) but not Esau, and wishes all people to be saved (1 Tim. 2:4) but not Esau. (For positive comments concerning God's attitude toward Esau, see Deut. 23:7–8; Amos 9:12; cf. also more-general statements like Mal. 1:11 and Acts 14:16–17). Understood as an idiom, this saying makes better sense. God chose (he "loved") Jacob/Israel (cf. Deut. 4:37; 7:6–8; 10:14–15; etc.), but he did not choose (he "hated") Esau/Edom. Thus, despite God's judgment coming upon Judah in the destruction of Jerusalem in 587 BC and their exile in Babylon, God never forgot his covenant with his chosen people and led them back to the promised land. Edom, however, experienced a judgment that led eventually to losing its geographical and ethnic identity in the fourth century BC, becoming absorbed into the Idumean empire, and ceasing to exist as a nation (Lam. 4:22; Jer. 49:7–22).

In my own struggle in trying to understand Malachi 1:2–3 and Luke 14:26 ("If anyone comes to me and does not hate his own father and mother and wife and children and brothers and sisters, yes, and even his own life, he cannot be my disciple" [cf. Luke 16:13]), it was only when I came to recognize the idiomatic nature of the love-hate language in these passages that they finally made sense. The key passage that helped me see this was Genesis 29:30–31: "So Jacob . . . *loved* Rachel *more* than Leah . . . When the LORD saw that Leah was *hated* . . ." Note here that in the ESV, which translates the Hebrew literally, the opposite of "loving more" is "hating." To love someone (Rachel) more than another (Leah) is in the Hebrew idiom to love one (Rachel) and hate the other (Leah). Other translations, rather than giving a word-for-word translation as the KJV, RSV, and ESV do, seek to provide a thought-for-thought equivalent and translate the contrast "loved more—not loved" (NIV) and "loved . . . more [or 'much more' or 'rather']—unloved" (NRSV, NLT, REB). The actual terminology used in the Hebrew text, however, is "love" and "hate." Yet surely the writer of Genesis knew that Jacob did not hate Leah. We know this because he describes their relationship as producing six sons and a daughter. Something other than hatred must have been involved in their relationship. Jacob did love Leah, but he loved Rachel *more*. Thus, according to the Hebrew idiom, Jacob *loved* Rachel and *hated* Leah.

The idiomatic nature of the love-hate contrast can also be seen in Deuteronomy 21:15–17. None of the modern translations provides a literal word-for-word translation of this passage; they choose rather to give a thought-for-thought one. However, the KJV translates the idiom in this passage word for word as follows:

> If a man have two wives, one beloved, and another hated, and they have born him children, both the beloved and the hated; and if the firstborn son be hers

that was hated: Then it shall be, when he maketh his sons to inherit that which he hath, that he may not make the son of the beloved firstborn before the son of the hated, which is indeed the firstborn: But he shall acknowledge the son of the hated for the firstborn, by giving him a double portion of all that he hath; for he is the beginning of his strength; the right of the firstborn is his.

Modern translations, recognizing the idiomatic nature of this contrast, translate the passage using such contrasts as "loves one but not the other" (NIV), "one loved and the other disliked" (RSV; cf. NRSV), "one loved and the other unloved" (REB, ESV), "loves one and not the other" (NLT). Again, the issue is not that one wife is loved and the other is hated/unloved/disliked. The idiom speaks rather of one wife being loved more than the other. This does not mean that the less-loved wife is hated and loathed. It means rather that she, like Leah, is loved less. However, the way that this was expressed in the Hebrew of that day was by the idiom of one wife being loved and the other hated.

The same idiom also appears in Proverbs 13:24,

> Whoever spares the rod hates his son,
> but he who loves him is diligent to discipline him.

In Luke 14:26 to "hate" one's father and mother means to love Jesus more. This is evident from the parallel in Matthew 10:37, "Whoever loves father or mother more than me is not worthy of me, and whoever loves son or daughter more than me is not worthy of me." Whereas Luke provides a word-for-word translation of Jesus's actual words, Matthew has given us a thought-for-thought one. What Jesus demands of his followers is not hatred toward their parents. On the contrary, those who place Jesus before everything else will love their parents, wives, and children even more than before. However, the followers of Jesus must always place their love and commitment to Jesus above their love for family. Jesus demands not lesser love for family but greater love for him, and love for family will increase continually even as our love for him increases.

Other Biblical Idioms

Another idiom that has caused great difficulty is found in Psalm 137:8–9:

> O daughter of Babylon, doomed to be destroyed,
> blessed shall he be who repays you
> with what you have done to us!

> Blessed shall he be who takes your little ones
> And dashes them against the rock! (cf. Ps. 109:6–15)

The repulsive nature of the imagery is evident to all. How could the psalmist wish this upon the children of Babylon, even if they were his enemies? Yet the idiomatic nature of the saying means something different than a mere desire for bloodthirsty vengeance. The imagery used here was tragically enough all too common in ancient warfare and had become an idiom to describe the judgment of a nation (2 Kings 8:12; Isa. 13:16, 18; Hosea 10:14; 13:16; Nah. 3:10; cf. Luke 19:44). What the psalmist is describing, however, is not a desire for vicious revenge upon the children of Babylon but rather a desire for divine justice to take place. He wishes for God's righteous judgment to fall upon the evil kingdom of Babylon. In his desire for divine justice he uses the imagery of his day to describe the overthrow of nations. It is interesting to note that in several ancient illustrations of a king's reign we find that the son of the king is sitting on his father's lap and the defeated and subject peoples are depicted beneath not the father's feet but the son's. Thus, the judgment of the king of Babylon must also involve the judgment of his sons. Only in this way will the evil dynasty be judged and destroyed. This idiom therefore should be understood and interpreted in light of the imagery of its day and what the author is seeking to describe by the use of this imagery. The author is longing for divine justice to manifest itself in the overthrow of this evil empire. (For other imprecatory psalms, see p. 129.)

Other idioms found within the Bible include

"our hearts melted" (Josh. 2:11; 5:1; 7:5; 14:8; 2 Sam. 17:10; Ps. 22:14; Isa. 13:7; 19:1; Ezek. 21:7; Nah. 2:10) for the loss of courage;

the stars, sun, and moon not giving light (Isa. 13:9–11; 24:23; Ezek. 32:7–8; Joel 2:10, 31; 3:15; Amos 8:9; Hab. 3:11; Acts 2:14–21) for divine intervention in history, whether for blessing or judgment;

"weeping and gnashing of teeth" (Lam. 2:16; Matt. 8:12; 13:42, 50; 22:13; 24:51; 25:30; Luke 13:28) for experiencing severe sorrow and loss;

"not a man was left" (Josh. 8:17; Judg. 4:16; 2 Kings 10:21; cf. Num. 21:35; Deut. 3:3) for winning a great military victory;

to "make the ears tingle" (1 Sam. 3:11; 2 Kings 21:12; Jer. 19:3) for bringing shocking news to those who hear;

to "blot out one's name" from God's book or from under heaven (Exod. 32:32–33; Deut. 9:14; 25:19; 29:20; 2 Kings 14:27; Ps. 9:5; 69:28; 109:13–14; cf. Exod. 17:14) for experiencing God's judgment;

"the apple of his eye" (Deut. 32:10; Ps. 17:8; Prov. 7:2; Zech. 2:8) for
being precious in God's sight; and

"girding up one's loins" (Exod. 12:11; 1 Kings 18:46; 2 Kings 4:29; 9:1;
Job 38:3; 40:7; Jer. 1:17; Nah. 2:1 NRSV; Luke 12:35; Eph. 6:14 RSV,
NAB) or "girding up the loins of one's mind" (1 Pet. 1:13 KJV, NAB)
for preparing oneself for action.

In modern translations of the Bible, numerous idioms are rendered according to their meaning rather than literally. (Cf. 1 John 3:17, where "bowels"
[KJV] is translated "heart" in modern translations, even in formally equivalent ones; and 1 Sam. 25:22, 34; 1 Kings 14:10; 16:11; 21:21; 2 Kings 9:8,
where one "that pisseth against the wall" [KJV] is translated as "male.")

Questions

1. Can you think of a present-day idiom whose meaning is quite different from the literal meaning of the words?
2. How do idioms demonstrate that meaning is not a property of the
   text?
3. How do idioms demonstrate that the etymology of words is of little
   value in understanding the meaning of the text?

12

The Game of Comparison

Parables

Probably the best-known literary form found in the Bible is the parable. Approximately 35 percent of Jesus's teachings are found in the form of parables, and such parables as the good Samaritan and the prodigal son are well known to Christians and non-Christians alike. Defining exactly what a parable is in the OT (*mashal*) or NT (*parabolē*), however, is difficult. These terms can refer to a proverb (1 Sam. 24:13; Ezek. 18:2–3; Luke 4:23 [the shortest of Jesus's parables is "Physician, heal yourself," which may have been a common saying in his day]; 6:39); satire or taunt (Pss. 44:14; 69:11; Isa. 14:3–4; Hab. 2:6); riddle (Pss. 49:4; 78:2; Prov. 1:6); figurative saying (Mark 7:14–17; Luke 5:36–38); extended simile or similitude (Matt. 13:33; Mark 4:30–32; Luke 15:8–10); story parable (Matt. 25:1–13; Luke 14:16–24; 15:11–32; 16:1–8); example parable (Matt. 18:23–25; Luke 10:30–37; 12:16–21; 16:19–31); and allegory (Ezek. 17:2–10; 20:45–21:5; Mark 4:3–9 [note 4:13–20]; 12:1–11 [cf. Matt. 21:39; Luke 20:15]; Matt. 13:24–29 [note 13:36–43]; 22:1–14). The two biblical terms possess a broad semantic range of possible meanings, but basic to each is the idea of a comparison between two different things. Something is likened to something it is not.

The real, lifelike quality of the parables, especially the parables of Jesus, has frequently caused interpreters to forget that the parable is a fictional literary form. This literary form consists of two parts: a picture part, or the story proper, and a reality part, or the comparison to which it is likened. (Other terms used are "vehicle" and "message"; "signifier" and "signified"; "illustration" and "illustrated"; *Bildhälfte* and *Sachhälfte*.) The picture itself does not describe an actual historical event. It is a fictional creation that came into being out of the mind of its author. We should not confuse a parable with biblical narrative, for in a biblical narrative the picture describes a historical event that actually happened. Thus, with respect to a biblical narrative, it is perfectly legitimate to ask questions such as, "Why did Joseph tell his brothers about his dream?" (Gen. 37:5–11); "Exactly what was it that defeated the armies of Sennacherib, the king of Assyria, as they laid siege to Jerusalem?" (2 Kings 19:35–37); "Why did Paul and Barnabas disagree about taking John Mark on a second missionary journey?" (Acts 15:36–41); "What happened to Paul when he was tried in Rome?" (Acts 28). It may not be possible to answer such questions, but they are legitimate because they are being asked with respect to a historical narrative.

On the other hand, we cannot raise such questions with respect to parables. We cannot ask, "In the parable of the prodigal son, why was the older brother out in the field when the prodigal returned?" (Luke 15:25). There is no historical answer to this question. The two brothers never had historical existence. They are simply the literary creations of Jesus. The older brother was out in the field because Jesus wanted him out in the field, and this is his story. Similarly, we cannot ask, "How was it that the father saw his younger son while he was still at a distance?" (Luke 15:20); "Was it by chance or was he continually searching for him?"; "Did he have good eyes?" Nor can we ask: "How did the older brother respond to his father's appeal?" (Luke 15:31–32); "Did he eventually repent of his attitude and accept his younger brother?" And we cannot ask, "Who took care of the ninety-nine sheep while the man searched for the one that was lost?" (Luke 15:4). Such questions confuse the genre of parable with that of historical narrative. The father saw his younger son while he was still at a distance because Jesus wanted him to. The older brother could not respond to his father's appeal because he never existed in real life. He was only a fictional character, and his fictional existence ceased when the parable ended. As to who would take care of the ninety-nine sheep: Jesus, the storyteller, would take care of them!

Thus, we must not confuse a lifelike parable, which is a fictional creation, with a biblical narrative referring to a historical event. Of course, the reality to which the picture part of a parable refers is real and historical. In other words, the meaning Jesus intended and its various implications continue, but we must not address the picture part of a parable, which is fictional, with questions that are appropriate only to nonfictional literary forms such as biblical narrative.

Because of the fictional nature of parables, it is not surprising that at times we find unreal elements in them. We thus find unusual exaggeration, as in the parable of the unforgiving servant who was forgiven ten thousand talents (Matt. 18:24). (Herod the Great's entire annual income was only nine hundred talents.) At times we also find unusual circumstances: all ten maidens fall asleep (Matt. 25:5); all the invited guests, after accepting the first invitation, decline the final invitation to come to the banquet (Luke 14:18). Yet except for one or two OT parables (Judg. 9:7–20; Ezek. 17:2–10), the parables of the Bible, especially the parables of Jesus, portray everyday experiences of the real world.

Basic Principles for Interpreting Parables

Many of the early church fathers brought with them in their study of the Bible the idea that the biblical text contained a fourfold meaning. These four levels are the literal, the moral, the spiritual, and the anagogical or eschatological meaning. Thus a biblical text that refers to Jerusalem was understood as referring to four things: a specific city in Judah (the literal meaning); the human soul (the moral meaning); the church (the spiritual meaning); and the heavenly abode of the saints, the heavenly Jerusalem (the anagogical or eschatological meaning). To find the nonliteral meanings of these texts one needed to apply an allegorical method of interpretation. It was especially in the area of parable interpretation that this method of interpretation was applied. According to this method, specific details in the picture part of a parable are understood as representing corresponding points of comparison in the reality part. In so doing interpreters treated as an allegory what the authors did not intend to be an allegory. A striking example of this is Augustine's interpretation of the parable of the good Samaritan. According to Augustine the picture parts of the parable correspond to the following realities:

The man going down to Jericho	=	Adam
Jerusalem, from which he was going	=	City of Heavenly Peace
Jericho	=	The moon, which signifies our mortality (there is a play here on the terms "moon" and "Jericho," which look and sound similar in Hebrew)

Robbers	=	The devil and his angels
Stripping him	=	Taking away his immortality
Beating him	=	Persuading him to sin
Leaving him half dead	=	Due to sin, he was dead spiritually, but half-alive due to his knowledge of God
Priest	=	Priesthood of the OT, that is, the Law
Levite	=	Ministry of the OT, that is, the Prophets
Good Samaritan	=	Christ
Binding up of his wounds	=	Restraint placed upon sin
Oil	=	Comfort of good hope
Wine	=	Exhortation to spirited work
Animal	=	Body of Christ
Inn	=	Church
Two denarii	=	Two commandments of love
Innkeeper	=	Apostle Paul
Return of the Good Samaritan	=	Resurrection of Christ

The basic issue with an allegorical interpretation such as this does not involve whether such an interpretation reflects a true biblical theology. (Some of the early church fathers required that an allegorical interpretation not conflict with the biblical teachings taught in the Bible and by the church. Some even insisted that alleged allegorical teachings found in the text must be explicitly taught elsewhere in the Bible to be valid.) The fundamental issue rather involves whether the parable truly teaches the alleged allegorical interpretation. While reading true Christian teaching into a parable is not as bad as reading a nonbiblical falsehood into it, it is best not to read into it (eisegesis) anything at all. Scripture does not need the help of interpreters who seek to have it say things that the biblical authors did not intend. What it needs are interpreters who seek to understand what its authors meant by their texts and the legitimate implications contained in that meaning.

Rule 1: A Parable Generally Teaches One Basic Point

It has already been pointed out that the term "parable" covers a broad range of meanings in the Bible. Basic to all, however, is a comparison of two dissimilar things. In an extended comparison, such as the parable of the good Samaritan, should we look for a string of various comparisons or a single, basic comparison? In other words, should we seek to interpret a biblical parable like an allegory, looking for specific meanings in the various details, along the lines of Augustine and the other early church fathers, or should we seek to interpret it as an extended picture that tries to establish a single, basic point of comparison (cf. Luke 10:29, 36–37)?

In the parable of the good Samaritan, is it important that the man was going "down" from Jerusalem to Jericho? It does not appear so. Jericho lies approximately 3,500 feet below Jerusalem, and the meaning of the parable would not change if the man had been going "up" from Jericho to Jerusalem. Would the meaning of the parable change if the innkeeper had been given three denarii rather than two? No doubt if he had, the allegorical method of interpretation would have seen in this a clear reference to the Trinity, but the meaning of the parable would not have changed. These details were added to the parable in order to provide local color and interest. They are not intended to be interpreted as referring to a corresponding reality. These additional details do not make a parable into an allegory. Similarly in the parable of the prodigal son, such details as the returning son being given a robe, a signet ring, and a fatted calf for a feast do not correspond to something else. It is true that the early church saw in them the return of the original righteousness that Adam lost (the robe), Christian baptism (the ring), and the Lord's Supper (the fatted calf and the feast), but the Pharisees and scribes in Jesus's audience would never have interpreted the parable in this manner, and the parable was addressed to them (Luke 15:3). These picture parts demonstrate the great love of the father and his full acceptance of his son. Thus, they help illustrate an aspect of the point of the parable (God's love for the outcasts), but they do not possess any specific meaning in themselves. Furthermore, we should be careful to focus our attention on what is said in the parable and not on what is not said.

This understanding receives support from the way metaphors and comparisons function. If someone were to ask the question, "What is God like?" I might reply, "God is like a loving Father who . . ." In so doing, I would have a basic point of comparison in mind. If someone, however, asked, "Well, then who is God's wife?" this would illegitimately press the point of comparison further than was intended. There was only one basic comparison I was seeking to illustrate by this metaphor. Ultimately any comparison will break down when pressed. The only comparison that will not break down is something like "God is like God." But this is no longer a comparison and serves no purpose. Every comparison of two unlike things must sooner or later break down. The fact is that the purpose of an analogy is to convey a basic point of comparison between the picture and the reality to which it corresponds.

If we keep this in mind, we will be less troubled by those parables in which characters exhibit questionable, if not immoral, behavior. For instance, in the parable of the unjust steward the behavior of the steward is clearly immoral. (Note that he is called "dishonest" only after the activities described in Luke 16:4–7.) The commendation of the unjust steward, however, is due to his shrewdness, not to his dishonesty. The point of the parable involves acting decisively in preparing for the coming judgment. (In the setting of Jesus this probably referred to the crisis caused by the arrival of the kingdom of God.) If we do not press the details of the parable but are content with its one basic point of comparison, the parable does not cause confusion. Even shrewd thieves can illustrate a basic point. Similarly, in the parable of the wise and foolish maidens (Matt. 25:1–13) the fact that the wise maidens were selfish and did not share their oil with those in need (v. 9) should not be pressed. The main point of the parable is clear enough: be prepared, as the wise maidens were. Needless to say, Jesus assumed that his hearers would know from his other teachings how to be prepared. Matthew also assumed that his readers would know this from having read Matthew 1:1–24:51. The same is true with respect to the deceitful character of the man who discovered treasure hidden in a field (Matt. 13:44). In this parable Jesus simply seeks to emphasize that there is nothing more important and that there is no cost too great when it comes to entering the kingdom of God.

In the study of parables therefore we should seek the main point of the parable and not press its details. This does not exclude the possibility that details in the picture part of a parable at times may refer to a corresponding reality. (Cf. such allegorical parables as Mark 4:1–9 [note vv. 13–20]; 12:1–11; Matt. 13:29–30 [note vv. 36–44]; 22:1–14; Luke 14:16–24 [note v. 23]; 20:9–18 [note v. 15].) Nevertheless, the greater danger for most interpreters is to see too much meaning in specific details rather than too little. It is sad to note that the allegorizing of the parables that was popular among the early church fathers has come back into vogue once again. (This is especially true with interpreters who follow a reader-response hermeneutic.) Whereas allegories should be interpreted allegorically, parables that are not allegories should not be allegorized. Radical parable interpreters have been especially prone to return to this methodology, for it permits them to read into the parables their own inclinations and interests. There is a significant difference, however, between Augustine's and the early church fathers' allegorical interpretations and that of the recent allegorizers. The former read into the various details of the parables the theological content of the Bible and the teachings of the church, whereas modern allegorizers tend to read into these details their own ideological emphases that are often far from being biblical or theological. The early church at least was correct in seeing that the focus of the parables is theocentric, centering on God and the arrival of his kingdom. They are not focused on Freudian psychology, existential thought, political revolution, economic transformation, feministic and sociological agendas, ecological concerns, and so on, as found in much modern-day allegorical interpretation. Such rewriting of the parables and reconstruction of the contexts in which the parables were originally spoken usually reveal far more about the agendas of their creators than about the Jesus of history and his teachings.

It has been argued by some that we cannot translate the point of a parable into a nonparabolic statement, for when we do so, the powerful affective impact of the parable is lost. This objection is well-taken. No one can deny that the parable of the good Samaritan (Luke 10:30–35) has more persuasive power than the summary, "We should love our neighbor who is in need just as the good Samaritan loved the man who fell among thieves." Similarly, the parable of the prodigal son (Luke 15:11–32) impacts the reader far more forcefully than the statement, "In this parable Jesus is defending his ministry among the outcasts of Israel and challenging the Pharisees and scribes to enter into the joy of God's salvation coming to these outcasts."

The difference between a parable and its interpretation, however, lies not in their meaning (assuming the interpretation is valid) but in their ability to affect the reader or hearer. A parable consists of commissive language, whereas a statement of its meaning consists of referential language (see pp. 68–69). The two differ in their ability to elicit response. If meaning is primarily cognitive, involving the mind and understanding rather than the will and significance, then a parable's meaning can be restated as a point using referential language. If we redefine the meaning of a parable as consisting of both the principle found in this literary form and its power to affect response (i.e., its ability to affect significance), then a restatement of the parable's meaning will always be incomplete. By definition it will always be incomplete, because it lacks the persuasive dimension and affective power of commissive language. In so doing we must remember, however, that we are now no longer using the terms "meaning" and "interpretation" as we defined them in chapter 2.

A parable is able to disarm its hearers and divert potential resistance and opposition in a way that referential language cannot. Consequently, the prophet Nathan did not approach King David requesting an appointment to talk to him about his adultery with Bathsheba and his murder of her husband Uriah. Instead he told David a parable that deflected any possible resistance until the parable's interpretation was given (cf. 2 Sam.

11:1–12:15). Only when David vented his anger at the terrible injustice portrayed in the parable did Nathan say, "You are the man!" (2 Sam. 12:7). Now the affective power of the parable fell in full force upon David, and his conscience and heart led him to repent. This came about due to (1) the persuasive and disarming nature of the parable's literary form and its ability to engage the hearer (the picture part), (2) the divine truth encapsulated in this form (the reality part), (3) the convicting work of the Holy Spirit, and (4) the human response of David resulting from the effects of 1, 2, and 3. In this respect over twenty parables of Jesus begin with a question that seeks both to disarm his hearers and to assist them in interpreting the parable.

Rule 2: Discover the Point Jesus Sought to Make

If meaning is determined by the author, we possess in the parables of Jesus two possible authors. One is Jesus (Meaning^{SM}), who created the parables; the other is the Gospel writer (Meaning^{Text}), who in his work interpreted Jesus's parables for his readers. Both have willed a meaning in telling the parable. (This should not be confused with those who argue that the parables are polyvalent or plurisignificant, having multiple meanings, and that these meanings are the property of the text or of the reader, not of Jesus or the Gospel writer.) Here we recognize that the Gospel parables have two authors, and both willed a meaning. These meanings, although possessing a similar principle, tend to be addressed to different audiences and to emphasize different implications.

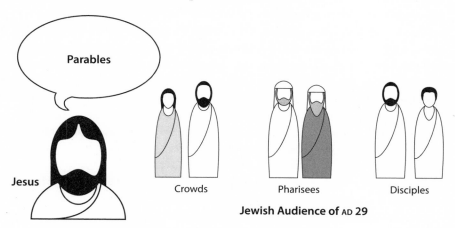

Jewish Audience of AD **29**

When the parables are interpreted in their original setting, the situation of Jesus, they become exciting and alive. Instead of being viewed simply as timeless illustrations, they are now seen, as one writer has stated, as weapons of warfare with which Jesus battled his opponents. This can be illustrated from the parable of the good Samaritan. Years ago when my daughter was about ten years old, I asked her to play a game with me. I asked her to answer my questions without reflecting on how she should answer. She was simply to tell me what immediately came into her mind. When she agreed, I said to her, "Samaritan." She responded with terms such as "good," "Jesus," "loving," "Christian," and "hospital." When I said, "priest," the terms tended to be somewhat negative. Probably many, if not most, people would respond in a similar way, at least with respect to the term "Samaritan." The result is that for most people the parable of the good Samaritan is a pleasant tale of a good man who did a good deed whereas bad men did not.

On the other hand, if we could ask Jesus's audience to respond to these terms, they would respond very differently. For the Jews in Jesus's audience, the Samaritans were hated and cursed, and this attitude was mutual. They were so hated and despised that if people wanted to insult someone they could say, "Are we not right in saying that you are a Samaritan and have a demon?" (John 8:48). Hatred between Samaritans and Jews had been festering for nearly a thousand years. It began in 922 BC upon the death of King Solomon, when the ten northern tribes of Israel (later named Samaria, after its capital city) separated from Judah (consisting of the tribes of Judah and Benjamin) and thus divided the nation into two parts. This hostility increased two hundred years later when the city of Samaria fell and those who were not taken into exile intermarried with the Gentiles who settled in the land. Thus, for Jews, they now added to their rebel status that of being half-breeds. The refusal of the returning Jews from Babylon under Haggai and Zechariah to permit the Samaritans to assist in the rebuilding of the Jerusalem temple, and the subsequent destruction of the Samaritan temple on Mount Gerizim by the Jews in 128 BC only heightened their animosity toward one another, as did the Samaritan desecration of the Jewish temple with the bones of dead men in the first decade of the of the Common Era.

The result of all this was that Jews wanted nothing to do with Samaritans (John 4:9). For example, when traveling north or south between Jerusalem and Galilee, devout Jews tended to cross the Jordan River and walk through Perea and the Decapolis until they passed Samaria and could enter Galilee. For a Jew to speak of a "good Samaritan" was a contradiction in terms for Jesus's audience. It would be like talking about a square circle or a faithful adulterer. On the other hand, priests and Levites in general were thought of positively. Jesus purposely shaped his parable knowing that it clashed with the established values of his audience. As a result, his parable is not a pleasant tale with expected results. On the contrary, it is a damning indictment directed against the social attitudes of his listeners. Their heroes are portrayed by their actions as villains and their villains by their actions as heroes.

I came across an example of such a role reversal when I read about the "Rape of Nanking," which took place in 1937. In this horrible atrocity Japanese soldiers raped, tortured, and murdered more than 300,000 helpless Chinese. The only place of safety for fleeing Chinese was the International Safety Zone created by the foreign community in Nanking whose nations were not at war with Japan. Two men whose bravery and courage stood out and saved tens, perhaps hundreds, of thousands of lives from the slaughter were Robert Wilson and John Rabe. Wilson was a devout Methodist physician, the son of Methodist missionaries. During this period he was the only surgeon at the University of Nanking hospital who never left the hospital. Some 200,000 to 300,000 Chinese fled to the Safety Zone. No person played a greater role in protecting the helpless Chinese seeking protection in the Safety Zone than John Rabe, the head of the International Committee in Nanking. He organized the housing for the many refugees, drove trucks outside the city to bring food into the Zone, met with Japanese officials, and stopped individual acts of murder and rape. Often his only safety lay in his arm band. It was his Nazi arm band—Rabe was the leader of the Nazi party in Nanking. He was the neighbor, the good Samaritan, dubbed "The Nazi who saved Nanking."

When we interpret other parables in the setting of Jesus, they also take on a new life and vitality. The parables of the lost sheep (Luke 15:4–7), the lost coin (Luke 15:8–10), and the prodigal son (Luke 15:11–32) must be understood as addressed to those who "grumbled, saying, 'This man receives sinners and eats with them'" (Luke 15:2). Thus, the emphasis is not on the demonstration of God's love for the outcasts but on the reaction of the older brother to such love. If these parables were directed to tax collectors and sinners (Luke 15:1), their main point would be to illustrate God's great love toward them. But since the audience to which these parables were aimed was the Pharisees and scribes, the point is different. Jesus appealed to them through these parables, as if to say, "Why are you not rejoicing in what God is doing? (Luke 15:7, 10, 24, 32). The lost are being found; the lame walk; tax collectors and sinners are entering the kingdom. Why, like this older brother, are you not joining in the banquet celebration?" The parable of the laborers in the vineyard (Matt. 20:1–16) makes the same point.

The second basic rule for interpreting the parables seeks the meaning of its original author. It can be stated as follows: seek the meaning of the parable that Jesus intended (Meaning^SM). The interpretation of any of Jesus's parables should be undertaken in the context of his entire teaching, of course. It is important that a parable of the kingdom (the part) should be interpreted in light of what Jesus says elsewhere on this subject (the whole).

Rule 3: Discover the Point the Evangelist Sought to Make

It has become increasingly clear that the Gospel writers were not simply recorders of the Jesus traditions but interpreters of them as well. They believed that God had called them not only to share the teachings and acts of the Son of God but to interpret them and reveal some of the implications for their readers. Consequently, although there is only one gospel, we possess that gospel in four forms: the Gospel according to Matthew; the Gospel according to Mark; the Gospel according to Luke; and the Gospel according to John. It is not surprising therefore that our Gospels are both similar and different. Each evangelist felt free to explain, clarify, apply, abbreviate, reorder, or omit (cf. John 21:25) these materials as the Spirit of God led him. In so doing each provided an inspired record and interpretation of the Jesus traditions for his readers.

On several occasions the Gospel writers took parables of Jesus aimed at one audience and interpreted their various implications for a different one. This was necessary because many of Jesus's parables were addressed to such groups as the Pharisees and scribes, and these were not the audiences for whom the Gospels were written. Thus Luke in writing his Gospel had to interpret the parables and traditions of Jesus that were originally spoken to one audience to a new audience (Theophilus and his other readers [Luke 1:1–4]). We find several examples of this in his Gospel. In the parable of the four soils, Luke applies this parable to the needs of his particular audience and singles out certain dangers that they need to avoid (believing for only a while [8:13]; the danger of riches and pleasures of life [8:14]) and certain qualities they need to nurture (an honest and good heart, perseverance [8:15]). These Lukan emphases (Meaning^{Text}) can be seen most clearly by comparing them to the form of the parable found in Mark 4:3–20.

Another example of this is found in Luke 16:1–8, where we find a parable of Jesus that teaches the need for resolute action and decision. Originally this parable was probably directed to a different audience and involved the need to repent in light of the coming of the kingdom of God. It is now applied by Luke to the believing community, and other sayings of Jesus have been added at this point. These sayings illustrate how Luke's readers can prepare for their time of accounting by a wise stewardship of their possessions (vv. 9–15).

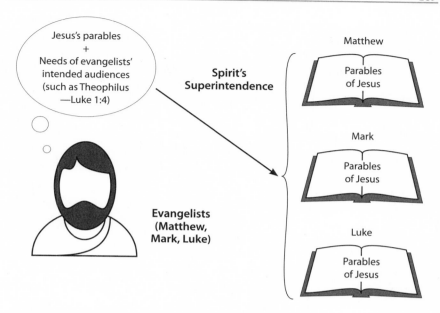

Matthew also illustrates this principle in his version of the parable of the lost sheep (Matt. 18:12–14). Whereas the original audience consisted of Pharisees and scribes (Luke 15:1–3, 4–7), Matthew applies the pattern of teaching found in this parable to his Christian audience (18:1, 5–6, 10, 14). As a result, the problem sheep is not described as "lost" (cf. Luke 15:4, 6) but as "gone astray" (Matt. 18:12–13), and the application or reality part involves the need of the Christian community to seek out those members, the "little ones," who are going astray. They must be sought and brought back into the fold. Both the meaning of the parable willed by Jesus and that willed by Matthew involve the same principle: God loves outcasts, whether within or outside the believing community, and they should be sought and welcomed.

If the evangelists have interpreted the parables in this manner, they are now also authors of the parables. Thus, even as we have sought the meaning of the parable that Jesus intended (Meaning^{SM}), we should also seek the meaning of the parable that the Gospel writers intended (Meaning^{Text}).

Guidelines for Arriving at a Parable's Main Point

In seeking to arrive at the main point of a parable, there are several questions that prove useful.

Who Are the Main Characters?

In parables where several characters are mentioned, there are always two or three characters who are most important. Usually it is quite easy to narrow down the multiple characters to three. For instance, in the parable of the prodigal son the three most important characters are clearly the father, the prodigal son, and the older brother. In the parable of the laborers in the vineyard (Matt. 20:1–16) there are again three: the landowner, the first-hour laborers, and the eleventh-hour laborers.

Parable of the Laborers in the Vineyard

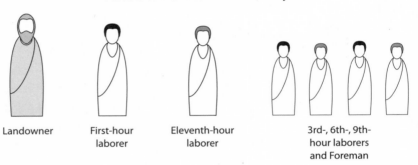

| Landowner | First-hour laborer | Eleventh-hour laborer | 3rd-, 6th-, 9th-hour laborers and Foreman |

In the latter parable, it is evident that the third-, sixth-, and ninth-hour laborers are relatively unimportant because they do not appear later in the evening accounting. Asking which two of these three characters are most important is helpful in drawing our attention to the particular characters Jesus and the Gospel writers wanted to emphasize. It is incorrect, however, to assume that each main character represents a separate truth taught in a parable.

What Occurs at the End?

In *Interpreting the Parables*, A. M. Hunter has referred to this guideline as the "rule of end stress" ([Philadelphia: Westminster, 1960], 11). It is based on the fact that good storytelling builds up and focuses interest on the conclusion of the story. A good mystery holds the reader in suspense until the very end, when everything is explained and becomes clear. This is why we dare not miss the closing minutes of a television episode of "Murder She Wrote" or "Crime Scene Investigation," or of a Sherlock Holmes, Agatha Christie, or Alfred Hitchcock movie. Even as a good comedian does not give away the punch line of a joke until the very end and a good mystery writer does not give away the solution until the end, so a good story builds up and concentrates the attention of the hearers on the final conclusion.

In a similar way, the emphasis and point of a parable comes at the end of the story. The point of the parable of the laborers in the vineyard (Matt. 20:1–16) would be very different if the conclusion read something like this:

> And when evening came, the owner of the vineyard said to his foreman, "Call the laborers and pay them their wages, beginning with the first up to the last." When those hired first came, each of them received a denarius. Now when those hired last came, they expected to receive less, but each one of them also received a denarius. And on receiving it, they marveled and said of the master of the house, "Truly this is a generous man."

If Jesus had told the parable in this manner, the focus would fall on the end action of generosity. The purpose of the parable would then be to illustrate that God is generous and kind. But Jesus did not teach the parable in this manner. He ended the parable with the grumbling of the first-hour laborers. This is where he wanted to focus his hearers' attention. The point of the parable for Jesus therefore centers on the reaction of the first-hour laborers. This part of the picture is emphasized because the reality to which Jesus was pointing involves the unwillingness of the grumbling Pharisees and scribes to accept and rejoice in God's gracious offer of salvation to the lost. Similarly, the focus of attention in the parable of the prodigal son is on the father and the older, grumbling brother who is unwilling to accept and rejoice in his father's forgiveness and acceptance of his prodigal brother (cf. Luke 15:2).

What Appears in Direct Discourse?

If a parable contains a conversation, this focuses the reader's attention on what is being said. Thus, it should be noted that in the parable of the laborers in the vineyard, no conversation takes place between the landowner and the eleventh-hour laborers. Yet an extensive one takes place between the landowner and the first-hour laborers (Matt. 20:11–15). Similarly, there is no conversation between the father and the prodigal son. True, the son has memorized his prepared speech and repeats it (Luke 15:18–19, 21), but the father does not respond verbally to him in any way. However, there is an extensive conversation between the father and his older son (vv. 29–32). In both these parables Jesus uses direct discourse to focus his hearers' attention on this part of the parable.

Who Gets the Most Space?

When telling a story, we usually spend more time describing the important characters. By the criterion of proportion, minor characters receive less attention; major characters receive more attention. In the parable of the laborers in the vineyard it is evident by the amount of space devoted to the first-hour laborers (Matt. 20:1–2, 10–15) that they play a more important role in the parable than the eleventh-hour laborers (vv. 6–7, 9). This great discrepancy in space clearly indicates that the point of the parable involves the first-hour laborers' response to the landowner. The issue is not as clear in the parable of the prodigal son. The space devoted to the prodigal involves thirteen verses (Luke 15:12–24), whereas the older brother is referred to in eight (vv. 25–32). This, however, is outweighed by the rule of end stress (the older brother, not the younger, appears at the end of the parable) and by the fact that the only dialogue found in the parable involves the older brother and his father.

Conclusion

The key to interpreting the parables is to remember that they are not extended allegories but that they tend to teach a single basic point. We should therefore focus our attention on the basic analogy in the picture part and on its corresponding point in the reality part. For example, in the parable of the prodigal son the analogy is that just as the older brother will not accept and rejoice in the loving forgiveness that his father has extended to his brother, so the Pharisees and scribes are unwilling to accept God's loving forgiveness of tax collectors and sinners through the ministry of Jesus. This, however, does not make the parable an allegory, because there is present only a single basic analogy, and every parable, metaphor, or simile contains a basic analogy.

At times in the search for the basic point of the parable, the following questions prove helpful: Who are the two main characters? What comes at the end? Who is involved in a dialogue? To whom or what is the most space devoted? To whom was the parable addressed? After having correctly understood the meaning of Jesus and/or the Gospel writer, however, our task is not over. The most important aspect of interpretation still lies ahead. We must now seek those implications that are most relevant for us and act on them. What ultimately does it profit us if we have learned the meaning of a parable without allowing that meaning and its implications to affect our lives?

In light of various recent interpretations of Jesus's parables, one additional guide may prove helpful. Interpretations of Jesus's parables that are long on sociological, psychological, political, and/or economic emphases and short on theological ones should be viewed with suspicion. All too often such interpretations betray the personal agendas of modern scholars, a general agnosticism toward the ability to recover the actual teachings of the historical Jesus, a radical reader-response hermeneutic, and a disinterest in theology in general. The author of these parables summarized the quintessence of human existence as involving love for God and love for one's neighbor (Mark 12:28–31). As a result, even a parable such as that of the good Samaritan is not simply a sociological teaching on human brotherhood and the evils of racism, but is based on the commandment "You shall love . . . your neighbor as yourself" (Luke 10:27). This command in turn is not based on an anthropological or sociological truth but on the fact that this has been commanded by God. Thus the essence of this parable of Jesus is ultimately theological in nature.

Questions

1. Keeping in mind the definition of meaning in chapter 2, why must Augustine's interpretation of the parable of the good Samaritan be incorrect? (Note Luke 10:29, 36–37.)
2. What is the difference between an allegory and a parable?
3. Read the parable of the laborers in the vineyard (Matt. 20:1–16) and compare it with the parable of the prodigal son (Luke 15:11–32). How are they alike?
4. To whom did Jesus address the parables of Luke 15:4–32? How does the audience to whom Jesus spoke affect our understanding of his main point? In other words, if these parables were addressed to "the tax collectors and sinners" (Luke 15:1), would the main point be different than if he had addressed them to "the Pharisees and scribes" (Luke 15:2)?

13

The Game of Exaggeration

Overstatement and Hyperbole

As has been noted on several occasions, the Bible contains a great deal of exaggerated language. Poetry, proverbs, and prophecy by their very nature use exaggerated language (see chapters 7, 9, and 10), as do most forms of commissive language (see pp. 68–69). Some Christians find it difficult to believe that there is exaggeration in the Bible. They associate exaggeration with inexactness and imprecision. Worse yet, in the minds of some, exaggeration is a synonym for falsehood.

Hyperbole and overstatement, however, are perfectly acceptable literary forms when shared by writer and reader. When used in this way, they are powerful literary forms that enable the writer to convey not just factual information but feelings and emotions as well. In fact, it is very difficult to communicate certain things apart from exaggeration. How do two people in love express their love to one another? Certainly not in the precise language of science. On the contrary, they may use poetry that is filled with metaphor and hyperbole. Or they may use prose, but this, too, will be filled with hyperbole. The one form they will certainly not use is the literal precision of a chemistry lab report. In the communication of people in love, whether between a man and a woman or between the psalmist and his God, exaggerated language is often necessary.

Love Letter

January 1, 2011

My dearest Joan,

_____ heart
aches _____
_____ die unless
I see you soon.

_____
_____
can't live without you _____
_____ hold my
breath until I see you _____
_____
_____
_____
_____

Chemistry Lab Report

Student's Name   Date
P.O.#   Instructor

Column Chromatography
_____
_____

Reaction
Fluorine $\underset{CH_3COOH}{\overset{Na_2Cr_3O_7}{\rule{0pt}{0pt}}}$ fluorenene
_____
_____

Procedure
Dissolve some fluorine in 25 ml. acetic
acid _____
heat at 80° for 15 minutes in a water bath
_____

Observations
_____
_____

What makes hyperbole or overstatement an illegitimate literary form is when the writer does not indicate to his readers that he is using this form of language. Unless shared, this form of language is frequently deceitful and dishonest. When a man tells his beloved that he is sick and would die if he never saw her again, this conveys the truth that he deeply loves and misses her, even if he feels perfectly well at the time. On the other hand, for an employee who feels perfectly well to phone in and state that he or she cannot come to work because of being seriously ill is to lie, and a bank teller who exaggerates bank accounts is likely to be charged with fraud. The acceptability of this literary form of communication depends on its being shared. When shared, exaggerated language is a powerful and effective form of communication. When not shared, it can be a bad example of miscommunication, incompetence, or deceit.

Exaggeration can be subdivided into two types: overstatement, in which what is said is exaggerated but literally possible; and hyperbole, in which what is said is so exaggerated that it is literally impossible. We shall not concern ourselves in this chapter with this distinction. The issue facing the biblical interpreter is not so much _if_ there is exaggeration in the Bible but _how_ to detect it. Its presence in the Bible is clear from the following examples:

You blind guides, straining out a gnat but swallowing a camel! (Matt. 23:24)

Why do you see the speck that is in your brother's eye, but do not notice the log that is in your own eye? Or how can you say to your brother, "Let me take the speck out of your eye," when there is the log in your own eye? You hypocrite, first take the log out of your own eye, and then you will see clearly to stake the speck out of your brother's eye. (Matt. 7:3–4)

Children, how difficult it is to enter the kingdom of God! It is easier for a camel to go through the eye of a needle than for a rich person to enter the kingdom of God. (Mark 10:24b–25)

> I am poured out like water,
>   and all my bones are out of joint;
> my heart is like wax;
>   it is melted within my breast. (Ps. 22:14; cf. Lam. 2:11)

And all the people went up after him [King Solomon], playing on pipes, and rejoicing with great joy, so that the earth was split by their noise. (1 Kings 1:40)

Clearly none of the above was meant to be taken literally. In the first example, which is a pun in Aramaic, Jesus's mother tongue (gnat = *galma*; camel = *gamla*), it is obvious that a person cannot swallow a camel. Similarly, a log cannot fit in someone's eye. And despite all the unsuccessful attempts to find a gate in Jerusalem called "the eye of a needle," the saying about a camel going through the eye of a needle was intended by Jesus to be interpreted as an example of hyperbole. The psalmist also did not intend for his readers to think that his heart had changed from a solid to a liquid, nor did the writer of 1 Kings want his readers to believe that an actual earthquake took place when Solomon was anointed king because of the shouting and singing of the people. These are all examples of exaggerated language.

Most people are intuitively able to determine if a passage contains exaggerated language. They just "know" that such passages should not be interpreted literally. This is especially true with respect to the use of hyperbole. Yet in the history of the church there have been numerous examples where individuals have not recognized the exaggerated nature of this literary form, and this has led to drastic results. During the 1970s, several groups within what was known as the Jesus Movement argued on the basis of Luke 14:26 that their members were to "hate" their parents. In supposed obedience to the biblical teaching (and in ignorance of the exaggerated nature of the idiom contained in this verse and of the clear teachings of the Bible elsewhere) young people actually believed they should hate their parents. At other times in history, some have mutilated themselves due to a misinterpretation of Matthew 5:29–30. (In the context of lust these verses speak about gouging out one's right eye and cutting off one's right hand in order to avoid the damnation of hell.)

There are a number of helpful rules that enable us to recognize if a statement in the Bible contains exaggeration.

1. The Statement Is Literally Impossible

The passages listed above are all examples of this. They are simply impossible. The realities of life do not permit them to be true in a literal sense. Compare also:

> I will surely bless you [Abraham], and I will surely multiply your offspring as the stars of heaven and as the sand that is on the seashore. (Gen. 22:17)

Other occurrences of the phrase "as the stars of heaven" include Genesis 26:4; Exodus 32:13; Deuteronomy 1:10; 10:22; 28:62; 1 Chronicles 27:23; and Nehemiah 9:23 (cf. Gen. 15:5; Jer. 33:22; Nah. 3:16). Similar exaggerated descriptions of things that are numerous compare them to the sand on the seashore (Gen. 32:12; 41:49; Josh. 11:4; Judg. 7:12; 1 Sam. 13:5; 2 Sam. 17:11; 1 Kings 4:20, 29; Job 6:3; Isa. 10:22; 48:19; Jer. 15:8; 33:22; Hosea 1:10; Heb. 11:12; cf. Job 29:18; Ps. 139:18; Isa. 48:19; Hab. 1:9) and to "the dust of the earth" (Gen. 13:16; 28:14; 2 Chron. 1:9; cf. Num. 23:10; Job 27:16).

> Saul and Jonathan, beloved and lovely!
>   In life and in death they were not divided;
> they were swifter than eagles;
>   they were stronger than lions. (2 Sam. 1:23)

In these cases, the authors expected their readers to recognize the nonliteral nature of the statements and to interpret them as expressive examples of certain truths (i.e., God would bless Abraham and his descendants and multiply their number; Saul and Jonathan were mighty warriors). These truths were conveyed through the use of hyperbole.

2. The Statement Conflicts with What the Speaker Teaches Elsewhere

This can be shown most easily in the case of Jesus. Note the following examples:

> If anyone comes to me and does not hate his own father and mother and wife and children and brothers and sisters, yes, and even his own life, he cannot be my disciple. (Luke 14:26)

> But when you pray, go into your room and shut the door and pray to your Father who is in secret. And your Father who sees in secret will reward you. (Matt. 6:6)

It is clear that a literalistic interpretation of Jesus's statement about hating parents conflicts with his teachings in Mark 7:9–13 and 10:19, which speak of honoring parents. It also conflicts with his teaching concerning loving enemies (Luke 6:27), for if we were to hate our parents, this would make them enemies and thus qualify them to be recipients of our love. (For the idiomatic nature of this language, see pp. 153–55.) Similarly, a literalistic interpretation of his statement to pray privately in one's room conflicts with the very prayer he taught his disciples, which is corporate in nature ("*Our* Father . . . Give *us* this day *our* daily bread, and forgive *us our* debts . . ." [Matt. 6:9–13]). Thus, whereas one should pray privately rather than ostentatiously, like the hypocrites Jesus criticized, there are times when Christians will also pray nonprivately, as when they pray with other believers, "*Our* Father . . ."

Other examples of this can be found in Isaiah 11:6–9 (cf. 65:25) and 35:8–10, both of which cannot be literally true, for in the first instance lions are present in the kingdom of God and in the second they are excluded (see pp. 144–45).

3. The Statement Conflicts with the Actions of the Speaker Elsewhere

It is true that religious teachers can contradict their teachings by their conduct. Jesus referred to this when he said, "The scribes and the Pharisees sit on Moses' seat, so practice and observe whatever they tell you—but not what they do. For they preach, but do not practice" (Matt. 23:2–3). Good teachers, however, seek to demonstrate through their actions what they mean by their teachings. Thus, if Jesus makes a statement that conflicts with his actions, this may be an indication that his statement contains overstatement or hyperbole. Here are some examples of this:

> Again, you have heard that it was said to those of old, "You shall not swear falsely, but shall perform to the Lord what you have sworn." But I say to you, Do not take an oath at all, either by heaven, for it is the throne of God, or

by the earth, for it is his footstool, or by Jerusalem, for it is the city of the great King. And do not take an oath by your head, for you cannot make one hair white or black. Let what you say be simply "Yes" or "No"; anything more than this comes from evil. (Matt. 5:33–37)

Do not think that I have come to bring peace to the earth. I have not come to bring peace, but a sword. (Matt. 10:34)

In the midst of the debate among his contemporaries as to when oaths had be kept and when they did not have to be kept, Jesus states that people should not swear an oath at all. Their character should be such that a simple yes or no ought to be sufficient. If they lack such character, all the oaths in the world would be irrelevant. Although some Christians interpret these words of Jesus literally and refuse to swear an oath even in a court of law, it is evident that Jesus was using exaggeration in this statement. One reason is that Jesus in practice accepted the legitimacy of such oaths. This is seen in the account of his trial. During his trial Jesus remained silent until he was placed by the high priest under an oath: "I adjure you by the living God, tell us if you are the Christ, the Son of God" (Matt. 26:63b). According to Leviticus 5:1 (cf. also 1 Kings 22:16; Prov. 29:24), a person was obligated to respond when placed under such an oath. To remain silent was to admit guilt. Jesus reveals that he accepted the legitimacy of this oath, because at this point he broke his silence (Matt. 26:64).

With respect to the saying in Matthew 10:34, it is obvious from Jesus's nonresistance at Gethsemane (Mark 14:43–50) and his forgiveness of his enemies (Luke 23:34) that this saying is an example of exaggeration. Sayings of Jesus such as those found in Matthew 5:9; 10:12–13; Mark 5:34; and Luke 19:42 also reveal that this saying should not be interpreted literally (see rule 2 above). Likewise, Jesus's sayings about praying in private (Matt. 6:6) and hating parents (Luke 14:26) conflict with his behavior in Mark 6:41; 8:6–7; 14:22–23, 32–42; Luke 6:12; 9:28; Matthew 19:13 and in John 19:26–27; Luke 2:51 respectively.

4. The Statement Conflicts with the Teachings of the Old Testament

Jesus's understanding of the OT can be seen from two of his statements. In the first he says,

Do not think that I have come to abolish the Law or the Prophets; I have not come to abolish them but to fulfill them. . . . Therefore whoever relaxes one of the least of these commandments and teaches others to do the same will be called least in the kingdom of heaven, but whoever does them and teaches them will be called great in the kingdom of heaven. (Matt. 5:17, 19)

The second is found in Jesus's summary of the greatest commandment, where he responds to the question, "Which commandment is the most important of all?"

The most important is, "Hear, O Israel: the Lord our God, the Lord is one. And you shall love the Lord your God with all your heart and with all your soul and with all your mind and with all your strength." The second is this: "You shall love your neighbor as yourself." There is no other commandment greater than these. (Mark 12:29–31)

It is clear that Jesus saw his teachings as being in harmony with and in fulfillment of the ethical teachings of the OT (cf. also Mark 10:17–19). If there are exceptions (Mark 10:1–12), these are rare and simply prove the rule.

If we therefore find a saying of Jesus that clearly and radically conflicts with the OT, this suggests that Jesus may be using exaggeration. Thus, Jesus's saying about hating parents (Luke 14:26), which clearly violates the teachings of the OT and the Ten Commandments (Exod. 20:12; cf. also Lev. 19:18; Deut. 6:5), is an example of exaggeration, as is his prohibition against swearing an oath (Matt. 5:33–37; cf. Lev. 5:1; 19:12 [cf. Exod. 20:7]; Num. 30:2–15; Deut. 23:21–23; note also those instances when God himself swore an oath: Deut. 1:8; Pss. 110:4; 132:11; Isa. 14:24).

5. The Statement Conflicts with the Teachings of the New Testament

In rule 4 we pointed out that Jesus's ethical thinking was based on the teachings of the OT. Thus, we can expect them to be alike, and knowledge of the teachings of the OT will help us understand Jesus's teachings. Similarly, the teachings of the NT closely follow those of Jesus and will therefore likewise provide assistance in our attempt to understand the meaning of Jesus's teachings. As a result, if we find a statement of Jesus that tends to conflict with the teachings of the NT, this should give us pause and cause us to question whether we may have an example of exaggeration in the statement. It would be strange indeed if Jesus's contemporaries and followers had radically misunderstood or misinterpreted the teachings of their Lord. For the Christian, this possibility is even more unlikely, since the writers of the NT are understood as the divinely inspired interpreters of Jesus's teachings. Thus, if we find a saying of Jesus that appears to conflict with the teachings of the NT, this may be a clue that Jesus was using exaggeration.

As an example of this, we can again examine Jesus's teaching about not swearing an oath. This stands in sharp conflict with the practice of Paul (Rom. 1:9; 2 Cor. 1:23; Gal. 1:20; Phil. 1:8), who swears such oaths, and with the fact that God is referred to as having sworn oaths (Acts 2:30; Heb. 6:16–17; 7:20–22). Other examples include Jesus's command to hate parents (Luke 14:26; cf. Eph. 6:1–3; Col. 3:20; 1 John 3:10–11; 4:7; etc.) and the following:

> Give to the one who begs from you, and do not refuse the one who would borrow from you. (Matt. 5:42)

> Judge not, that you be not judged. (Matt. 7:1)

It is clear that Paul knew of instances when one should not give to the one asking, for he reminds the Thessalonians, "For even when we were with you, we would give you this command: If anyone is not willing to work, let him not eat" (2 Thess. 3:10). As to the prohibition on judging, similar teaching is found in Romans 14:10 and 1 Corinthians 4:5, but Paul judges in 1 Corinthians 5:3 and rebukes the church in 1 Corinthians 6:1–6 for not judging in a particular instance. And how can someone rebuke (1 Tim. 5:20; 2 Tim. 4:2) without judging? The NT therefore understands Jesus's teachings as prohibiting the negative and critical judgment of others. Yet in the context of love and the purity of the church, judgment is at times necessary.

6. The Statement is Interpreted by Another Biblical Writer in a Nonliteral Way

There are a number of instances when a biblical author interprets a saying found elsewhere in a manner that indicates that he understood the original saying as being an exaggeration. This can be seen quite clearly when we compare the Matthean and Lukan versions of Jesus's statement about hating parents:

> If anyone comes to me and does not hate his own father and mother and wife and children and brothers and sisters, yes, and even his own life, he cannot be my disciple. (Luke 14:26)

Whoever loves father or mother more than me is not worthy of me, and whoever loves son or daughter more than me is not worthy of me. (Matt. 10:37)

What we have in these two statements are probably two versions of the same saying of Jesus. Most scholars believe that the Lukan version is closer to the actual words Jesus said. (The reason for this is the difficulty of the saying in Luke. It is easier to understand Matthew explaining Jesus's harder original saying [the Lukan version] than to understand Luke making Jesus's easier original saying [the Matthean version] more difficult.) What we have in these two accounts are variant philosophies of translation by the Gospel writers. Luke was led to provide his readers with a literal translation of Jesus's saying. He did so by using a word-for-word translation. Matthew, however, was led to give a thought-for-thought translation of Jesus's teaching. Both sayings properly understood, however, convey the same meaning of Jesus. One (Luke) in his word-for-word translation retains to a greater extent the original exaggerated saying; the other (Matthew) in his thought-for-thought translation seeks to explain more fully for his readers what Jesus meant by this saying.

Another example of this is found in Jesus's teaching on divorce, found in five distinct places in the NT:

Whoever divorces his wife and marries another commits adultery against her. (Mark 10:11)

Everyone who divorces his wife and marries another commits adultery, and he who marries a woman divorced from her husband commits adultery. (Luke 16:18)

To the married I give this charge (not I, but the Lord [i.e., this command was given by Jesus]): the wife should not separate from her husband (but if she does, she should remain unmarried or else be reconciled to her husband), and the husband should not divorce his wife. (1 Cor. 7:10–11)

In the Matthean version of this teaching, we have the following:

But I say to you that everyone who divorces his wife, *except on the ground of sexual immorality*, makes her commit adultery, and whoever marries a divorced woman commits adultery. (5:32, italics added)

And I say to you: whoever divorces his wife, *except for sexual immorality*, and marries another, commits adultery. (19:9, italics added)

In my understanding what Matthew has done by his famous "exception clause" is to reveal that he understood Jesus's teaching to be exaggerated in nature. In the Pharisaic discussion of what the legitimate reasons for divorcing a wife (Mark 10:2) were, Jesus replies that all divorce is wrong. There is no such thing as a "good" divorce. Divorce always reveals a failure of the divine purpose. To enter into a discussion concerning the legitimate reasons for divorce would have misdirected the focus of his hearers from God's hatred of divorce (Mal. 2:16 NIV) to a discussion of those instances when divorce may be the lesser of two evils. In the context of Jesus the former was by far the more important. In the context of Matthew, however, the evangelist as an authoritative interpreter of Jesus's words indicates that there is an instance when divorce is permissible, although not demanded. Paul in 1 Corinthians 7:10–11 may give another.

The following is another example of where a biblical writer indicates he believed that a saying of Jesus found elsewhere is hyperbolic:

> Do not think that I have come to bring peace to the earth. I have not come to bring peace, but a sword. (Matt. 10:34)

> Do you think that I have come to give peace on earth? No, I tell you, but rather division. (Luke 12:51)

Here Luke has eliminated the exaggerated metaphor, which could possibly be misinterpreted as political in nature, and translated the word *sword* according to its meaning. What Jesus meant was not that he had come to bring political insurrection, the sword of rebellion, but that he had come to be God's divider, the divine watershed, who would divide all humanity into two parts: believers/unbelievers, Christians/non-Christians, sheep/goats, saved/unsaved. We can also note how Matthew interpreted Jesus's saying about not judging in Matthew 7:1 by such statements as 7:6 (how can we recognize those before whom we should not throw our pearls unless we make some sort of judgment about them?) and 18:15–17 (how do we perform church discipline without judging?).

7. The Statement Has Not Been Literally Fulfilled

At times we encounter a saying of Jesus that has not been fulfilled in a literal sense. Here are some examples:

As he came out of the temple, one of his disciples said to him, "Look, Teacher, what wonderful stones and what wonderful buildings!" And Jesus said to him, "Do you see these great buildings? There will not be left here one stone upon another that will not be thrown down." (Mark 13:1–2)

Ask, and it will be given to you; seek, and you will find; knock, and it will be opened to you. For everyone who asks receives, and the one who seeks finds, and to the one who knocks it will be opened. (Matt. 7:7–8)

Have faith in God. Truly, I say to you, whoever says to this mountain, "Be taken up and thrown into the sea," and does not doubt in his heart, but believes that what he says will come to pass, it will be done for him. Therefore I tell you, whatever you ask in prayer, believe that you have received it, and it will be yours. (Mark 11:22–24)

Despite the appalling destruction of Jerusalem and the temple in AD 70, there still exist stones that stand on one another. Thus, if we interpret Jesus's saying literalistically, this saying has not been fulfilled. Some have consequently argued that Jesus's prophecy referred only to the temple proper and not to the entire temple complex. Yet, in light of the terrible devastation that the city and the temple complex experienced, the use of exaggerated language to describe this is perfectly understandable. Only exaggerated language can do justice to the tremendous destruction that the temple and the city of Jerusalem experienced at that time. (Contrast the loss of literary power and emphasis if Jesus had said something like, "Only 4.2 percent of these stones will still be standing on one another.") Would anyone criticize a person for saying that in the attacks of September 11, 2001, the World Trade Center in New York City was "flattened," since a very small part of it remained standing?

As for the sayings on prayer, in my life I know of prayers that have not been answered. Most Christians will admit the same. James, in fact, says this when he writes, "You ask and do not receive, because you ask wrongly, to spend it on your passions" (4:3). James states that one of the prerequisites for God answering prayer is that the motives must be correct. In Mark 11:22–24 another prerequisite is listed: praying in faith. Needless to say, Jesus did not intend his hearers to interpret his saying in Matthew 7:7–8 as a guarantee that any prayer would be answered, regardless of how absurd and dishonoring to God it might be. Jesus assumed that all such asking/seeking/knocking would be done with the right motives and according to the will of God. He assumed that his followers would always pray, whether expressly stated or by implication, "Yet not what I will, but what you will" (Mark 14:36). (For additional prerequisites for having one's prayers answered, cf. Prov. 28:9; John 9:31; 1 Pet. 3:7.) However, to include in Matthew 7:7–8 such requirements or qualifications would have detracted from what Jesus was seeking to teach. In this saying Jesus wanted to assure his followers that their Father in heaven was eager to hear and answer their prayers. To list various conditions or assumptions in this poetic saying would have detracted from the point he was making and would shift the focus of attention from God's desire to answer the prayers of his children to the preconditions for God answering prayer. Jesus did not want to do this and therefore used overstatement to reveal his point.

Similarly, has not experience taught us concerning Mark 11:22–24 that believers have often prayed in faith to God and not had their prayers answered (cf. the psalmists' cries in various lament psalms such as 13:1–2; 22:12; 28:1–2; 88:13–18)? Certainly for many, "whatever you ask in prayer, believ[ing]" has not always been granted. Our very attempts to explain why this happens demonstrate the fact that the language used in this passage is not meant to be interpreted literalistically but to be understood as exaggerated language encouraging us to pray.

Another example of this rule can be found in the proverb of Jesus in Matthew 26:52, "For all who take the sword will perish by the sword." Not all mercenaries and warriors die violently. Some profit quite nicely from war and live peacefully to an old age. Nevertheless, if this saying had been read to the German and Japanese people after World War II, would any in the audience have found fault with its exaggerated nature?

8. The Statement Would Not Achieve Its Desired Goal

It is apparent that if some sayings were carried out literally, they would not achieve what the speaker intended. Removing the right eye (Matt. 5:29–30) would not solve the problem of lust (note Matt. 5:28). People can still lust with the left eye or without any eyes. It is what comes out of the heart that defiles a person (Mark 7:20–23). Surely Jesus knew that such self-mutilation would not bring about the goal he sought. As a result, this must be an example of exaggeration by which Jesus sought to demonstrate the importance and necessity of repenting in order to enter the kingdom of God. The commissive nature of this saying emphasizes that there is no sin worth perishing for in hell. It is better to repent, no matter how painful this may be.

9. The Statement Uses a Literary Form Prone to Exaggeration

We have already pointed out that there are certain literary forms, such as proverbs, prophecy, poetry, and idioms, that are prone to exaggeration. Without duplicating what has already been said in previous chapters concerning these forms, we call attention to the examples of hyperbole and exaggeration in the following:

Proverbs: Proverbs 3:9–10; 10:3–4; 13:21; 15:1; Matthew 6:21; 10:24; 26:52; Mark 6:4; Luke 16:10

Prophecy: Isaiah 13:9–11 (describing the destruction of Babylon); Jeremiah 4:11–13, 23–26; Mark 13:2, 13a, 14–19, 24–25

Poetry: Exodus 15:1–21 (cf. Exod. 14:21–29); Judges 5 (cf. Judg. 4); Matthew 5:39–41; 6:5–6, 24; 7:7–8; 10:34

Idioms: Deuteronomy 21:15–17; Joshua 2:11; 5:1; 7:5; Malachi 1:2–3; Matthew 8:12; 13:42, 50; 22:13; 24:51; 25:30

10. The Statement Uses Universal Language

Although terms like "all," "everyone," and "no one" can be used in a literal sense (cf. Luke 13:3, 5; Rom. 3:10, 23; 2 Cor. 5:10), there are times when the unqualified use of such terms suggests that what is being said is an exaggeration. Some examples of this can be found in the following:

> For from the least to the greatest of them,
>   *everyone* is greedy for unjust gain;
> and from prophet to priest,
>   *everyone* deals falsely. (Jer. 6:13)

And Jesus said to him, "'If you can'! *All* things are possible for one who believes." (Mark 9:23)

Give to *everyone* who begs from you, and from one who takes away your goods do not demand them back. (Luke 6:30)

John appeared, baptizing in the wilderness and proclaiming a baptism of repentance for the forgiveness of sins. And *all* the country of Judea and *all* Jerusalem were going out to him and were being baptized by him in the river Jordan, confessing their sins. (Mark 1:4–5)

It is evident that in the first example "everyone" is an exaggeration, for Jeremiah himself was a prophet and he was not guilty of the charge. Similarly, it is evident that "all things" are not possible for the Christian: The believer cannot become God. He cannot cause God to cease to exist. And what Christian parents would tolerate giving their children everything they beg for? Love would deny things that would harm them. As for the reaction of people of Judea and Jerusalem, Mark certainly does not want his readers to believe that every man, women, and child, even the ill and dying, went to be baptized by John, so that not a single person could be found in the entire region of Judea and the city of Jerusalem. What he wants his readers to understand is that the appearance of John the Baptist on the scene caused a great stir and that *everyone* (note the exaggeration) went out to see him!

Ultimately, whether universal terms should be interpreted literally or not should be determined by the biblical context, the literary genre (does the term appear in a genre prone to exaggeration [see rule 9 above], human experience, the realities of life?), and similar considerations. The use of universal language should warn us of the possibility that what is being said is exaggerated. For other examples, see Matthew 10:32 (cf. 7:21–22); 23:3, 35; Mark 2:21–22; 10:11–12; 13:30; Luke 5:39. Note also how "all men" (*pantas anthrōpous*) in Romans 5:18 is paralleled in 5:19 by "the many" (*hoi polloi*).

Conclusion

The use of exaggerated language in the Bible is evident. The degree to which it is used is not always acknowledged, but it is more extensive than most people realize. The recognition of such language in the biblical text, however, is not the end of the interpretative process. It is actually only the beginning. We must also seek to understand the meaning this language endeavors to convey as well as its implications. At times the meaning of the saying is self-evident once we recognize its exaggerated nature (Matt. 6:6; 10:34; Mark 10:25). And at times we are assisted by the immediate context in which the saying is found (cf. Matt. 7:3–4 with 7:1; Matt. 10:34 with 10:35–36), or by the larger context of the author's (Jesus's) teaching (cf. Luke 14:26 with Matt. 10:37) or the Bible's teaching in general (cf. Luke 14:26 with Exod. 20:12; Matt. 5:42 with 2 Thess. 3:10).

Once we have understood the meaning of the exaggerated statement, we must also ask why this meaning was framed in this particular literary form. At times this form may have been used as a mnemonic device, to help the hearers/readers remember the saying. It is clear that Jesus's statement about hating parents (Luke 14:26) is not easily forgotten! We furthermore dare not dismiss the meaning of such statements. On the contrary, the presence of exaggeration is a clear indication of the importance that the author places on what is being said. We tend to use exaggerated language to emphasize what is important. We do not exaggerate trivial matters. Rather, we use such language when we seek to convey something that we think is especially significant. As a result, we need to pay special attention when we find this literary form in the Bible. When we come across such examples, we need to ask ourselves, Why was this teaching so important in the mind of the author that he used exaggeration to express what he meant? Thus, the meaning of such a statement should be especially important for the reader and the spoken or implied action carefully heeded.

Questions

1. Can you recall when you recently used exaggeration in speaking or writing to someone? How did you let your audience know that you were exaggerating? Why did you use exaggeration?
2. In which of the following situations would you tend to expect exaggeration: a grandparent describing his or her grandchildren; a person in an accident reporting what happened to a policeman; a patient describing an illness to a doctor; a person telling of the fish he caught on vacation; a witness testifying in a court; a poet reading his or her poetry; giving a description of the addition to the house that you want a carpenter to build?
3. How is the issue of truth related to the use of exaggeration?
4. Is Matthew 17:20 hyperbolic? How about Luke 10:19?

14

The Game of Correspondence

Epistles and Letters

In the NT the dominant literary form is the epistle or letter. Technically, a letter is a less literary and more personal form of communication that tends to address a specific situation or problem and builds on an established relationship. The occasional nature of Galatians, 1 Corinthians, Philippians, and 1 Thessalonians is apparent from the very start. An epistle is more artistic in form and is intended as a self-explanatory treatise to a wider public. The distinction between them can be blurred, however. Paul's writings seem to lie somewhere in between, with Philemon resembling more a letter and Romans an epistle. Most were addressed to a church community and were expected to be obeyed (2 Thess. 3:14), exchanged (Col. 4:16), and considered as a word from God to them (1 Cor. 14:37–38; 1 Thess. 2:13). Thus from the beginning Paul's letters were considered normative and authoritative not only for the churches and individuals specifically addressed but for the church as a whole, even for congregations he did not personally establish (2 Pet. 3:15–16).

Even as present-day letters possess a conventional literary form (date, address, salutation, body, conclusion, name), letters in biblical times also possessed a conventional literary form.

The Form of an Ancient Letter

Within ancient letters we usually find the following:

Salutation: This consists of a reference to the sender ("Paul and Timothy, servants of Christ Jesus") and the recipient(s) of the letter ("To
all the saints in Christ Jesus who are at Philippi, with the overseers
and deacons") along with a greeting ("Grace to you and peace from
God our Father and the Lord Jesus Christ" [Phil. 1:1–2]). The Pauline
salutation conforms to the conventions of his day. The main difference is that whereas the more traditional greeting of the time would
use "Greetings" (*chairein*), as in Acts 15:23; 23:26; and James 1:1,
and a Jewish greeting would use "Peace" (*shalom*), Paul uses a more
distinctly Christian greeting: "Grace [*charis*] and peace." In 1 Timothy
1:2 and 2 Timothy 1:2 we find "Grace, mercy, and peace." On several
occasions Paul uses his salutation to explain why he has written the
letter (Rom. 1:5–6; cf. 15:15–29) and to prepare his readers for his
argument in the body of the letter (Gal. 1:4; cf. 1:11–2:21).

Thanksgiving and/or prayer: This is found in all of Paul's letters except
Galatians, where its omission is significant.

Body: This is frequently the largest part of a Pauline letter, as can be
seen from Romans 1:18–11:36; Galatians 1:6–4:31; cf. also 1 Corinthians 1:10–4:21.

Exhortation and instruction: Note Romans 12:1–15:32; 1 Corinthians
5:1–16:18; Galatians 5:1–6:15.

Conclusion: This can include a wish for peace (Rom. 15:33; 2 Cor.
13:11; Gal. 6:16; Eph. 6:23; 1 Pet. 5:14; 3 John 12); a kiss (Rom. 16:16;
1 Cor. 16:20; 2 Cor. 13:12; 1 Thess. 5:26; 1 Pet. 5:14); a concluding
autograph (1 Cor. 16:21; Gal. 6:11; Col. 4:18; 2 Thess. 3:17; Philem.
19); a benediction (Rom. 16:20; 1 Cor. 16:23–24; 2 Cor. 13:14; Gal.
6:18; Eph. 6:24; Phil. 4:23; Col. 4:18; 1 Thess. 5:28; 2 Thess. 3:18;
1 Tim. 6:21; 2 Tim. 4:22; Titus 3:15; Philem. 25); a doxology (Rom.
16:25–27; 2 Pet. 3:18; Jude 24–25); greetings to various individuals
(Rom. 16:3–16; 1 Cor. 16:3–16; Col. 4:17; 2 Tim. 4:19, 21; Titus
3:15); greetings from those accompanying Paul (Rom. 16:21–23;
1 Cor. 16:19–20; 2 Cor. 13:13; Phil. 4:21–22; Col. 4:10–15; 2 Tim.
4:21; Titus 3:15; Philem. 23–24); prayers (Rom. 15:33; 1 Thess. 5:23;
2 Thess. 3:16; 1 Pet. 5:14); prayer requests (Rom. 15:30–33; Eph.
6:18–20; Col. 4:2–4; 1 Thess. 5:25); and news and the travel plans

of Paul and his team (Rom. 15:22–29; 1 Cor. 16:1–12; Eph. 6:21–22; Col. 4:7–10; 2 Tim. 4:20–21; Titus 3:12–13).

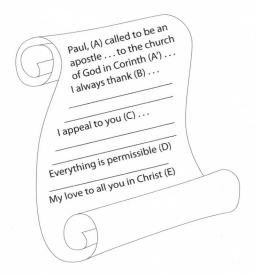

January 1, 2011
Dear Joan, (A')
It was good hearing from you. I am glad that everything is going well (B) . . .
Let me share with you some of the things that have been happening (C) . . .
Don't be discouraged, but keep looking up (D) . . .
Love, (E)
Bob (A)

An author was not enslaved to this form, but it is usually important for the interpreter to note those instances when the author chose to deviate from it. In Galatians Paul omits a thanksgiving and/or prayer and thus reveals his anger and frustration over what was happening in the church. He simply could not find anything to be thankful about in the recent turn of events. At times Paul also used the thanksgiving to prepare his readers for what he was about to write in the body and exhortation of the letter. In 1 Corinthians 1:5–7 he refers to the "speech," "knowledge," and "spiritual gifts" of the Corinthian church and deals with these at length in 1 Corinthians 1:18–4:21 and 12:1–14:40. We can also see in the thanksgiving in Philippians 1:4–5 the themes of joy and the Philippians' common partnership with Paul in the gospel that are referred to later in the epistle. The latter is referred to in 2:19–30 and 4:10–19, and the former is found scattered throughout the letter (1:18, 25; 2:2, 17–18, 28–29; 3:1; 4:1, 4, 10). The unusual addition of material to the salutation, such as we find in Galatians 1:1b–d and Romans 1:1b–6, likewise reveals a great deal about Paul's purpose in writing these letters.

In a similar way, Paul at times uses his conclusion as an opportunity to recapitulate the material in the body and exhortation of his letters. This can be seen in Galatians 6:11–16, where he qualifies his normal benediction, and in 6:17, where he summarizes the defense of his apostleship (cf.

1:11–2:21). Another example of this can be seen in 1 Thessalonians 5:23–24, where we have an exhortation to holy living (5:23a; cf. 1:3; 3:11–13; 4:1, 3–7; 5:8), a reference to Christ's return (5:23b; cf. 1:3, 10; 2:19; 3:13; 4:13–18; 5:1–11), and perhaps a word of reassurance in times of persecution (5:24; cf. 1:6; 2:2, 14; 3:2–4).

Understanding the Words of Scripture

In seeking to understand how an author like Paul used a particular word, we can assume, unless stated otherwise, that the meaning he intended lies within the semantic range of possible meanings available to his audience (see above, pp. 24–25, 49–52). Thus, we can know the range of possible meanings of these words. This range of possibilities is available to us today in a Bible dictionary or, for those with facility in the biblical languages, in a Hebrew or Greek lexicon. The issue for the interpreter is how to narrow down these possibilities to the specific meaning of the word that the author intended his readers to understand. (Although on occasion an author may intend a double meaning, as in a pun, such occurrences are relatively rare.)

It is obvious that not all words are equally important in an author's argument. Some play a more critical role. For instance, the term "counted" is clearly a key term in Romans 4 due to its frequency (along with "count" and "counts," it occurs eleven times). Similarly "wisdom" is also a key term in 1 Corinthians 1:17–2:16, where it occurs fifteen times. At times, the knowledge of a particular word's meaning is especially important because of the critical role it plays in the argument. At other times, knowing the specific meaning of a word is important because of the theological significance that it bears in the argument. It is on the meaning of such critical terms that we must focus our attention.

The Value of Etymology

Frequently in the past, interpreters investigated the etymology of words in order to understand their meanings in sentences. No doubt most of you have heard someone refer to the "root meaning of a word." I have personally heard someone elucidate the meaning of a biblical word by appealing to the root meaning of the English word used in translation. Apparently the speaker did not realize or reflect upon the fact that the biblical author did not write in English and that the English language did not exist at the time.

The fallacy of seeking to discover the particular meaning of a word by means of its etymology can be seen by reflecting on how we use language.

In the last twenty-four hours (or even week or month), when have you thought about the etymology of any of the words that you used in speaking or writing? When we speak or write, we are almost always concerned with only the present meaning of the words we are using. In other words, we are interested not in what these words meant when they came into existence and how they were used in the past (their diachronic meaning) but in what they mean at the time they are spoken or written (their synchronic meaning). Does anyone today use the word *nice* with an awareness of the fact that in the eighteenth century it meant "precise" or that it comes from the Latin *nescius*, which means "ignorant"? Of course not. Or does anyone use the word *let* because it comes from an old Dutch word *lette*, which means "to hinder"? Not today, but the King James translators did in Romans 1:13, when they wrote, "Now I would not have you ignorant, brethren, that oftentimes I purposed to come unto you, (but was let hitherto,). . . ." Even when we use the word in this old sense in calling a tennis serve a "let," which means the game is hindered from proceeding, very few people think that we are using the word *let* according to its old, etymological meaning. When the Cambridge Platform of 1648 defined a church as "a company of professors" and the New Hampshire Confession of 1833 denounced "superficial professors," both were referring here to Christians or "professors" of the Christian faith, not to faculty members of a university. Two other examples of words whose present-day meanings are quite different from their root meanings are *generous*, from the Latin *generosus* ("birth, race, class"), and *asbestos*, from the Greek *asbestos* ("inextinguishable").

The etymology of a word is of little value in biblical interpretation. It is only useful in two instances. One is in those instances when we have little or no idea of what a biblical word means because it is found very seldom, or not at all, elsewhere. An example of this involves the word *daily* (*epiousios*) in the Lord's Prayer. This Greek word is found only three times in ancient Greek literature. (Someone claimed to have found a fourth instance in a papyrus fragment, but the fragment can no longer be found.) The three instances are in the Lord's Prayer in Matthew, the Lord's Prayer in Luke, and the Lord's Prayer in an early church writing called the Didache! In desperation scholars have referred to the possible root meaning of this word. (Help is also sought from early Greek translations of the NT in the hope that perhaps an early translator may have known its meaning.) We also find instances in the OT in which a word is found only once or twice and nowhere else in the literature of the ancient Near East, and we do not know what it means. In such instances we appeal out of desperation to a hypothetical etymological meaning, because we have nothing else to go on. In all such instances, however, we must be aware that we are essentially grasping at straws, and we should never place great weight on this hypothetical root meaning.

The second instance in which a word's etymology is useful involves biblical names. Frequently, names were intentionally chosen because of their root meaning. The most famous example of this is found in Matthew 1:21, where Joseph is told to give Mary's baby the name "Jesus [Heb. *yehoshua'*], for he will save [Heb. *yasha'*] his people from their sins." The name given to Mary's son is carefully chosen based on the etymology of the name. "Jesus," which is the Greek equivalent of the Hebrew "Joshua," has as its root meaning "Yahweh is salvation." Two verses later in Matthew, Mary's son is called Immanuel, which has as its root "God is with us." We find numerous instances in the OT where people are intentionally named due to the etymology of the name. This was because of the common idea that people were/would be as they were named: Genesis 3:20 (Eve); 4:1–2 (Cain), 25 (Seth); 17:5 (Abraham); 21:3–6 (Isaac); 25:25 (Esau), 26 (Jacob); Hosea 1:9 (Lo-Ammi [NRSV]; the ESV translates the Hebrew term as "Not My People"). Sometimes the name has an etymological significance that is not explained: Elijah (Yahweh is God), Shemaiah (The Lord has heard [the prayer of his parents]), Eliezer (My God is my help). The importance of etymology in names is seen especially in the names of God: Yahweh or Lord ("I am" or "I cause to be"), El Shaddai (God Almighty), El Elyon (God Most High), El Olam (God of Eternity), El Berith (God of the Covenant). Outside of this rather limited usage, however, the etymology of a word provides little assistance in understanding what an author meant by the words he used. This is especially true in those instances in which words have taken on an idiomatic meaning.

Understanding a Word's Meaning through Its Usage by Similar Authors

If the key resource for obtaining the possible meanings of a particular word is a dictionary or lexicon, the key resource for understanding its specific meaning is a concordance. By seeing how a word is used elsewhere, we can eventually come to understand how the author is using it in the particular instance we are studying. What do people who think like this author mean when they use this term? Who are the people who think most like this biblical author, and what do they mean when they use this term? It is evident that Paul thought more like classical Greek writers than like modern-day writers, even modern-day Greek writers. Thus when Paul refers to wine in Ephesians 5:18, it is probable that he thought more like ancient writers in their understanding of this word than like people today who use this word. It is probable that Paul meant by this word the same mixture of water and what we today call wine that the ancient Greek writers did (cf. Homer, *Odyssey* 9.208–9; Pliny, *Natural History* 14.6.54; Plutarch, *Symposiacs* 3.9; and especially Athenaeus, *Learned Banquet*, book 10).

We can come even closer to what Paul meant by asking how the writers of the Greek OT (the Septuagint, LXX) understood a term, for Paul thought more like them than like the Greek classical writers. In addition, since the Septuagint was the Bible of his churches, Paul tended to use his words in a manner similar to how they were used in his readers' Bible. Even more helpful would be to understand how Paul's contemporaries, who wrote the other books of the NT, understood the term he used. More helpful still would be to find how the same author uses this term elsewhere in his letters. For instance, when Paul says in Philippians 1:29, "For it has been granted to you that for the sake of Christ you should not only believe in him but also suffer for his sake," his use of the term "granted" elsewhere sheds light on what he means here. The Greek word Paul uses is *echaristhē*. When Paul speaks of the grace of God and being saved by grace, he uses the noun form (*charis*) of this verb. Thus, when Paul speaks of suffering in Philippians 1:29, he is not speaking of something that a Christian may be forced to bear or obligated to endure. On the contrary, suffering for Christ is a gracious privilege. Christians, Paul says, may be "graced" with the privilege of suffering for Christ. Clearly, understanding how Paul uses this word and its noun form elsewhere is helpful in understanding how he is using it in Philippians 1:29.

We also are helped in understanding what Paul means in Philippians 2:12 ("work out your own salvation with fear and trembling") by comparing how he uses the term "work out" elsewhere. This is not the term Paul uses in his discussion of justification by faith when he seeks to establish that justification is not by works. There Paul uses the noun *ergon* and the verb *ergazomai*. Here he uses the verb *katergazomai*, which appears a total of twenty times in Paul's letters. In none of these twenty instances, however, is there present any idea of meriting or earning something. The sense in which Paul uses this term can be seen in the following two passages:

The signs of a true apostle *were performed* among you with utmost perseverance. . . . (2 Cor. 12:12)

For I will not venture to speak of anything except what Christ *has accomplished* through me to bring the Gentiles to obedience—by word and deed. (Rom. 15:18)

The verb translated "were performed" and "has accomplished" is *katergazomai*, the same verb Paul uses in Philippians 2:12. In these two examples it is clear that Paul is not speaking about meriting or earning anything. The signs of an apostle were not earned by Paul but were manifested or demonstrated. Likewise, Christ did not earn or merit the salvation of the Gentiles through Paul's preaching. From Paul's use of the term in these and other instances, it is apparent that in Philippians 2:12 we should not interpret this verb to mean "earn, work for [your salvation]" but rather "manifest, carry out the implications of [the salvation that you already possess]."

There are times when we can ascertain the particular meaning of a word by comparing how the author uses it within the same book. We already saw an example of this when we discussed the meaning of the word *folly* in 1 Corinthians 2:14. It was evident from the way that Paul uses the same term in 1 Corinthians 3:19 and a related term in 1:20 that by "folly" he meant "rejected as foolish" and not "incomprehensible" or "incapable of being understood" (see above, pp. 60–62). Another example of this is the meanings of the terms "justify," "justification," and "righteousness" in Romans 3:21–4:25. Much has been written on the subject, and the forensic dimension of these terms is minimized or ignored by some. However, in Romans 8:33–34 it is evident that justification is the opposite of condemnation and from Romans 4:6–8 that it involves forgiveness. On the other hand such terms in Matthew possess a mostly ethical meaning (cf. 1:19; 5:45; 6:1; 20:4; 25:37; etc.).

Another example of how this works is found in the parable of the sheep and the goats in Matthew 25:31–46. The key issue in this account involves how we are to understand the expression "my brothers" in verse 40. Does Matthew by this term refer to the needy of the world, whether they are believers or not? Does he refer to fellow believers? Or does he refer here to the disciples and early missionaries of the church? Within the NT the expression "brothers" or "brethren" was frequently used as a description of the believing community (e.g., Acts 1:15–16; 15:13; Rom. 1:13; 7:1, 4; 1 Cor. 1:10–11). Far more valuable for understanding what this expression means in Matthew 25:40 is the fact that Matthew uses this same expression metaphorically four other times in his Gospel—three times in 12:48–50 and once in 28:10 (cf. v. 8)—and that in each of these instances it refers to the disciples. It is most likely therefore that it refers to them in 25:40 as well. This is supported by the fact that the best analogy to this parable in the Gospel is found in 10:40–42, where the Christian community is told that receiving "these little ones" (cf. 10:42 with 25:40 "least of these my brothers") means receiving Jesus (cf. 10:40 with 25:35–40). (Cf. also the giving of "a cup of cold water" in 10:42 with "I was thirsty and you gave me drink" in 25:35, 37.) Thus, from within Matthew itself we find sufficient evidence to conclude that the expression "these my brothers" refers to the prophets (10:41), apostles, and early missionaries of the church. The reason rejecting them is so serious is that they are Jesus's messengers, and to reject his messengers is to reject him. One's attitude toward the gospel is clearly seen and reflected in how one treats those who proclaim the gospel. We need only compare the different treatment Paul received from the Philippian jailor before his acceptance of the gospel (Acts 16:23–24) and after (vv. 30–34).

Another example of how an author in his usage of a word elsewhere in the same work reveals what he means by a term is found in the three words "born . . . brought up . . . educated/instructed" found in Acts 7:20–22 and 22:3. In Acts 7:20 "brought up" describes the first three months of Moses's life after birth. After this he is then "brought up," according to 7:21, by Pharaoh's daughter. (Note how she seeks the help of a wet nurse to feed the baby Moses [Exod. 2:3–10].) In Acts 22:3, where the same terminology is used, Luke indicates that Paul was not raised as a child in Tarsus, but after being born there, he was "brought up" from infancy in Jerusalem, where he was later "educated" at the feet of Gamaliel.

There are times when the specific meaning of a word becomes clear from the very paragraph in which it is found. There has been a great deal of confusion as to how James 2:14–26 can be reconciled with Paul's explicit teachings that justification is not by works but by grace alone. Within the semantic range of possible meanings of the two terms, however, "grace" and "works" can mean several things. If we investigate what James and Paul specifically mean by these terms, it becomes evident that they are not referring to the same thing. The faith that cannot save is described by James as a faith that "does not have works" (2:14), a faith that can ignore the naked and hungry in the believing community (2:15–16), a dead faith unaccompanied by good works (2:17, 26), an intellectual faith that believes a fact such as there being one God (2:19a), and a faith that even demons can possess (2:19b). James himself reveals that he does not accept this kind of mental assent as true faith when he says in 2:14, "Can that faith save him?" Note that he does not say, "Can faith save him?" but rather

"Can *that* faith, the kind of faith I just described, a faith that has no subsequent good deeds, save him?" The answer of course is No, that kind of faith, which even the demons have, cannot save anyone. From within the semantic range of possible meanings of the term "faith," James chooses "mere mental assent," such as even demons possess. Demons know, they mentally accept, they "believe" in the sense in which the word is used in James 2:14–26. Yet the "faith" that Paul talks about is not mere mental assent but wholehearted trust and dependence on God and his saving grace. It is a "faith working through love" (Gal. 5:6).

What James means by "works" is also quite different from what Paul means. For Paul, works allow boasting, earning favor, and placing God in one's debt (Rom. 4:2–4). In Romans and Galatians they involve "works of law" and have as their focal point the Gentiles being circumcised, keeping the Sabbath and religious festivals of Judaism, and keeping Jewish food regulations. They are focused on what we would today call ritualistic rather than ethical issues. On the other hand, when James speaks of works, he refers to clothing the naked and feeding the hungry (2:15–16). Works reveal a person's faith (2:18) and involve obedience to God, as in the case of Abraham (2:21–23) and Rahab (2:25). They are faith's loving response to the needs of others. They are the natural and necessary result of faith's desire to please God. It is evident that the paragraphs in which James and Paul use the terms "faith" and "works" assist the reader to understand exactly what they meant by these terms.

Several additional examples in which insight into the meaning of a term is found in the immediate context are as follows: the term "gospel" in 1 Corinthians 15:1–2 is explained by the "for" clause in verses 3–8; "justifies" in Romans 8:33 is shown to be the opposite of "condemns" in verse 34; what Jesus meant by "temple" in John 2:19 is explained by the Gospel writer in verse 21, who also explains in 7:39 what Jesus meant by "rivers of living water" in the previous verse; "counted to him as righteousness" in Romans 4:3 (cf. v. 6) is explained in verses 7–8.

Sometimes the explanation of a term can be found within the sentence itself. An example of this is found in Hebrews 5:14, where the author explains what he means by "for the mature" with the following relative clause, "for those who have their powers of discernment trained by constant practice to distinguish good from evil." Compare also how in Genesis 24:2 "chief servant" (NIV) is explained in the same verse by "the one in charge of all that he had," how in Romans 4:11 the expression "sign of circumcision" is explained by the following appositive ("as a seal of the righteousness that he had by faith while he was still uncircumcised"), and how "sexual immorality" in 1 Corinthians 5:1 is explained by the appositional clause that follows it ("of a kind that is not tolerated even among pagans, for a man has his father's wife"). Another way that a speaker or author defines the meaning of a term or expression is by the use of synonymous parallelism. In Luke 6:27b, "Love your enemies" is explained by the threefold parallelism that follows in 6:27c–28, and in Matthew 6:9c, the meaning of the petition "hallowed be your name" is clarified by the following two petitions in 6:10.

Understanding the Propositions of Scripture

Words in isolation cannot possess a specific meaning. It is only within sentences that they possess specific meanings. Whereas the first step in seeking to know the meaning of a biblical text involves knowing the meaning of the individual words (the parts), the next step is to observe how these words function within the sentence (the whole). (Actually, the procedure is not as simple as this, for we cannot understand the specific meaning of a word without simultaneously understanding the meaning of the sentence in which it is found. This is another example of the hermeneutical circle.)

Whereas the key tools for understanding what words mean are a dictionary/lexicon and a concordance, the key tool for understanding the meaning of a sentence is a grammar. For the readers of an English translation of the Bible, this means they must have the same understanding of English grammar that the translators possessed. For those who possess the ability to read the Hebrew OT or the Greek NT, this means they must possess knowledge of the grammar, the syntax, of the biblical language. It goes without saying that, because grammar changes, we must be sure we are dealing with the same grammatical rules that the translators or authors worked with at the time. In interpreting the works of Paul, we must know the grammatical rules not of Classical Greek or Modern Greek but of the Greek that Paul and his readers shared in common, called Koine Greek. Similarly, when seeking to understand the KJV, we must know late sixteenth- and early seventeenth-century English grammar, whereas in interpreting modern English translations of the Bible, we must know late twentieth- and early twenty-first century English grammar.

A sentence consists of a combination of words (verbal symbols) used by their author to make some sort of a statement. When strung together, these sentences make up an argument. To decipher what the author meant by the sentence, we must know how the words within them relate to each other. In English, word order is most important. The words "Bob loves

Joan" in any other order ("Joan loves Bob," "Loves Bob Joan," "Loves Joan Bob," "Bob, Joan loves," "Joan, Bob loves") possess a different meaning. In Greek, however, word order plays a lesser role because the endings on the word determine what is the subject and what is the object. Thus, we can have: "Bob*us* agapei [loves] Joan*ēn*" or "Joan*ēn* agapei [loves] Bob*us*," and there is no real difference. Both mean "Bob loves Joan."

When interpreting the Bible, readers often pay insufficient attention to how parts of sentences and clauses relate to one another. For example, the relationship between "you are saved" and "faith" will be radically altered if we use various words such as "because of," "before," "after," "despite," "since," "apart from," "regardless of," and "for." Most readers of the Bible pay far too little attention to how such phrases and clauses relate to each other. The following is a description of some of the ways in which parts of sentences can relate to each other. (It should be noted that formal-equivalent translations such as the NASB, NRSV, and ESV generally reveal these relationships more clearly than thought-for-thought translations such as the NIV, NLT, and REB.)

1. Cause

In this kind of relationship, effect A is because of B; that is, B is the cause of A: "The man died [A] *because of* his wounds [B]." Some of the terms used to describe this kind of a relationship are "because," "for," "since," by," and "on account of."

> What then? Are we to sin [A] *because* we are not under law but under grace [B]? By no means! (Rom. 6:15)

> Therefore, my beloved, as you have always obeyed, so now, not only as in my presence but much more in my absence, work out your own salvation with fear and trembling [A], *for* it is God who works in you, both to will and to work for his good pleasure [B]. (Phil. 2:12–13)

> You do not have [A], *because* you do not ask [B]. You ask and do not receive [A], *because* you ask wrongly, to spend it on your passions [B]. (James 4:2c–3)

We have discussed in the previous section that the Greek term translated "work out" does not refer to earning or meriting something and thus cannot refer to achieving salvation through works. This is revealed even more clearly by the causal relationship of Philippians 2:13 with what has preceded. The Philippian Christians are to work out their salvation *for* God is already at work in their lives. It is because they are already the recipients of God's grace and salvation that the exhortation is given to "work out" this salvation they now possess. "Working out" their salvation is based on the fact that they already possess this salvation from God. (Cf. in the discussion of covenant and law, how the gracious establishment of the former precedes the latter [p. 107].) For other examples of a causal relationship between clauses, see Romans 11:20 ("because of" introduces the cause), 30 ("because of" introduces the cause); 12:1 ("by" introduces the cause); 1 Corinthians 1:21 ("for since" introduces the cause); 2 Corinthians 2:13 ("because" introduces the cause); Galatians 6:12 ("for" introduces the cause); Ephesians 2:8 ("by" introduces the cause); 1 Thessalonians 5:8 ("since" introduces the cause).

2. Result

In this relationship, B is the result of A: "The man was wounded [A], *so that* he died [B]." Some of the terms used to describe this kind of a relationship are "so that," "that," "as a result," "therefore," "accordingly," "consequently," and "so as."

> And if I have prophetic powers, and understand all mysteries and all knowledge, and if I have all faith [A], *so as* to remove mountains [B], but have not love, I am nothing. (1 Cor. 13:2)

> And it is my prayer that your love may abound more and more, with knowledge and all discernment [A], *so that* you may approve what is excellent, and so be pure and blameless for the day of Christ [B]. (Phil. 1:9–10)

> For not only has the word of the Lord sounded forth from you in Macedonia and Achaia, but your faith in God has gone forth everywhere [A], *so that* we need not say anything [B]. (1 Thess. 1:8)

For other examples, see Romans 1:20 ("so" expresses the result); 7:3 ("accordingly" expresses the result); 1 Corinthians 9:24 ("that" expresses result); 2 Corinthians 8:5–6 ("accordingly" expresses result); Galatians 2:13 ("so that" expresses the result); 3:17 ("so as" expresses the result); 5:17 ("to [keep]" expresses the result); 1 Thessalonians 5:4 ("for" expresses result).

3. Purpose

In this relationship, B is the purpose of A: "He allowed himself to be wounded [A] *in order that* he would be sent home [B]." Purpose and result are quite similar, for if we are successful in what we have purposed, what results is the purpose. Purpose, however, refers to the intention of the action. Sometimes the distinction between purpose and result is both clear and important. The difference between the charge of manslaughter and first-degree murder is not the result but the intention. Shooting someone accidently or intentionally may have a similar result, the death of the victim, but the law recognizes that they are to be treated differently. This is true in the OT, which permitted cities of refuge (Num. 35) for those whose actions resulted in killing someone but who did not purpose to do so. Some of the terms used to describe this kind of relationship are "in order that," "so that," "that," "to" plus an infinitive, "lest" (in order not to), and "rather."

> For I long to see you [A], *that* I may impart to you some spiritual gift [B¹] *to* strengthen you [B²]. (Rom. 1:11; there are two purpose relationships in this verse, marked B¹ and B²)

> Now we know that whatever the law says it speaks to those who are under the law [A], *so that* every mouth may be stopped, and the whole world may be held accountable to God [B]. (Rom. 3:19)

> All Scripture is breathed out by God and profitable for teaching, for reproof, for correction, and for training in righteousness [A], *that* the man of God may be competent, equipped for every good work [B]. (2 Tim. 3:16–17)

For other examples, see Romans 5:20 ("to" expresses the purpose); 7:4 ("so that" expresses the purpose); 1 Corinthians 9:12 ("rather than," that is, "in order not to," expresses the purpose); 11:34 ("so that" expresses the purpose); 2 Corinthians 8:9 ("so that" expresses the purpose); Galatians 1:4 ("to" expresses the purpose); 6:12 ("in order" expresses the purpose); 1 Thessalonians 3:5 ("to learn about" expresses the purpose); 1 Timothy 4:15 ("so that" expresses the purpose).

4. Condition

Here, A is the condition of B: "*If* he were wounded [A], he would have been sent to the field hospital [B]." Some of the terms used to describe this kind of relationship are "if," "if . . . then," "if while," "except," and "unless."

> You, however, are not in the flesh but in the Spirit [B], *if* in fact the Spirit of God dwells in you [A]. [*If*] anyone . . . does not have the Spirit of Christ [A] [, he] does not belong to him [B]. (Rom. 8:9)

Therefore, *if* anyone is in Christ [A], he is a new creation [B]. The old has passed away; behold, the new has come. (2 Cor. 5:17)

But *if* you are led by the Spirit [A], you are not under the law [B]. (Gal. 5:18)

For other examples, see Romans 8:13 (the two "ifs" express two conditions); 11:12 (the two "ifs" express the condition), 21 ("if" expresses the condition); 1 Corinthians 7:11 ("if" expresses the condition); 13:1 ("if" expresses the condition); Galatians 5:25 ("if" expresses the condition); Colossians 3:1 ("if" expresses the condition).

5. Concession

Here, B takes place despite A: "*Even though* he was wounded [A], he did not die [B]." Some of the terms used to describe this kind of relationship are "despite," "even though," "although," "though," "yet," "apart," "if," and "even if."

For *even if* I made you grieve with my letter [A], I do not regret it [B]. (2 Cor. 7:8)

But *even if* we or an angel from heaven should preach to you a gospel contrary to the one we preached to you [A], let him be accused [B]. (Gal. 1:8)

Have this mind among yourselves, which is yours in Christ Jesus, who, *though* he was in the form of God [A], did not count equality with God a thing to be grasped [B]. (Phil. 2:5–6)

For other examples, see Romans 3:21 ("although" expresses concession); 5:10 ("if while" expresses concession); Galatians 6:1 ("[even] if anyone" expresses concession); Philippians 2:17 ("even if" expresses concession); Philemon 8 ("though" expresses concession); Hebrews 5:8 ("although" expresses concession), 12 ("though" expresses concession); 1 Peter 1:6 ("though" expresses concession).

6. Means

A is the means by which B is accomplished: "*By* helicopter [A] the wounded were brought quickly to the field hospital [B]." Some of the terms used to describe this kind of relationship are "by," "with," "by means of," "through," and "in."

For if you live according to the flesh you will die, but if *by* the Spirit you put to death the deeds of the body [A], you will live [B]. (Rom. 8:13)

For by grace you have been saved [B] *through* faith [A]. And this is not your own doing; it is the gift of God, not a result of works, so that no one may boast. (Eph. 2:8–9)

Knowing that you were ransomed from the futile ways inherited from your forefathers [B], not *with* perishable things such as silver or gold [not by, A¹], but *with* the precious blood of Christ [but by, A²], like that of a lamb without blemish or spot. (1 Pet. 1:18–19)

It is easy to confuse means and cause. In the examples given above it should be noted that the wounded man was not brought to the field hospital *because of* a helicopter but *by means of* a helicopter. The cause for being brought to the field hospital was his wounds. Similarly, in Ephesians 2:8–9 the believer is not saved *because of* faith. Faith is not the cause but the means of salvation. All the faith in the world could not save a person if Jesus had not died for the sins of the world. The cause of salvation is God's grace in Christ; that is, it is *by* or *because of* grace (in Greek this is an instrumental of cause). The means through which this salvation is appropriated is *through* faith. The purpose (so that) is that no one should be able to boast before God. (If a person is saved from a life-threatening disease by means of an antibiotic, that person is saved *because of* the antibiotic that was administered *by means of* a hypodermic syringe. A person could be stuck day and night with the syringe, however, and not become better. It is not the syringe but the antibiotic that is the cause of the healing. The syringe is the means.)

For other examples, see Romans 5:15 ("through" expresses means); 1 Corinthians 2:13 ("in" expresses means); Galatians 5:16 ("by" expresses means); James 2:18 ("by" expresses means); 1 Peter 2:24 ("by" expresses means); 1 John 2:3 ("by this" expresses means).

7. Manner

In this relationship, A is done in the manner of B: "He served his country [A] *by* enduring numerous wounds [B]." Manner describes how the action of the verb takes place. Some of the terms used to describe this kind of relationship are "by," "with," "by means of," "in," and "from."

If I partake [A] *with* thankfulness [B], why am I denounced because of that for which I give thanks? (1 Cor. 10:30)

Because our gospel came to you [A] not only *in* word [B], but also *in* power
[B] and *in* the Holy Spirit [B] and *with* full conviction [B]. (1 Thess. 1:5)

For the Lord himself will descend from heaven [A] *with* a cry of command
[B], *with* the voice of an archangel [B] and *with* the sound of the trumpet
of God [B]. And the dead in Christ will rise first. (1 Thess. 4:16)

For other examples, see 1 Corinthians 9:26 ("aimlessly" and "beating the
air" express manner); 11:5 ("with" expresses manner); Galatians 6:11
(the first "with" expresses manner); Philippians 1:18 (the first three "ins"
express manner).

There are other kinds of relationships that clauses and phrases can
have, but these are some of the most important. It should be observed
that in the norms of language the same word can introduce a number of
different relationships. For instance, "so that" can be used to introduce
purpose or result; "by" can introduce cause, means, or manner. The specific
relationship is decided by the meaning the author has willed through the
surrounding context. It is from the context that the range of possibilities
permitted by the semantic range of possible meanings can be narrowed
down to the one specific meaning intended by the author. This is true not
only in the original Greek and Hebrew text in which the author has expressed his meaning, but also in the English version being used. Here also
the authors reveal how they want their readers to interpret the relationship
of their clauses and phrases by means of the literary context they provide.
To understand the reasoning of the biblical authors, we must pay careful
attention to how they relate the clauses and phrases they have written. This
is true not only of the Epistles but of all parts of the Bible. It is especially
important, however, with respect to the Epistles because it is within this
literary form that we encounter the most carefully reasoned arguments
found in the Bible.

The Danger of a Mirror Reading of the Epistles

It is immediately apparent in reading the Epistles that their occasional
nature assists the reader in reconstructing the situation in life for which
they were written. By reading Galatians we can come to a reasonably good
understanding of the Galatian problem, and by reading 1 Corinthians we
can identify some of the troubles occurring in the Corinthian church. There
is a danger, however, of interpreting every command or prohibition and
every teaching in an epistle as reflecting a particular situation within the

church. Such a "mirror reading" is unwarranted. Not every command or prohibition need reflect a present problem in the church; not every teaching need reflect a present doctrinal issue. Rather, they may serve prophylactic and preventative purposes, reflecting common problems and issues in life or encountered in Paul's ministry elsewhere. (Should a church visitor hearing a sermon on "Thou shalt not steal" assume that this church congregation has a particularly high percentage of thieves? Or could this sermon be due to it being a part of a series on the Ten Commandments or being the next passage in the book of the Bible through which the pastor is leading the congregation?)

Some indicators that a mirror reading is perhaps legitimate are references to

specific problems in the church being referred to (1 Cor. 1:10–17; 5:1–5; 6:1–20; 11:7–34; 15:12–56; 2 Cor. 10:1–12:21; Gal. 1:6–9; 5:2–12; 1 Thess. 4:13–18);

specific questions having been asked by recipients of the letter (1 Cor. 7:1–24, 25–40; 8:1–13; 12:1–40; 16:1–4); and

unusual emphasis on certain issues (1 Cor. 1:18–3:23; Gal. 1:11–2:21; 3:1–5:1).

In the attempt to understand the situation in the church concerning which Paul and the other writers of NT letters wrote (the why), we need to remind ourselves that this, like the mental acts of the author, involves a hypothetical reconstruction. It is also not the same as seeking to understand the communicative intention of the authors in these letters (the what). We possess the latter in the text that they have provided for us, and this should always be the primary goal of our study.

Conclusion

In seeking to interpret the Epistles, the person able to study the Bible in its original languages possesses two distinct advantages over the person studying the Bible in translation. One is that there are certain grammatical insights that can be gleaned from the author's writings that are not available to the person who must read them in translation. For instance, knowing that the verbs "will continue" and "cannot go on (sinning)" in 1 John 3:9 are in the present tense helps in translating this difficult verse. Since the present tense more often than not gives the sense of continual action, this helps us to understand that John is not saying that the Christian never sins, which would contradict what he has already said in 1 John 1:9–2:2, but that the Christian does not continually abide in sin. The ESV ("makes a practice of sinning . . . keep on sinning"), NIV ("will continue to sin . . . go on sinning"), NLT ("do not make a practice of sinning . . . keep on sinning") have translated this in helpful ways, but the KJV ("doth not commit sin . . . cannot sin"), RSV ("commits sin . . . cannot sin"), NRSV ("do not sin . . . cannot sin"), and REB ("commits sin . . . cannot sin") unfortunately confuse the reader. Even as in the teaching of Chinese or French literature the teacher who possesses facility in these languages has an advantage over the one who does not, so the student of the Bible who has facility in the biblical languages has an advantage over the one who does not.

The second advantage of knowing the biblical languages involves a difference in the goal of interpretation. Whereas the interpreter of Romans who has facility in Greek can seek as his or her goal the discovery of Paul's meaning, the reader of a translation cannot. The goal of reading a translation of the Bible is to understand the meaning of the translators. This can be demonstrated rather simply. If we do not understand a word in an English translation, where do we look? In a contemporary English dictionary. But Paul did not know English. Thus, we are not looking at what Paul meant by this English word but what the translators meant. A reader of the Bible in translation is a step removed from the meaning of the biblical writer, whereas those who have facility in the original languages have direct access to the text of the author.

Having said this, it should be pointed out that the translators of such versions as the ESV, NIV, RSV, NRSV, NLT, NAB, and REB possessed a remarkable grasp of the biblical languages and the meaning of the biblical authors. In addition, they also possessed a facility for expressing well their understanding of this meaning. Thus, we can have great confidence in the translations we are reading. Their accuracy is remarkable, and of all the countries of the world we are most blessed with numerous, highly accurate translations of the Bible. In my library, I have several dozen such translations. In those instances in which we are carefully studying a particular text or passage, it is advantageous to compare several translations.

Questions

1. Why would a departure by Paul from the normal epistolary form be more significant than his following it?

2. Why would understanding the meaning of various words in the Greek OT (LXX) be more helpful in studying Paul's use of these words than understanding the meaning of these words in classical Greek or modern Greek writers?

3. Look up two or three references in points 1–7 of "Understanding the Propositions of Scripture" in this chapter, and observe how the context given by the authors helps in understanding the grammatical relationship between the clauses.

4. What is the advantage of knowing Greek and Hebrew in the study of the Bible?

5. Where can a person who does not know the biblical languages go to find assistance in interpreting the Bible?

Appendix 1

Answer Key to Chapter 2 Exercises

1. *Subject matter*. Note that Luke and his willed meaning are not the focus of the statement. The center of attention is information about the early church.
2. *Understanding*. The statement involves having arrived at a correct cognitive grasp of Paul's meaning.
3. *Implications*. This states an inference or submeaning of the willed principle of Paul's meaning.
4. *Interpretation*. This is a verbal expression of the speaker's cognitive understanding of Paul's meaning.
5. *Mental acts*. This is a hypothetical reconstruction of Paul's thinking process as he was writing.
6. *Semantic range*. This deals with the range of possible meanings the participle can have in this context and the way it interacts with other words to shape the overall meaning of the sentence.
7. *Subject matter*. Although the word *meant* is used in this statement, it does not involve meaning as defined in this chapter, for Jesus is not the author of this text. The author who wrote the text is the evangelist Mark. The statement involves the subject matter of the text (i.e., Jesus and his teachings). What the author Mark meant by the Greek words he wrote in Mark 12:17 involves the meaning of the text. What Jesus meant by the Aramaic words he spoke in AD 30 involves the subject matter of the teachings of the historical Jesus (or Meaning^SM).

8. *Literary genre*. The statement involves the rules of a particular genre (perhaps poetry, proverbs, or prophecy), and that genre involves exaggerated or figurative language in this passage.

9. *Specific meaning*. The statement involves proceeding from the possibilities or semantic range of a specific term contained in the statement to its specific meaning. It does so by investigating how Paul uses the term elsewhere (the context). It is also possible that the speaker is thinking of the *context*.

10. *Implications*. The speaker is seeking to understand a possible unconscious meaning or inference that Moses was unaware of but that fits with his willed principle.

11. *Subject matter*. In this statement we are not seeking to understand what John meant by telling this story about Jesus but stating that in the life and ministry of Jesus this was his first miracle.

12. *Implications, significance*, or *subject matter*. If the statement appeals primarily to the understanding (i.e., it is cognitive in intent), it is an implication. If it deals with the will (i.e., it is volitional in intent) and refers to a response of the speaker, it involves significance. If it refers primarily to the teachings of the historical Jesus, it involves subject matter. An additional statement or two is needed to be more specific.

13. *Semantic range*. The statement refers to the possible meanings of the symbols (words) found in the text.

14. *Subject matter* or *genre*. This is best described as a reference to the subject matter of this passage. No mention is made of Paul and what he meant by this early church creed. This could also be referring, however, to this material being in the genre of an early church creed and that it should be interpreted accordingly.

15. *Significance*. The statement involves an evaluation (that it has no value) of one's understanding (that it is interesting) of what Paul meant by the text.

Appendix 2

Answer Key to Chapter 3 Exercises

1. *Semantic range*. The statement deals with the range of possible meanings allowed by the verbal symbols Paul used. The interpretation given ("what you say") lies outside that range of possible meanings.
2. *Genre*. The issue at hand involves the literary form of the passage and the rules governing that form.
3. *Interpretation*. This is a verbal expression of the speaker's understanding of Luke's meaning.
4. *Understanding*. This describes the eureka moment of grasping an author's meaning.
5. *Implications*. This deals with a possible unconscious meaning of Moses and whether it fits within his consciously willed principle or pattern of meaning.
6. *Subject matter*. We are trying to understand how Jesus's audience reacted to Jesus's words. Note that the author of the Gospel is not in view.
7. *Semantic range*. We are dealing with the various possibilities of what a verbal symbol meant in the author's day.
8. *Significance*. "Accept" is a volitional term, so we are not dealing with mental issues (understanding, implication) or verbal issues (interpretation) but with a volitional issue (a response to Isaiah's meaning).

9. *Meaning.* The statement refers to a lack of interest in Paul's original meaning. It can also refer to *significance*, since it involves a response to that meaning.

10. *Implications.* The statement reveals a concern for present-day implications of what Paul meant. That concern probably involves a cognitive understanding of how what Paul said applies today.

11. *Semantic range.* The statement deals with the limited possibilities of meaning contained in the language used by the biblical author.

12. *Subject matter.* We are learning information about the life of Jesus. Note the lack of concern for what Matthew was seeking to teach about this incident.

13. *Implications.* This is not concerned about the specific conscious meaning of Paul, but with the unconscious submeanings found within Paul's principle.

14. *Significance* or *implications.* It is uncertain whether the statement reveals an action that the speaker now wills to follow or whether this is simply a cognitive understanding of how people should behave if they want to obey this command.

15. *Interpretation.* This is the verbal expression of one's understanding of Paul's meaning.

Appendix 3

Answer Key to Chapter 4 Exercises

1. *Implications.* The statement deals with a possible inference or sub-meaning that the author may have meant. If the statement involves not so much a cognitive understanding of a possible implication but rather a volitional action that the reader should perform, then it would involve *significance*. If instead of "Mark meant" the statement said "Jesus meant," this would involve the *subject matter*.
2. *Subject matter.* The statement is not concerned with understanding what the author is seeking to teach by this information but with simply acquiring knowledge about ancient hospitality.
3. *Specific meaning.* Whereas a lexicon or dictionary is useful for learning the semantic range of possible meanings of a particular term, a concordance is useful for seeing how the author uses a word elsewhere is his writings and thus in ascertaining its specific meaning in a particular passage.
4. *Understanding.* By its explanation of the text, the commentary helped the reader arrive at a correct mental grasp of the author's meaning.
5. *Subject matter.* We are here acquiring information about an event recorded in Acts. Note that this does not involve the author and his communicative intention in recording the event.
6. *Understanding.* Explanation is cognitive in nature and seeks to explain the meaning of the text.
7. *Significance.* Exhortation appeals to the will and seeks to elicit a response.

8. *Interpretation.* Having arrived at an understanding of Paul's meaning, the speaker is not able to verbalize that understanding.

9. *Semantic range.* The statement deals with how the tense and mood of the verb shape the overall meaning of the sentence.

10. *Genre.* The statement makes a comment based on the rules governing the genre of letter writing.

11. *Subject matter.* This deals not with what the biblical author meant by this prayer found in his Gospel but rather with what one of the characters (Jesus) making up the subject matter of his Gospel meant by it.

12. *Meaning* or *interpretation.* The statement deals with the *meaning* of Luke, but by explaining it the person making the statement gives to us his *interpretation.*

13. *Implications.* The statement draws out a submeaning of Luke. Because it is explained, however, it can also be understood as an *interpretation.*

14. *Mental acts.* The statement seeks to reconstruct what Paul was thinking about when he wrote.

15. *Genre.* The statement refers to the particular genre of the story being discussed and the implications of this for the rules of interpreting it.

Glossary

application: The way meaning relates to the reader. The term is a combination of personal implications and significance.

author: The actual writer who penned the work being interpreted.

author-centered hermeneutic: A theory of literary interpretation that assumes that the author of a text determines the text's meaning.

communicative act or intent: Synonyms for the authorial meaning of a text emphasizing the communicative nature of texts in contrast to seeing a text as a work of literary art.

context: The author's willed meaning of the passages surrounding the text.

conviction: That work of the Holy Spirit that brings to the reader the assurance of the truthfulness of a biblical text's meaning and the persuasion of the need to respond.

Enlightenment: In biblical studies this refers to that period in history (primarily the late eighteenth and nineteenth centuries) when the historicity of the miracles recorded in the Bible began to be doubted and denied.

exegesis: The process of understanding and interpreting a text.

generic expectation: The interpreting of a text based upon a conclusion as to its literary form and the rules governing that literary form.

genre: See *literary genre.*

illumination: The special guidance that the Holy Spirit supposedly gives to believers in understanding the meaning of Bible.

implications: Those inferences contained within the meaning of a text that an author may have been unaware of but that nevertheless fall within his or her willed principle or paradigm.

inference: A synonym for *implications.*

intentional fallacy: An objection to seeking in a text the willed meaning of an author because of the belief that a reader can never relive the experiences of the author when he or she wrote (i.e., the mental acts) or because the author may not be able to express adequately his or her intended meaning.

interpretation: The verbal or written expression of a reader's understanding of the author's meaning contained in a text.

langue: A French word that is a synonym for *semantic range*.

literary genre: The literary form used by an author and the rules governing that form.

meaning: The principle that an author consciously willed to convey by the words (shareable symbols) used.

mental acts: The experiences that an author went through while writing a text.

mental experiences: A synonym for *mental acts*.

mirror reading: Reading a text with the assumption that the instructions and content within it reflect specific situations in the life of the original readers.

norms of language: A synonym for *semantic range*.

norms of utterance: A synonym for *specific meaning*.

parole: A French word that is a synonym for *specific meaning*.

pattern of meaning: The conscious willed principle of an author and all its implications contained in his or her text, a synonym for *principle*.

principle: The meaning that an author consciously willed to convey by the words (shareable symbols) he or she used.

reader-centered hermeneutic: A theory of literary interpretation that assumes that the reader of a text determines the text's meaning.

semantic range: The limit of possible meanings allowed by the words (verbal symbols) of a text.

shareability: The common understanding of the language of a text shared by both the author and the intended readers.

shareable symbols: Literary markings containing meanings shared by the author and reader.

significance: How a reader responds to the meaning of a text.

specific meaning: The particular meaning that an author has given to a word, phrase, sentence, etc., in the text.

subject matter: The content or "stuff" talked about in a text.

submeaning: A synonym for *implications*.

subtype: A synonym for *implications*.

text-centered hermeneutic: A theory of literary interpretation that assumes that the text itself determines the text's meaning.

unconscious meaning: A synonym for *implications*.

verbal symbols: Literary markings that convey meaning.

Select Bibliography

Adler, Mortimer J. *How to Read a Book*. New York: Simon & Schuster, 1940.

Brown, Jeannine K. *Scripture as Communication: Introducing Biblical Hermeneutics*. Grand Rapids: Baker Academic, 2007.

Caird, G. B. *The Language and Imagery of the Bible*. Philadelphia: Westminster, 1980.

Cotterell, Peter, and Max Turner. *Linguistics and Biblical Interpretation*. Downers Grove, IL: InterVarsity, 1989.

Fee, Gordon D., and Douglas Stuart. *How to Read the Bible for All Its Worth*. 3rd ed. Grand Rapids: Zondervan, 2003.

Green, Joel B., ed. *Hearing the New Testament: Strategies for Interpretation*. 2nd ed. Grand Rapids: Eerdmans, 2010.

Hirsch, E. D., Jr. *Validity in Interpretation*. New Haven: Yale, 1967.

Kaiser, Walter, and Moisés Silva. *An Introduction to Biblical Hermeneutics: The Search for Meaning*. Rev. and expanded ed. Grand Rapids: Zondervan, 2007.

Klein, William W., Craig L. Blomberg, and Robert L. Hubbard Jr. *Introduction to Biblical Interpretation*. Rev. and updated ed. Nashville: Nelson, 2004.

Lewis, C. S. "Fern-Seed and Elephants." In *Fern-Seed and Elephants: And Other Essays on Christianity*. Edited by Walter Hooper. Glasgow, Scotland: Fontana/Collins, 1975.

Osborne, Grant R. *The Hermeneutical Spiral: A Comprehensive Introduction to Biblical Interpretation*. Rev. and expanded ed. Downers Grove, IL: InterVarsity, 2006.

Pelikan, Jaroslav. *Interpreting the Bible and the Constitution*. New Haven: Yale, 2004.

Plummer, Robert L. *40 Questions about Interpreting the Bible*. Grand Rapids: Kregel, 2010.

Ryken, Leland. *How to Read the Bible as Literature*. Grand Rapids: Zondervan, 1984.

Sandy, D. Brent. *Plowshares & Pruning Hooks*. Downers Grove, IL: InterVarsity, 2002.

Schreiner, Thomas R. *Interpreting the Pauline Epistles*. 2nd ed. Grand Rapids: Baker Academic, 2011.

Silva, Moisés. *Biblical Words and Their Meaning: An Introduction to Lexical Semantics*. Rev. and expanded ed. Grand Rapids: Zondervan, 1994.

Tate, W. Randolph. *Interpreting the Bible: A Handbook of Terms and Methods*. Peabody, MA: Hendrickson, 2006.

Vanhoozer, Kevin J. *Is There a Meaning in This Text? The Bible, the Reader, and the Morality of Literary Knowledge*. Rev. ed. Grand Rapids: Zondervan, 2009.

Virkler, Henry A., and Karelynne Gerber Ayayo. *Hermeneutics: Principles and Processes of Biblical Interpretation*. 2nd ed. Grand Rapids: Baker Academic, 2007.

Subject Index

Scripture Index

Old Testament

Genesis

Exodus

Leviticus

Numbers

Deuteronomy

Joshua